KISS THE GIRL SAVE THE WORLD KILL THE BADDIE

JULIAN STAN

Editing: Gabriel Stancu
Cover & Interior Design: Julian Stan
Background Cover Photo: Kevin Kurek via Unsplash
ISBN: 9798846271975

Julian Stan
www.arkdian.com
contact@portocal.app
Insta: @arkdian
www.linkedin.com/in/julianstancu
www.portocal.app
Twitter: @arkdianOfficial
Spotify: @arkdian
For Life Coaching Packages contact Julian directly via the channels above.

18+ Contains explicit language

*Note that this book is under no way licensed medical advice. For actual data and facts please see References. Some fictional chapters are pure theories of the author, which need further debating. How you decide to live your life is solely your responsibility. The author is not liable for any misinterpretation.

Contents

ABOUT THE AUTHOR

Julian Stan is a British/Dacian (Romanian) writer, influencer and entrepreneur living in London. He grew up and studied in the beautiful seashore city of Constanta, close to the most famous resort on the Black Sea, Mamaia, also called the "Miami of Europe". He owns a bachelor's degree in Economics from Ovidius University - Constanta, and a post-grad in Border Force Tactics, Travel Documents, and International Law.

Before deciding to permanently move abroad, he served as a Border Force/Coast Guard officer for almost a decade. In the UK he worked for three years in biotechnology, as laboratory technician in the large scale fractionation of the human blood plasma, with Bio Products Laboratory. He decided to become self-employed in 2020, in order to expand his businesses.

He is also the author of the one-of-a-kind novel **"This is my Electronica"**, about his love for electronic music, DJing, and Ibiza. This work is unique in his native country.

There are countries that lead, and countries that serve. This is how you know where your conspiracies have their operational headquarters. Never forget that Governments are there to serve you, and not the other way around.

PROLOGUE

Why are we here? Going to biased schools used as brain washing systems, work our asses off clinging to the idea of pension, and then to start living life when our bodies are ready to retire from this life? I find this ideology highly unsettling. This is my life, what I used to be, and a part of what I still am, what I've become. Even normal people have something interesting to say, sometimes maybe more than people in the public eye, or even people focused on gaining experience. You'll find way less usual people that are corrupt, than your everyday superstar.

This is the most sincere book I've ever written. No events have been altered, but some names had to be changed for obvious reasons. I hope this book will tickle you in all the right places. If you have difficulties digesting some of the events, don't worry, go on and live your own beautiful – great things will happen to you too, one way or another. The more you oppose, the less books you will write. Say *yes* more, be unique, and try to see and understand the truth around you. It's not easy, but it will change you for good. Remember that understanding is paramount. You can see a car on the street, but knowing how it works is a totally different dimension. I never thought I had an interesting life, as I was delayed in growing up, maybe I still am. But at some point in time something amazing happened to me, called *enlightenment*. I didn't ask for it, but it chose me too. Watch yourself, and be aware of your surroundings. You'll discover bad people among your friends, good people among your enemies, and a multitude of unexplored colours to what we call life. Enjoy realities you probably didn't know they existed. They're all intense and fun. Give yourself to life!

CHAPTER 1

SUMMER BLUES AND COUNTRY MUSIC

Music for this chapter
The Cinematic Orchestra - Arrival of The Birds & Transformation
Zack Hemsey - The Way (Instrumental)
Thomas Newman - American Beauty

Who the fuck is Johnny K?

During late childhood years I started going to my parents' farm during the hot summers, times when I was looking for the sea like a mad man. Me helping my mother with the crops and the animals was paramount. During the scorching heat, all you could do was staying in the shade. I was never one to stay put, so in my search to find an occupation I decided to start growing rabbits. Building the cages was nothing, as I've always had innate carpentering skills. I bought a beautiful doe, then borrowed a buck for good genes. In a couple of years, by the age of 12, I already had about 50 pieces of fine rabbits, which I was taking outside on the plain fields to graze freely. *"Weren't they running away?!"*, you're probably asking yourself. The answer is no. They were all grazing inside the *zone*, and actually fighting me when slapping their *loins*. Playful little fellas they were, and when I was trying to scare them away, to see what happens, they were actually going back to their cages, while throwing their hind legs up into the air, jumping and prancing, enjoying their temporary liberty. Give freedom to caged animals, and they'll surprise you with their definition of safe. I guess it's the same with humans. All the villagers that were passing by during the day were amazed at how a city boy was handling the rabbits, acting curious about why they didn't run away. We knew a couple of villagers that tried to let their rabbits loose. They had trouble with the animals splitting into all directions when they saw the cage door open. It then took ages to catch them. I guessed they didn't show them too much affection, hence their wild nature. I was living a fairytale, a beautiful episode of my childhood.

In the beginning, after I managed to breed my first batch of little rabbits, I chose one male that was standing out among the others, in order to use him for future inseminations. Living in the countryside you deal with the sexual of life almost every day, and from an early age, because you are closer to nature than anyone living outside that environment.

I named the male Johnny K.

He was a combination of white and grey, with a pattern that stood out. I also had to isolate him fast when reaching puberty, or he would have impregnated all the females in one day. That had been the first sign of him being perfect for the task. It seemed that, after I've chosen him to be the main specimen for breeding, he turned into an even bigger porn star. The countryside people have a belief that if you name an animal, it will take your character and energy. I was laughing, seeing Johnny K's behaviour, and it couldn't actually be true, as I was just a kid. I didn't really understand what that meant anyway. You know, when kids start laughing with the adults, but they never got the joke because they're too young? Everyone wanted to see him in action so, when I was taking him to a female for an entire day, everyone was spying on them. He seemed like the perfect choice for breeding, and his offsprings were works of art. With his help, I managed to actually grow a farm of rabbits in record time, although when I started I knew nothing about how to take care of them.

The moment I named him Johnny K we became best friends, and wherever I was going when they were all out on the fields, he was following me, knowing that if I was around he would be safe. As reward for being the best I was taking him to the ladies. When just spotting me going towards his cage, he was starting to run around, and by the time I was there he was circling the cage, running on the walls without even touching the floor. After opening the door he used to stop suddenly, following my hand with his eyes, waiting to grab him by the back of his neck. He looked so happy, and the moment he was out of the cage, his breathing was becoming a race - he knew I was prepping him to go on a date. The female was terrified by him at first, but by the end of the day she would groom his long ears, licking him all over his fur and sleeping really close to him. I don't know why but, as I'm writing this, it kind of sounds familiar...
Great story, end it already!

The Johnny K story ends something like this. One day, after about a year from his first lady, I went to his cage to take him to another one. While he was running inside the cage like crazy I spotted something pink bulging out from his fur, on both sides of his fluffy, jiggly tail. I was worried a bit. When I opened the cage door, he suddenly stopped as usual. I picked him up gently. He wasn't struggling. When I lifted his tail, I could see what the problem was. It wasn't anything wrong with him, but the sight shocked me. I didn't know that something like that could ever occur. It was actually a good but terrifying consequence of his *unorthodox regular activities*. He had developed pink testicles the size of AK 47 bullets. Honestly, I'm not joking! I've handled AK47 bullets. By any standards, this is not actually normal for male rabbits. Who knows what the cause might have been, he was otherwise a really healthy rabbit, eating only the best foods. If you could find the explanation for this, please share it with the world. Everyone in the family came to see him, as he was the funniest abnormality we've ever seen in the animal kingdom. We kept on laughing at the sight, while he was relaxing lazy, probably on his balls as pillows, just being himself, the eternal Johnny K.

He lived a really long life, for a rabbit. When I was 19-20 years old, I visited my sister in the countryside. By then he was definitely 8 years old. Upon moving there she continued to take care of the last rabbits. Johnny K was still there, and alone... During a close checkup, we determined that his *cohones* had receded to normal measurements. His love life had a massive downfall after I moved back to the city. That was the last time I've seen him, before joining the army.

People living in the countryside know that once you choose an animal to be yours it will take your character, and also it might give you clues about how you'll become later in life. I hope you're alright up there, Johnny K, you've lived a nice life. Good boy! By the way, you were right...

The horse whisperer

At the age of 17 my mother asked me to come to the farm for a very special mission. Their chores had become too big of a burden to be manageable without a horse. She wanted me to go with my father, and find a good horse that she could handle as well. I was trusted by her to chose right, more that she trusted her husband. In the *Dacian* (Romanian) countryside horses are still widely used for working the crops, especially in remote small villages. We knew that close by, on the island formed by the two courses of the Danube river, the largest mass of farmland on continental Europe, villagers still have pure blood horses, or at least combinations of good breeds. I found the task quite exciting. Walking for 20 km at 35°C with my silent father was not as fun.

We crossed the water on this ancient raft doing regular crossings, to a time forgotten land. The villages there are still so remote, that many don't have television sets. Finding a good horse was not easy business. I was overly confident though. My father had the money, but I was the one with the power of decision. It felt nice. Power... He wanted a calm and docile horse, I was aiming for one with strength and personality. You don't want to beg it to pull the weight in the middle of the cornfield. We started asking the farmers about people that were looking to sell a horse. As we progressed with seeing different specimens, from one family to another, we kept on receiving tips about other opportunities. I had a list of about two decent horses that could meet the criteria, but I wasn't convinced about any of them. We eventually ended up at this farm with a lot of trees, next to this horse that wasn't moving. "Psst! Hey, you, horse! Yo, dude, are you home? Want some hay?" He didn't react to anything. Only his bottom lip was alive, moving a bit from reflex. My father was actually thinking that we might've struck gold with that one. "I don't think so!" Back then I wasn't allowed to say *fuck*. It was already evening when we heard about this old man, wanting to get rid of his horse because he could not handle it anymore. It sounded interesting, and also against my mother's requirements. Despite my father thinking we shouldn't go, I wanted to see the horse. The man received us with open arms, and took us into his garden, where the horse was feasting on some cane. The moment I saw it, I got hooked. This foxy mare with golden hair had everything we were looking for. I was walking towards her without thinking, when the owner advised me to be careful because she was feisty with strangers. I could see her watching me, while pretending to eat. I measured her lead to make sure she cannot reach me, then I moved forward slowly. I didn't get too close, when she pulled her ears back and charged straight at me. As the lead stopped her, she turned her back towards me, getting ready to hit with the hind legs. I didn't take that into consideration when judging her reach. My pupils got dilated at the sight, and I tripped during my quick pullback. I could also hear her shouting *neigh* at me, as I was trying to stroke her. Her whinnying said it all. "Easy, girl, easy...this is our horse!", I told my father straight away. Her owner was asking us if we thought we could handle her. I knew that was a problem, but I didn't care. Something was telling me she was perfect for the job. My father wanted to see more horses. I didn't want to hear it. "We'll buy this one!" She had fire in her eyes, and the way she was defending herself was beautiful. Despite being tamed, her spirit was still free. I loved it! The way she charged at us made my heart start pumping at a high rate. Because we disturbed her, she didn't care about eating anymore. We could see her just wanting to break free to get us. I had no chance of petting her. We paid for her, shook hands, then we left. My father would come back with another villager's carriage, to tie her behind it and take her to our farm. There was no way we could've handled her with just a rope, for such a big distance and over a wide river. Plus, her owner warned us that she was afraid of water.

Bummer! After deciding the transaction, I remembered this beautiful story from a vinyl of my childhood years.

There was this prince that got word from a witch, of a world of eternal youth and life without ending. He couldn't stop thinking about it. He had to find it! For that task he needed a good horse, which he should pick using a plate of live coals, as dictated by the witch. As a royal he had loads of horses, but the one that would dare to take a bite at the fiery embers was the right horse. He wasn't happy when the most courageous horse was an old skinny stallion. From this point onwards the story starts having no meaning for what I'm trying to say. The whole experience of finding a good horse had been somewhat similar with the story. Choose a horse that's ready to take a chance at you, at life. I know that if you're a woman reading this you won't like it, but as a man, you have to choose a woman that bites, that stimulates you to become better and sharper, not one that says *yes* straight away. Same as choosing a good horse. It might be similar for women too although, no matter how this world is telling you think, men and women are different. That is the beauty of it. A good movie to understand what I mean by this is *Legends of the Fall.*

Soon she would eat sweets from the palm of my hand. Everyone was impressed with her, and our best hay was hers to enjoy. The big surprise came when we put her to work. She couldn't stand being touched with any whip. Our voice was enough for her to know what to do. "C'mon girl!" And she'd start pulling any weight with minimum of effort. She had a tall and proud attitude that attracted the attention of most villagers. You can spot the good genes of a horse just by looking at it. Her youth was probably amplifying the beauty too. Every time I was going back to the farm she'd recognise me, and start whinnying and snorting to give her something.

She never lost her way of testing you, to see if you're paying attention, by charging at you with the ears pulled back. Unlike the first time, she'd not hurt me. She never liked it when I was leaving, giving me long looks. Maybe she was thinking, *"bring back some chocolates! I will eat your fingers if you don't..."*.

Her most outstanding trait though was the way she was approaching hills. Even if there was a tonne of weight behind her, corn, grains, hay, you name it, she would first assess the incline of the slope, then charge at the hill with all her strength. We later found out that she was only trying to make her job easy. When it first happened we didn't know what was going on. No one could hold her back. We thought she was trying to kill us, but she would not stray from the main road. Trying to restrain her with the reins was pointless. When the villagers were seeing our horse before a hill, they would stop to watch her go. Once on the other side of the hill she was behaving normal, like nothing happened. She hated going uphill at a normal pace, with huge weight behind her or without. And it made sense. Following her rapid assessment, she'd start galloping from afar, just enough to get her through to the other side, with the least amount of resources. Short term pressure is better than long term burden. In no time, many villagers started promising any amount of money to my parents just to have her. It was tempting, but especially my mother, who initially wanted a manageable horse, didn't even want to hear about selling her. She was part of our family. The amount of work she was doing for the farm was immense. When my parents split, she was one of our most adored animals that suffered a great deal. The moment my mother left the farm, the horse looked at her sad, whinnying and snorting. She kinda knew that my mother would never return to feed, talk to her and stroke her. Whenever we remember our animals, tears are involuntarily being shed. You've been a beautiful, hard working girl! Everyone is missing you big time... Happy *neigh*!!!

A tomato apocalypse

People living in the city think their world is real, and countryside folk believe that it's their world that's better. If you've lived only in the city, it's highly unlikely that your one is the real thing. Humans come from nature, not artificial. There is a level of indoctrination and self-education in both groups, but only one is right. I'm not saying that artificial is bad, because it promotes creativity, but irresponsible artificial is deadly. When in the city, I was always busy with going shopping, looking for a summer job, meeting with friends, avoiding traffic, watching tv, drinking poor quality liquors, eating junk food, breathing pollution, etc.. At the farm, I could hear my pulse for once, I could hear the lamb breathing, the birds chirping, the dogs barking at wild animals, while my brain was switching to meditation mode. I was expanding in a corruption free environment, while enriching a relationship with nature that needed no effort or sacrifice. We were one. This is why socialism and capitalism alike want to put people in cities. In a city you're forever trapped and constantly busy, on an exponential slope. Why are drugs so predominant in urban settings?! City life can be amazing, but depending on it is dangerous.

Have you ever tasted a natural tomato? No, not the orange vegetable you can find in the supermarket. I'm talking about the intense red one that grew in a garden, in clean fertile soil, without any interference from chemicals or pesticides. A tomato coming from a real seed, developed in the previous year's crop, in an outstanding ripened tomato, left to age enough to capture the highest potency of the expression of the tomato genes. The connection between natural plants and humans is greater than you might think. We've all been brought up together by a subliminal interdependence, mastered during billions of years. When you modify a seed in the lab, or grow it artificially or forced, the connection between it and who it should feed is interrupted at a quantum level, the one that actually dictates the finite from chaos. This is why the energy (aura) of a natural tomato is radiating, compared to a modified or artificially grown one (by the way, before acting all crazy, this can be proven scientifically). A biologist promoting GMOs is another modern terrorist, using updated tools and weapons he/she should not have access to, in the context of that mentality. The increase in cancers is outstanding proof that all these scientists have lost the plot. GMOs should not be used in feeding the planet, same as plastic should not be used to bottle water. No matter the subject I'm approaching, somehow I end up in the same place: someone at the other end is forcing on us a lifestyle that we should all avoid.

A natural tomato smells divine. You can determine its acidity just by inhaling the oils on the surface of its red skin. When you pick it, it feels a bit firmer that a woman's breast. If it's properly ripened, you'd have no problem in crushing it in the palm of your hand. With a little bit of salt it would taste divine. Nature intended to keep you healthy, remember that. Why would it miss a gene?! It's also for other animals and bugs, if no humans are around to pick it.

I will remember the summer of 1998 my entire life. My mother received a plot of land close to the forest on the Danube river, a few miles away from the village. The soil there was considered the most fertile in the entire area. We decided to plant only tomatoes. All villagers were using their own seeds from the previous year's crop. It's been like that for thousands of years. Now, many are using seeds brought from the city. A lot of types of tomatoes have been lost because of these interferences from companies selling seeds, and wooing villagers with better resistance to pests and bad weather, mainly *acid rain*. That year was the year of the tomato for our family. When they started ripening, we could barely cope with the level of production. Each week we would harvest over half a tonne of divine tomatoes. The pleasure of picking them one by one was intense. You could compare it with how you feel when collecting eggs from the barn. Back then we had this little but strong donkey, that could carry any weight you'd put behind him. Powerful little animals. Considering their strength and size, I'd say they might be stronger than horses. Should I tell you about their stubbornness? Uphill we had to help him though, but he'd never stop or complain about anything. With a mountain of fresh red tomatoes behind him, he was cruising with the carriage towards the farm. On the way there, we would start fights with the softest vegetables, enjoying a childhood most people would envy. In the heat of the summer we were celebrating a successful crop, the apogee of every year at the farm. The mountain of tomatoes was growing fast, under this sour cherry tree. My mother started making tomato paste and juice, to avoid losing them. They were still too many, and considering the rate at which they were ripening, we were getting overwhelmed. The villagers coming to visit us were shocked at the level of production. Some that had lived their entire life in the countryside, were telling us that they've never seen such a big tomato pile. Tomato salad with thinly chopped shallots, cucumbers, spring onions and fresh cheese was a daily caprice. Even so, it wasn't something you could have enough of. Contrary to the idea promoted in big cities, that natural crops are not tasty, our tomatoes were absolutely scrumptious. I've lived in big cities most of my life, I know both worlds, so trust me when I say this: natural taste is the most intense. It's impossible to get it from vegetables grown in fertilised cotton balls, or fibreglass, or whatever they're using in artificial greenhouses, nor will it be as nutritious. You're being lied to. I've done natural farming for more that a decade, following methods used during millennia. Before the interventions from big cities, the people from my parents' village didn't know what cancer was.

We started taking part of our best tomatoes to the farmers market. Just e few villagers bought into our products, despite being the best there. Most of them have heard about the impressive size of our crop. They were just looking at our counter, and buying from merchants with products of lower quality, or from questionable sources. Even the gypsies, reselling someone else's merchandise, were making more money than us. The market was once a week, so we had to lose the product fast. It didn't happen, despite selling it with the same price as the others. They all wanted a cheaper price, but in a market you cannot *break* the price. You risk having conflicts with the other sellers. We tried pushing for a higher quantity discount, but it still didn't work. My mother knew everyone in the village, and concluded that they were envious of our products, of us city folk having such an amazing crop. We took the tomatoes to our city, where my mother made good money. In the same time, I had a stand in my borough, but sold almost nothing. We soon found out what the secret to selling was: do not try to sell to people that know you! Unconsciously or not, they don't want you to succeed. This is why we made no money in the village and in our borough, whilst my mother broke the record in the city's vegetable market. Soon we developed a problem with selling, as we had to deal with the crops. After making some money in the city, we gave up. It would've been way easier and financially viable to be able to sell in the village. People's attitudes were upsetting, but we didn't despair, and ramped up the production of tomato sauces. We also started to pick the unripened ones to marinate them. Have you ever had pickled green tomatoes? They're zesty, and so delicious with steak or sausages, that your taste buds will faint. That year we filled the cellar with hundreds of bottles and jars containing tomato byproducts. It was enough for three winters. We've abused the lycopene intake for a couple of years. You cannot overdose on health, can you?

CHAPTER 2

LONDON TO IBIZA

Music for this chapter
Fluke - Zion
Maceo Plex - Learning to Fly
Sasha - Xpander
The Shapeshifters - Lola's Theme

I bought my first car in London in December 2016. After finding an online ad about this 2000 Polo, that looked quite good for the price, I met with the owner, this 19 years old, who was trying to convince me that his vehicle was a Lamborghini. I knew the car was ok, right after driving it for 50 metres. I'm good at picking cars and women. My habit is to hold on to cars for longer though. Maybe I'm not as good as I think at picking women. I just needed a means of commuting to, and from work, and to have flexibility. No matter where you live, being able to travel unrestricted is a necessary luxury. Back then I was working on the production line for Kodak, the same company that is now presented as a negative example in Management schools around the world. I was living in Wembley at the time, and commuting to work with the awful Bakerloo line. It did smell and look like a loo. I never in a million years would have believed that London can be so dirty and beautiful at the same time. It took both to the rank of art. There are a few Underground lines in London with an *on the brink of something* feeling, and the line I was using was one of them. When you travel, intuition is telling you that anything can happen at any moment. I needed the car really bad. The Polo had been a good choice, as it behaved impeccable. After a few months of good friendship I started wondering if it can take us all the way to Ibiza. I never drove through Europe before, and the thought gave me butterflies in the stomach. Just imagine yourself, driving over 3,000 miles in temperatures exceeding 35°C, with no A/C, just to bathe for a second in the clear Balearic waters. *"Hell, yeah!"* Hop onto the hellish express to Heaven. "Can you take us there, girl?" The Polo didn't reply, so I took it as a *yes*. I asked two friends that were dumb enough to agree to such a perilous endeavour, and after they accepted, I stared planning everything. There's nothing wrong with planning the trip ahead, but soon I would find out how some options have to be kept open. The delays I took into consideration were marginal, and if something would've happened with our means of transportation, we could have lost a lot of money. I've always risked with a relaxed mind, and driven by intuition and belief. Consider the bigger risks, but don't overthink them. Also, don't take anyone prone to accidents with you in such an adventure. One of the friends was always on the negative side of thinking, and that was a bit worrying, the other was always relaxed, and agreeing to any stop or drink. That's the spirit! Just in case, we were three against one.

At the end of July 2017 we crossed the English Channel to Calais, and once on the French motorway we floored it. The Polo was behaving exceptional, despite carrying four hooligans, and a full boot. I was changing shifts with my brother every 150 miles. As we reached a toll point on the motorway I realised the unplanned. There was a way to avoid the tolls by taking the auxiliary roads, but the delay would've added another 12 hours to our journey. That was not an option. "Damn you, France!" We reached Paris before dark, and went to Mardin Çorba, one of the best soup restaurants in the French capital. It's located in Saint-Denis area, which is not such a great area of Paris. To be honest, most of that city is a dump anyway; only the ones living in the *high castle* are promoting it as marvellous. No offence, Paris, but don't worry, I love a lot of your areas too. You have to hit that soup location if you're in town. We filled our bellies with delicious tripe soup, and the next morning we started again towards Bordeaux. We knew that it is a great place to get drenched in good wine. Oh, how our expectations have been deceived. We had a few hours to burn, so we went to *La Maison du Vin*, in the centre of town. "*Bonjour! Je voudrai* to try *vous vin* tasting." I studied French for twelve years, therefore my use of it was flawless. Eventually we met half way, to get about five glasses of wine each. It was a mid-range tasting. We started sipping. "Hmmm! Do you think they've poured wine from the same bottle in all the glasses?" We just received them, without seeing the bottles the wine came from. When they brought them out, the early twenties sommelier just gave us the usual French blurb about each glass. *"Ok! Then where is the wine?"* Me and my brother have extensive experience in wine making, and we knew that that was not wine. It tasted awful. *"Guys, it's Bordeaux! Where is the goddamn wine?"* We knew from before that France has poor wine, and that experience confirmed it. We went there with hope in our hearts though. I wouldn't touch French wines, except a few Beaujolais, and a few Champagnes. After we departed, I could only hear a sad harmonica tune playing in my head. I washed down the bitterness of French sin with some Belgian beer. This one had sugar in it. "Who adds sugar to beer!!!" We switched to normal beer, to avoid getting diabetes. Our route took us for a night to one of our friends' aunt, who lives in La Roche Possay. Stop giggling! Those fields are idyllic. Nature at its best, and untamed manifestation of great French cheeses. We had all the reasons to get fat in pristine environment, and then we swam in a nearby river flanked by trees and French bushes. The latter are different than in other countries, they're more romantic. It was the authentic *Huckleberry Finn* experience, with dragonflies landing on my bald head. They loved it, something new and artificial in the middle of the river. Upon departure we filled our bottles with their magic healing water, for which the area is so famous, and then I bought some cosmetics for my British girlfriend. I knew she'd appreciate them more than I would.

Time was starting to press on our schedule. We began to feel tired, while the old Polo was mocking us. Our aim was to reach Grenoble. We spent a night there, and had discovered how boring that city is. The main information we got was that Schumacher used to ski there a lot. I'm guessing that he didn't do it on the city streets. At least our apartment was nice and comfortable. One of the guys wanted to see a stage from *Le Tour de France*, so we rushed towards the mountains. The disappointment was huge when we found out that the roads were closed to access by car, unless you lived in one of the hotels up the mountain. Typical *Jandarmerie* work, ruining people's day! That night we couldn't find accommodation, and we slept on the mountain.

There was nothing else left to do, than go to *Cime de la Bonette* summit, at 2860m. Could the Polo take it? Only one way to find out. One lad could not make it alive though. He was ill at those heights, so he stayed in the car, about a hundred metres down the summit. He was almost unconscious. At the top the views were out of this world. Not much to see, other than brown soil peaks. It was a desolate landscape, yet extremely beautiful. Touchdown! Descending from those heights, the brake discs started to burn. Easy tiger! We had to stop at different points to let them cool down. It worked. At the base of the mountain we were sticky, and needed a break. We found this rest area next to a clear river, at these coordinates: 44.5537460, 5.7666180. As soon as we stopped the car, we jumped in the cold mountain water. It felt divine and invigorating. We lingered there for a while, then with regret we continued on our way to Monaco. Having everything planned did not allow us to enjoy things more. By the time we got there everyone was irascible. We went to see the glamour after parking somewhere under the F1 circuit, next to a custom Lamborghini and a spacecraft. It all cost €0.90 for the whole night. Nice! No wonder the rich like living in Monaco, it's cheap. We took the rich air into our lungs, and the sparkle onto our retina, then we proceeded to finding an area where we could sleep. It was late at night when we barely found a parking spot, next to the sea. We camped on some loungers on the beach, then I fell asleep. My brother, also nicknamed *Gabriel de Grand Vitesse*, woke me up after about three hours. It was 3am and dark. "What the hell are we doing, man!" Our brains were twisted. It was my brother's turn to drive us to Cannes for the morning. I went back to sleep in the car.

I wake up at one point to see us stopped in the middle of the road, at a crossroads. My brother was arguing with this Arab looking guy, next to a Mercedes, in the night. Suddenly my instinct kicked in, got out of the car, and I was ready to jump on the guy. He was threatening to call the police, accusing my brother that he hit his car with the Polo. The Mercedes looked intact. "Get out of here, dude!" My brother was checking his car. "Did you touch him?" "No, I don't think so..." "Bro, his car has no scratch, fuck him!" "Ok, man, call le police!" "Lets go, get in the car, we're leaving."

The guy came to take a photo of the car and us. I took my phone out and did the same. "Yeah? What are you going to do with the photo?" "I will take it to police", he said. "Fuck off, *putain*!" My English and French were better than his. The other two buddies never moved from the Polo. We got in the car, and drove away. The guy had no chance, unless he would've taken a gun out. I was awake and attentive as a tiger. I could see the guy's elbow twisting the wrong way, and his knee bending sideways, while Liam Neeson, with his cinematic voice, was whispering what to do in my ear. Apparently my brother pressed the brake hard, and the guy had to swerve a bit, as he startled. My brother wasn't 100% sure about what happened. He couldn't tell if he'd actually caused an accident or not. He was driving, but connected to the *Matrix*. I asked him if he was alright to drive, and he approved. Whoever was driving was always saying, *"yes, I'm ok"*, anyway, no matter the level of tiredness. We were exhausted during the night. Getting out of Monaco had proven to be an adventure in itself. We drove for about half an hour, to end up in the same place, close to where the *accident* happened. We were like in a maze, and the online maps weren't helping us either. *"Maybe Cannes is a myth..."* The second time around we managed to get there. When we arrived we parked near a small park with palm trees, then crashed on the beach into a deep sleep. At dusk we jumped in the warm sea, together with some old ladies enjoying their second youth. They decided to skip their morning jello, to try and hit on us. They were getting too close... Cannes, you can do better that this. Also, there seems to be something wrong with your prices! We got dry, then left towards Barcelona. Driving during the night, with everyone else sleeping next to you, was a nightmare. I will never plan a trip like this again. Nights are for sex, party, or sleep. Preferably all three together. Luckily we reached Barcelona during the day, therefore we had a few hours to kill. We went on Barceloneta beach, where everyone goes, to find a very agitated sea. The waves were a menace, and breaking right on the beach. Two people were out swimming, and another was trying to surf, while the whole beach was watching them. I wanted to get in, but my survival instinct was telling me to stay put. I won! The thing with that type of sea is that it's easy to jump in, without thinking about how you'll get out. I swam for a while going three floors up and down, when the wave was forming, then I decided to get out. I was smiling at the guys on the beach, making it seem like I was enjoying the exit. I thought I was safe, when a massive wave rolled over me, and got me stuck to the beach. I was too slow, and now I had sand even in my ears. My back was hurting as well. When joining the group I was trying to make it look cool. What happened was the opposite. We had a whole night of driving ahead of us through the Spanish *mehico* all the way to Denia, for our ferry to Ibiza. When driving through Valencia I was trying to show the others the futuristic *Ciutat de les Arts i les Ciències*. They couldn't care less; I was talking to zombies. In the morning we *landed* in Denia. The Montgó was covered by clouds, while the ferries looking like spacecrafts from Star Wars were waiting in the dark. There was a cool peace in the air, in tune with our achievement. A photo on the Polo, a nap on the sand, and it was already time to board the Paradise Express.

"Hola, señores! Cómo estás?"

I was left alone with the car upon boarding, while the others had to go on the boat separately. Although I did not study Spanish for a single day in my life, I was doing great with the Coast Guard officers. My skill encountered a slight gap when

they started speaking fast, and in long phrases. It's been a while since my last Spanish holiday.
"Si…hablas Inglés?"
They suddenly showed bored. All I had to do is open the boot. I was praying they would not search our entire luggage, because it was a mess, and the car crammed. "Do you have weapons or drugs in the car?" I recognised this question, so I proudly answered, "no".
"Señor, no te preocupes, yo *fue* un agente de la guardia *costiera* de *Dacia* (Romania)."
"Bueno…"
The officer went inside the booth to counsel with his colleague, and tell him what I just confessed. I was scolding myself, *"what the deuce are you doing, you idiot? you don't say that to an officer at the border, hoping to get away from luggage search! Stupid! That would only attract more suspicion."* After working as a Coast Guard officer for some time, you feel like sharing this information in the most inappropriate situations. Some part of my brain probably got washed by the state programme. Nothing to be proud of there… The two officers had a swift and superficial look through our luggage, without unloading anything, then they wished me safe crossing.
"Gracias!"

Everything looked dodgy about the car and me, but they know that smugglers don't take drugs to the island like that. Everything is well organised and the *passage* is clear. So there is no need to hire Polos with UK number plates to carry it. I don't remember anything from the ferry, except our arrival in the port of Sant Antonio, the Brits' favourite destination. The whirling azure water around the propellors was the first sign of Paradise. A private catamaran was trying to beat us to the punch. Welcome to Ibiza, the land of eternal youth, crystal clear waters, and life without worries.

Our accommodation was in a *finca*, on the hilltops of Sant Miguel, an area where you can't even buy club tickets. The silence during the night was divine, and the crickets ravers. You wouldn't want to be anywhere else, at any moment in your life. It was a trip for relaxation, that did not get us any pussy. We didn't really plan to run after it, plus we weren't a compact pack that could collaborate successfully towards achieving this goal. One friend was afraid of deep water, and the other was not confident in his own abilities in deep water. Not the best gang to hit the beach with, nor the women. You feel like you're the only one having fun, like Stifler from *American Pie*. It was me and my brother really feeling it.

We went to Amnesia, one of the best clubs on the island, place where previously I've experienced a panic wave during an *espuma* party, on a sold out night. That was some scary stuff, having hundreds of people crashing on top of you. The two friends decided to split a pill, from a seller in the club. "Guys, come on, don't do it! You don't even know what it is…" "Chill out, man, it's all good." For about half an hour they were alright, until the pupils of one of them turned unequal. I'm not talking about the dilation or contraction of the iris, but about the whole pupil of the eye. One was bigger than the other. My brother searched online to see what that was, and it didn't sound good. After only half a pill! They took it well, although I don't really understand why someone would do that in a club, unless you don't like or understand the music, and don't care about your health or enjoying the company. That guy could've sold them cyanide, and get away with it. They could've got cocaine, which is really high quality there, unlike the shit 10%-20% one you can get in

London, if you're lucky. Also, why would you get synthetics in Paradise? It's like still searching for the truth, when you already found it. You get synthetics when you live a crap life, in a dumpster of a flat or house in Wembley, Dagenham or Enfield, to access different dimensions and better places, in order to bypass your condition, but not in Ibiza... Such a cliché! That place is the drug… Synthetics can also mess up with your brain so bad, that you might never be yourself again. If you want to see how bad a reaction can be, just visit the emergency department in Can Misses hospital. Give those doctors and nurses a break!

Time is so short there… By the time we finished a bottle of wine, way out into the sea, swam through a hidden cave, and enjoyed a secret gulf, lighted only by the stars, close to the beach that offers the best sunset in the world, we had to leave. See you soon *Julian Beach*!

Our way back was kind of a race, as we had to be on time for the ferry to Dover. The Spanish outbacks are utterly scary, when you have to get out of the car to pee during the night. It felt like we were in Mexico, hunted by the cartel. Maybe it was due to our sleep deprivation. One night it was my time to finish the 150 miles, after midnight, while everyone else was asleep. It was terrifying driving in that condition. As I reached the target, at about 4am, I parked in a petrol station's rest area, locked the doors, and went into one of the best sleep states I've ever experienced. I didn't move a muscle, till nine or ten in the morning. When I got out of the car, the stretch felt so good it almost gave me an orgasm, and I almost dislocated my shoulders. One lion roar later, and I was enjoying the hot coffee like a mad man. We felt sorry for the guys on the back seat. Upon reaching Calais we felt destroyed, barely talking anything. The whole trip was worth the compromise. Our car behaved impeccably, and I loved it.

During that time I was writing a travel blog, looking for ways to improve people's lives with my knowledge about the places I've been. It took a while, but during one of those moments before the deepest sleep occurs, the idea of an app came to me. I later released *Portocal*, an iOS app that can give you only the best locations from where you are, without the need to compromise. Many times we were, "guys, where should we go?" Then we'd search through all the options for about an hour, and probably land in the worst joint of a restaurant or pub. Good things come to you when you travel and relax.

Back in London, everyone we told about what we did thought we are mad to risk so much. That was probably true, but when did we stop being crazy. I could not wait to see my girlfriend, with her sexy British accent, after soaking under all that sun. When I scrapped the Polo, in 2019, I cried. It deserved a motor and a battery pack, with at least 500 miles range. I bought another car, which I was using for business, and had nowhere to keep the Polo. It didn't sell either, and it started creating issues when it found out that I was using another vehicle. It was *her* time. X193GBC, you will be missed. Thank you!

CHAPTER 3

THE VINEYARD

Music for this chapter
Paco de Lucia - Entre dos Aguas
Biel Ballester Trio - When I was a Boy
The Stool Pigeons - La Luna
Chet Baker - Almost Blue
Laufey - I wish You Love

I was born in a very old culture, a people that had dominated and shaped the European landscape for thousands of years. Even the Romans had admitted that they've returned to their roots, when they finally conquered half of the territory north of the Danube. We were always fighting with the Greeks, and thus borrowing from each other's customs. These are the lands where philosophy and religion were being taught in schools long before the Roman campaigns. Also, they are the realms of the fearless Thracians, tribes who've fought between each other, more than with the real enemies of the East and West. This trait can be spotted even today, between communities really close to each other. When emperor Trajan defeated Decebalus' army (around 60,000 Dacians and 40,000 from Germanic and Sarmatian tribes - impressive combat power considering that the Roman Empire could raise an army up to 200,000 soldiers), during a second campaign, and took over the southern part of Dacia, he also kidnapped the beautiful Dacian queen to be his wife. The story makes for one of the most beautiful love stories in ancient history. Ill and weakened, Decebalus committed suicide before being captured, as he could not live with double failure - to protect the kingdom and his wife. He was betrayed by Biciclis, one of his closest people, after being captured by the Romans. From what we know, his wife had lived a good life with her new Roman husband. Even today, foreigners keep on stealing superb Dacian women. You can see them lounging in the sun of Dubai, or sipping dirty martinis in Casino de Paris, in Monaco. When asked where they're from, they'd probably reply, *"from Transylvania"*. No *Dacian* actually likes the current name of the country.

Legend goes that this priest considered a god, Deceneu, came with ideas of reducing the vineyards, as their number was so high, it was attracting foreign aggressors. This is one of the reasons why, at one point, he influenced the king to burn a lot of vineyards. Even the Romans' have done it. A second reason was because the kingdom would always struggle to raise an army, as everyone was drunk and disobedient. This happened in the Middle Ages too, more than a millennia after. I've always believed that love, wine and treason, were invented in Dacia, a kingdom that stretched far and wide, covering the whole of Eastern Europe we know today. It has always been an area with some of the most fertile soils in the world, and for this reason, the kingdom had always been attacked from the East by migratory people, seen by these as the *promised land*, and by the Romans, considered the continent's pot of gold. Later on, the whole of Europe became targeted by the East. So, Dacia always had quality grapes, and as you might already know, they did not have the knowledge to engineer the vine, as it happens today all around the world. The Dacian vineyards were engineered by nature, and the people, stubborn enough to resist modern standards that make no sense. I like this type of stubbornness.

The Greeks called the Dacians *barbarians*. The word didn't have the meaning of today. It was due to them not speaking Greek language, and drinking *clean* wine, instead of diluting it with water, according to Platon's writings.

Dacia or old Thrace, was also considered the birthplace of Dionysus, the god of wine, due to the vast fields of vine. If you have the chance, speak with a Dacian, and see how they talk about wine.

In today's globalisation context, the European Union, for example, are trying to get rid of the types of vine that have made people's lives an exquisite paradise for thousands of years. This is the same Union that have strict standards against the US' chlorinated chicken, but which allowed its import by an EU country like *Dacia* (Romania), to sell it in French and German chain supermarkets. They also want to terminate the vineyards they consider non-productive, or if they are not *noble*, whatever that means. During my parents' appraisal of the farm with vineyard, in a court of law, the judge decided that the vineyard was old, non-productive, and of low quality vine. Really?! And this is how the wine adventure begins.

What is left of this once great kingdom is nowadays called *Romania*, a name that needs to be wiped out from the history books. It is like this because some uneducated and biased Italian historians concluded, sometime during the 19th century, that we come from Rome. Then, who did the Romans conquer?! It's the same as calling England *Romania 2*, just because the country had been conquered by the Romans. Although this wouldn't be far fetched. How many British people know, that the first farmers landed on their island from Eastern Europe, around 10,000BC? Back then there were only Thracian tribes, scattered around a vast area, outnumbering any other tribes living in Europe. They're not learning that in school, it would be outrageous... But that doesn't change real history. They even have a borough called *Dacorum* (belonging to Dacians), on the outskirts of London. Maybe England should be called *Dacia Too*. This time it would be based on real history.

When I was six my mother inherited the farm from her parents, and I moved there with her, for a while. Everything around was as natural and organic as you can get. All the seeds were as nature created them, and the crops tasted divine.

I can tell you, there is no tomato or pepper in London that tastes like what we were producing, may it be organic or not. Only once I could find the same tomatoes, in a Polish grocery shop. Because I was coming from the city, I loved nature in a more personal way, compared to someone that was raised only there. All the people should learn to love, both the city and the countryside. In the city you can live the human greatness, whereas in the countryside, you can relate with your origins. I learned how to grow things, and most times, my mini vegetable garden was ripe before my mother's.

Every April, before the buds started sprouting, we would prune the trees and the vineyard. I was listening to my mother explaining how you should do it, to help the vine grow healthy, to produce just the right amount of grape, depending on the type of vine. After the pruning the vine would start to *cry*, producing drops of water on the cuts. It is said that that water is good for the skin, and spells. It takes the vine approximately five years to reach maturity. Different types of vine need different soil conditions, but most grow perfectly in soil that does not keep the water for too long. We call it *yellow soil*. When this is not quite possible, if the vine is growing on an inclined plane, it can make all the difference. It's all about keeping the vineyard away from too much water, and *fat* soils. Under no circumstance should you use fertiliser or pesticides; you'd ruin years of work. The best wine is obtained out of a combination of different grapes. Remember this! Here, I'm talking about red wine that any person would like, from grapes engineered by nature during millions of years. We never produced white wine; these grapes prefer hills to flat terrain. I use to say that white wine is for getting sick, and red is for getting hard, if you know what I mean... And white wine is the easiest to fake. There are also grape types that have a really powerful aroma, which you don't mix with other grapes, if using them for the usual wine, as they would ruin the whole batch. You have to separate them. Really flavoursome grape types will take you to taste paradise, but they have to be squashed separately. Because of the specificity of the grape, the quantity of wine is not great, but it will impress your occasional guests, and also compliment specific dishes, more than normal red wine.

Most farmers in *Dacia* (Romania) also own vineyards. The positioning of the country on the Earth's map makes it perfect for any type of vine. It's a great pride to have thousands of square metres of vine in your backyard, composed of a carefully calculated vine combination, mostly variations of non-hybrid *vitis vinifera*, which appeared in Europe between 10,000BC-7,000BC, maybe way earlier than that, as no one can tell exactly. In our village there were some families that never had good wine, and everyone knew. People could tell just by looking briefly over the fence. When this art is inherited from many generations before you, the skill becomes instinct. All my grandparents liked booze more than life itself, so they made sure to plant their vines with outmost attention to detail and proportions. Their wine was exquisite almost every year. I say almost, because when it rained too much during the summer, or during harvest, they knew the crop would be lost, or at least compromised. The wine would taste awful, and have a short shelf life. Working the whole year, just to lose tonnes of spoiled must due to bad weather is devastating. Some people didn't know how to combine the grapes, and for this reason, they used to buy wine from the families that had really good one, for weddings and other family events. When visiting farmers with poor wine, we felt like bringing our own with us. That would have been inappropriate and rude, so we had to endure the blasphemy that their wine represented. If I despise something more than anything else in this world, it is bad wine and people that accept bad wine, just because they grew up with it. If you grow up with war, you don't like it just because of that, do you? You build taste in time, when you start discovering the real things. For example, when Americans visit Italy, a country with amazing food and experts in coffee, they act like they've seen Jesus when spotting a *McDougal's* place with poisoned burger menus, or a *Starboobs* watered down coffee joint. If these are your best finds in Italy, just because they complimented your formation years, you don't deserve Italy!

If you have a bottle of wine handy, look at the label and read the ingredients. You can't, can you? It's because wine is one of those products exempt from displaying the ingredients. Wine companies don't want you to know that you're drinking poison, with some grapes in it. Depending on the country, wine laws are different. Maybe a country doesn't have one. A wine law is setting the standards for wine production, to avoid having wines on the market with zero grape content. So legally, the government is allowing you to fake wine. Why would you need a wine law in the first place, if you are on top of things. Even so, I still believe that many wines on the market have never touched real grapes. During communism, people would get the death sentence for faking alcoholic drinks but now, we have wine laws to cover the big scammer wine companies. Corruption and coverup grow directly proportional with regulations. In 2015, the UK's then prime minister, David Cameron, passed a wine law, making sure that wines sold in the kingdom are at least 40% grape. What the rest is, I dread to think... What about before increasing the percentage? Producers add water, sugar, acids, additives, animal products for clearness, and sulphites, among the most known to people. Have you noticed how there is no bad year for your favourite wine brand? Ever wondered, *"how come the wine tastes the same every year"*? All this is due to lab engineering. You are enjoying wine that has been mastered, to satisfy a constantly increasing market. At the end they add sulphites to preserve it. You must develop cancer... They don't know that you can preserve wine using other natural methods, like cinnamon extract.

A while back, a research institute in *Dacia* (Romania) managed to synthesise cinnamon, to create a natural, healthy alternative to sulphites, but global wine companies didn't want to hear about it. No one bought into the new discovery. Maybe they do want you to drink poison. Why would they do it otherwise?

A bottle of natural 100% grape wine will cost you way more than what you pay for yours, but most of it is either inaccessible to you, or in private cellars, covered in dust. To make it clear, you have to be a really bad person to add water and sugar to wine. It should be made from 100% grape, and nothing else. Wine laboratories are doing titrations just to make wine taste the same, year after year after year. On that, you as a customer, are also losing on the flavours of different years. Keep this information with you, for as long as you live. Please, stop buying wines that are less than this, and do not support the extermination of natural vine, that is considered non-productive by the big wine companies and unions. Nothing farther from the truth. They control the governments, and are constantly pushing legislation to tackle the quality of private vineyards. Big companies don't like private producers because they're not buying from them. If you are a private vineyard owner, or you want to become one, go and explore the *Dacian* (Romanian) countryside, ask people with the best wines to give you their vine combination, and ask them for stalks. You will thank me for this advice because you'll be unique, and a wine boss in your community. In France, for example, you can see noble vineyards everywhere. I don't think they have one single vineyard made of vine types I grew up with. This is why they have such bad wines, including small owners. The big wine producers in *Dacia* (Romania), even managed to make better wines using French grapes. You go compare your favourite Pinot Noir with a Pinot Noir produced in *Dacia* (Romania), and see the difference. I can bet that 99% of you reading this book, have never heard about how good *Dacian* (Romanian) wines are. They're both far from being the real thing and 100% natural wines, but you'll understand the Dacian skill, when it comes to making wines.

I would like to see the ingredients of wine written on the bottles, but considering the sheer size of the wine demand worldwide, and the powerful people behind the industry, I doubt that this will ever become a reality. I have done the calculations of all the registered vineyards in the world, and of the worldwide wine consumption, and came to the conclusion that we would probably need ten times the current grape production, to satisfy the demand with 100% grape content, also taking into account the bad years for random areas. Just think how many litres of red China is drinking, of course accompanied by a can of cola... I heard red has become really popular there in recent decades. Wouldn't it be nice if nature offered only perfect conditions, and no disasters? You also have to consider, that many rich people keep a lot of the 100% grape wines for themselves. The known wine markets behave as if nature brings only good years for grapes. Considering the fact that disasters are part of our lives, we need to ask ourselves, where is all this wine we are drinking coming from. It's like a fountain without ever getting dry. You can find your favourite wine anywhere you'd go on this planet, in inexhaustible amounts. *"Yes, we do have Shiraz 2018! That was a really good year..."* Of course it was a great year, same as all the years before that!

During my London to Ibiza trip, in 2017, we stopped at this amazing looking vineyard in the French Alps. They had a shop open, where we bought a few bottles of red. The wine was puke, a total waste of money and work. Those people have never tasted real wine. What is the point of being a developed country, if you don't know the real thing, as nature intended? Plus, countries like France, US, Spain and New Zealand, etc., have educated generations to like bad wines. If you would have tasted the real one, you would have the same attitude towards these wines on the market. With every generation, we lose more and more important things that actually make us humans, while big organisations are doing everything in their power to destroy the natural, with obvious intention. We want a lot, and no quality.

The European Union will offer financial support to vineyard owners, only if the vine is recognised by them. All vines erroneously considered wild and non productive have to be destroyed. Once these types will disappear, they will take away true wine with them, forever. Then why are the

British royals stocking up wine from *Dacia* (Romania)!? Oh, you didn't know that, did you? Because of difficulties, people will run to get the free incentives from the Union, and in return, they will replace the good with the bad. True delicious wine will be forever extinct. Nature is powerful enough to hold on to its things for a while, but our abilities to destroy are no match, even for such an amazing *organism*. We are too advanced in the wrong context, for our own good. It would take hundreds of thousands of years to get the missing vines back.

The preparations for harvest were starting about a week before, with the cleaning of the oak barrels. That was a strenuous work, and weirdly enough, my mother dealt with it. You rarely see strong women like her. In most villages, the people set dates for grape harvest, in order to be able to help each other. This day we harvest mine, tomorrow we do yours. When producing wine, logic and chemistry become one science. You never harvest during two different days, and then mix the must together. That will spoil everything. September in *Dacia* (Romania) is still warm enough to start the fermentation in a matter of hours. In good years, the last rain fell at least one or two weeks before harvest. During all this time the excess water had to drain from the soil and grapes, to let the yeast rebuild on the skin of the grapes.

During a surfing trip in Portugal, in 2018, I visited this amazing vineyard, that used to belong to the royal family. In a few of their videos the grapes were trodden by men with hairy legs. Even so, they are allowed to sell their wines globally. Private vineyard owners in *Dacia* (Romania) have been sidelined for poor manufacturing practices, as well as for not knowing how to make wine. It's the same as telling the bee, that it does not know how to make honey. Besides the fact that the sommelier in Portugal did not know that

Dacia (Romania) is one of the best wine producers, I realised a big mistake that commercial *noble* wine producers are making, on top of cultivating the wrong, too engineered, single type grapes. Their vines are hanging on wires, with the grapes out in the open sun. This is a big mistake, because it's forcing them to have harvests during mid or late August! I have never heard of someone in our village to harvest in August, despite the hot summer temperatures. All villagers would think that you're crazy if you do that. The catch is this: grapes hit by direct sunlight for extended periods of time get ripened forcibly.

In *Dacia* (Romania), people have this amazing dish made of stuffed vine leaves with rice and meat, a culinary treat inherited from the Ottomans that kept on attacking us. Because they are Muslims, *Dacians* (Romanians) decided to add pork to the dish, to spite them, and so, they've created an addictive recipe. Vine leaves come from the vineyard, which are carefully chosen to be young leaves, but the ones that do not leave grapes out into the scorching sun. There would be grave arguments if one family member would go over the top, and leave the vine bald. The sun *cooks* the grapes early! I had a revelation in Portugal, a country with some really good wines, that put France at the bottom of my list. They are still commercial wines though, but probably with a higher grape content, and better engineering. The early ripeness of the grape causes the need to add sugar, water and everything nasty to the wine you are drinking. The acidity is higher too. When the grape gets ripe too early, due to the sun's rays, it does not have the right taste, nor the natural maturity of its chemical composition. It is more sour than sweet, with an underdeveloped palate, like a kid on steroids trying to hit on women, or having a fight with an adult. It's big and plump, but without brains, nor strength. A true wine expert can tell if you'll have good wine, only by tasting the grape. This forced ripeness would cause the brewers to intervene abruptly, to calculate the sugar and additives requirement, to take the alcohol to acceptable levels, control the acidity and clarity. Everything is taken care of with outmost attention, so you can enjoy an amazing hybrid red wine with your tender beef steak. Having a wagyu ribeye with engineered wine, loaded with water, additives, sugar and sulphites, is a great sin.

Here is another drink with sulphites, despite you ingesting them from many other sources. If you think that sulphites are not harmful, even in high doses, just look at the miners in sulphur mines. You rarely see them going past 40 years old, and they probably don't eat sulphur. Of course there is no comparison between you and them, but considering the quantities of bad wine you are consuming, I'd say you're getting pretty close. When I was 17, my sister used to work as an armed guard for a big commercial wine producer in my city. One day she brought home a bottle of white wine. I had a glass of the disgusting liquid, then went to sleep. I woke up with an amazing head ache, and an altered sense of balance. My centre of gravity seemed displaced, and I could not concentrate properly. My brother felt the same. The wine was the only reason for my state, despite being at an age when masturbation was religion. Sulphites are causing havoc in your body. I strongly believe this, without having any crooked scientist telling me different. Most times, our bodies know when the science is good or bad. They're too perfect to be wrong most of the times. Humans are the only animals that would eat and drink almost anything, even if the natural protection of the body says no.

Our vineyard was planted in 1954 by my mother's father. By any standards, it was a young vine, and knowing how to maintain it can keep it in shape for more than a century, easily, without needing replacement. The whole area with vine measured about 1,500 sqm, which translates into roughly 0.37 acres, or 16,145sq ft. In good years we could easily get 2,000 litres of must. In European standards, this is better than most noble vineyards. And we have never added sugar, acid or other additives to our wine. No one had the right to say that our vineyard was old and non-productive, when in 2008 it was producing this much wine, 54 years after it's been planted.

I just realised the weird numerical coincidence. The vine was planted in 1954, and in 2008 we harvested it for the last time, exactly after 54 years, before my parents' divorce.

This whole surface needed about 10-11 hard-working people to harvest by sundown. In good years, the more the people, the sooner we'd finish, in order to deal with the press. This device is what squeezes the must from the grapes, until the remains would get almost dry. You'd basically spin around the press full with dripping grapes, pulling a lever that screwed down on the threaded shaft, that was putting immense pressure on wooden logs, pushing down the load with minimum effort. The shaft was welded into the middle of a wide pan-like shaped steel collection tray with legs, and an inclined opening, to direct the must straight into the bucket. The shaft was surrounded by a bracketed round wooden guard, that had the purpose to hold the pulp inside when applying the pressure, leaving only the must to flow freely through the cracks. Beyond this point it was only chemistry. Nature knows exactly what to do with the magic liquid. During the harvest you'd bring the grapes to the *crusher*, but not before removing the green stems and bad, rotten grapes. The stems on which the grapes grow can ruin the wine, by releasing bitterness into the must during the pressing stage; they contain only bitter sap.

There are a handful of main reasons why you might get bad wines: poor combination of types of grapes or too much of a certain type in the combination; using one type of grape; fat soil - using fertilisers can mess up the vine for years to come; you can also have fat soil naturally - in this instance your vine has been planted in the wrong place; if it rains a lot when the grapes are almost ripe and close to/during harvest; spraying the vineyard with pesticides; picking the grapes before the morning dew dries out; when harvesting in two different days or more, and you're mixing the must to form one batch. An extra reason can be if you leave the crushed grapes to macerate/start fermenting before pressing the must out - this can increase the levels of methanol in the wine with up to 20%.

Our vineyard was composed of old types of vine, belonging to popular *Vitis Vinifera*, varieties like *tiras*, *jijileancă*, *ageleancă*, the hybrid *zaibăr* (created from European vines combined with lower quality American types to resist pests), and a few of *cudric* (white grapes with an addictive taste; they ended up being eaten). Some also have a type of vine called 1001. The latter is considered the most unproductive, but it definitely contributes to amazing wine. Basically most grape types come from Vitis Vinifera, but they've been engineered to resist harsh conditions, and to satisfy a constantly increasing market, with poor knowledge about wine and taste. The higher the demand and production, the lower the quality. The European Commission is offering incentives only if you kill your old vine types or hybrid, and plant their noble types. They want this world to have only about 10-20 types of wines, instead of thousands. But not the Beaujolais. You didn't know that this is a hybrid, did you?

The EU are saying that *Dacian* (Romanian) hybrids are producing wines high in methanol, which is an error in judgement and science; methanol depends on how grapes ferment. Considering that the Beaujolais is a French type, it mysteriously slipped past the European regulations, straight into the shops worldwide. *Dacia* (Romania) has been a paragon in wine making for thousands of years, but as time passed, the French went all queer, and created noble grapes for the gentile of the recent human timeline. France is one of the founding countries of the European Union, and this is a reason why they push for the destruction of the natural, and of the wrongly presumed unproductive. You have to buy only their wines. This is why you see French wines everywhere. You have to understand that the wines you are buying can be less than 50% grape content, or even zero percent. The current wine production is killing people. Red wines are supposed to help you live longer and healthier. They also don't want hybrid vines, because it is believed that these grapes produce a higher quantity of methanol, which is wrong; it's all about how the fermentation occurs. Methanol is toxic for humans in high concentrations. You get high methanol concentration if you ferment the must with the pulp and the skin. If you squeeze the must straight away after the crushing (before the fermentation begins), the levels of methanol will be insignificant at the end of fermentation. To me there is nothing more noble than natural vine. Noble is such a relative term, and in the case of wine, it does not mean quality, but maybe engineering and specificity, which for a true connoisseur is irrelevant.

To understand the level of grape engineering (grafting, genetic modifications, crossing different species of vine - hybrids) the big wine companies have achieved, I have to bring into discussion the *table grapes*. These are not used for wine, because they do not contain a whole lot of liquid, but more pulp. If they are grown and crossed naturally, they can be really delicious. One of my step grandfathers started being a guard for vineyards like this, when he reached pension age. At the end of his shift he was bringing loads of grapes home. One bunch was so big, that it could weigh up to five kilograms. They were quite pumped up grapes. We loved them, and it was difficult to stop from eating. If you were going away after that, and there was no toilet around, you would have been in big trouble. Most probably, before reaching the market, they were treated with sulphur, to slow down decay. We are lucky to have had the opportunity to enjoy them, before being spoiled for the shelves.

Nothing compares with the end of grape harvest day. A divine silence would come upon the village, disturbed only by the singing of the dripping wine press. Everyone would then sit down, and have an amazing dinner, washed down with natural fruit *ţuică* (traditional strong spirit) and fresh must. *"Long live our hosts and the owners of this vineyard, and may their wine be amazing and clear!"*

Everyone's hands and all the dishes were purple. When finished, the oak barrels used for fermentation were 80%-85% full, to allow the wine to swell. A few villagers were *burning* their barrels with sulphur, but everyone knew that due to that, their wine was not healthy. It gave you massive head aches. Plus, they were probably using too much sulphur for the quantity of wine. No one was doing any titration to calculate the proportions exactly. We called that *danger* wine, and when visiting, we didn't use to drink much.

The fermentation usually takes up to 40 days, give or take one or two weeks. This duration is followed like a religion. No oxygen had to be caught inside, and towards the end of the fermentation we'd use airlocks with the barrels full. When no carbon dioxide would get out anymore, the barrels would get completely sealed for preservation. In time, the wine would form a skin on the surface, to protect itself from turning into vinegar when in contact with oxygen. If the wine is sealed properly, there are almost zero chances of that happening. Then, we'd only get wine out through the tap. If you wanted to keep a barrel for more than a year, you would not fit a tap to it. Whoever was trying to take the cap off the barrel, and pull wine out the wrong way, they would get a massive scolding. *"Why did you break the skin of the wine!!!"* That was a definite no-no. This is how you know if wine makers know what they're doing. If they take you to a barrel, open the cap, dip the pipette in the wine, and pour some in your glass, you know that it is not 100% wine. A true wine maker would never do that. When I was a kid I used to grab my own mini cup, and dip it in the bucket of red, more often than my parents would have allowed me. It was extremely delicious, and it felt healthy.

After 20 years of experience with wine tasting and making, I realised that it all comes down to our connection with nature. Ok, maybe I was doing a bit more than tasting... Wine is sacred, and it should be drank like sinners do before receiving their punishment. Faking it is a grave sin!

The case I'm trying to make for wine is this: the vines not considered productive or noble have to be protected by any means. They're the rainbow of wines. Our vineyard was more productive, and easier to maintain than a Pinot Noir. If you plan to start your own vineyard, do not fall prey to crooked policies backed by the wine cartels. Visit *Dacia* (Romania) and surrounding countries with similar types of vine, educate yourself, read the regulations for commercial wines, taste different wines from locals, then decide your favourite combination. Be careful though. Not being used with natural wine can make you highly vulnerable to even one glass. You've been warned! Quality cannot survive without your active involvement. If you are passive, and refuse to take any action, it means that you agree with being forcibly educated to accept your decline as a species. Enjoy the sulphites! The wine you are currently drinking is most probably killing you. Why do you think there are no ingredients on the bottle? If you ever meet me, I'd love to take you on a wine tour in the ancient *Dacian* (Romanian) landscape. The more I am writing at this chapter, the more I'm getting disturbed by the soulless *aliens* behind the grand scheme of our existence, at the ill intentioned policy makers and the easily corruptible filth of a people called politicians. This world is not ours, we are its guardians, and so far we've done a shameful job. When I see organic wine I don't even know what it means, because if it's not made only from grapes, how can it be organic? I hope this gives you an idea of what *organic* means nowadays. Wine should only be organic, if the definition would mean what I think it should; you don't spray the vineyard with any *approved* chemicals. When there is a pest infestation, you carefully clean each vine. A common issue we had was caused by caterpillars, but it was easy to get rid of them. What is organic wine, and if there is such thing, what is non-organic wine? Recently I've seen a label saying *vegan Prosecco*. What the fuck is vegan Prosecco? Grapes are not animals, nor should you use animal products during wine making… Wine does or should not have animal products in it, ever! In the hope that all isn't lost, may God save natural vine and 100% grape wine!

CHAPTER 4

LOVE SEX FAMINE

Music for this chapter
Tangerine Dream – Love on a Real Train
Vangelis – Blade Runner Blues
Sebastian - Love in Motion
The Future Sound of London – Papua New Guinea
Káryyn – Ever

"A man who can read in a woman's eyes has nothing else left to learn."
WILLIAM SHAKESPEARE

I give you, Hilde. She's one of my former girlfriends, one that used to drive me crazy, mostly in a good way. It was around 2011 when we first met, in a shop close to where I was living. I can say the attraction was instant and mutual. She knew I was fresh in the neighbourhood, when she measured me head to toes, while I was buying things I didn't really need. Intrigued, I entered the shop after seeing her sexy body through the glass door, and feeling an amazing woman perfume from afar. I wanted to see if the two senses were matching. Later on into the relationship, I confessed my ability to smell her addictive scent from great distance. She enjoyed that, and it added to the overall craze. I always knew when she was on shift, just by walking in the area, probably at tens of meters away from the shop. I was right, over 99%

of the time. This made me better than a drug sniffing dog. When coming from work, slain and sweaty, my sense of smell was even more sensitive, when she was there.

During the first few weeks in my new apartment, I didn't have a specific plan to conquer her. My life as a Coast Guard Officer was degrading, and taking everything from me quickly; pursuing a lady was among the last things on my mind, especially a woman working in a grocery store. My standards were pretty high back then, thinking that I needed a girlfriend with an interesting job, whatever that meant. Needless to say, I wasn't ready for what I was seeing myself into. Little did I know, that no matter how educated or uneducated a woman is, she is still an expert in seduction. It's probably one of the biggest mysteries of human nature. For some time I was just happy to see her, and breathe in the pheromone-inebriated air. A perfume that was so intense and fine, it could steal your sleep. It happened to me quite sudden. There are some women on this planet, that descended from sensual heaven without leaving anything behind. They bring the whole set with them, including madness. What contributed to my change of heart, was a day when she leaned forward to grab something from the refrigerator. It might seem like a cheap and cheesy cliché to say that her amazing ass blew my mind, but this is the pure truth. In a split second I came to my senses and thought, *"fuck my professional standards, that ass is mine!"*. She had an amazing body, and a bit of a sexy slutty face. I don't mind that, if she's slutty only with me. At the time she was engaged in an ending relationship with a sailor. I was going to make sure it was going to end, if it didn't lead there. She wasn't happy either, and I could feel that; it wasn't difficult to see. There are so many jokes about sailors' wives and girlfriends, most of them true. Few about sailors' activity on the seas though. Probably because they cannot be proven wrong, due to their seclusion. Sailors say, *"what happens on the boat, stays on the boat"*, and their women go, *"what happens on land in your absence, well, you'll eventually find out when you come back, or over the phone"*. I mean, how can you keep a woman's natural urges under control and satisfied, when you're away for half a year or more, every year. You're condemning her to develop a fibroid. She wasn't sexually satisfied when he was home either. And by what she said, he was a former pimp; she didn't like that history of him. That was in another league compared to the most dangerous thing I'd ever done. Talking about living crazy lives... *"No, thank you!"* I started pursuing, and she was ready to give him the news; she stopped answering his calls from *Bermuda*, but he kept on doing it. Now, she was ready to end it. She changed her phone number. I was on land, and kept on stirring her up. I wanted her really bad.

She came into my life after a few sad years of abstinence, prostitutes, and a lot of alcohol. I'm not proud of that. No one should be abstinent, it's unnatural and sad. I loved her instantly, because she was actively involved in the passion between us, as if I was her first man. Not once did she look bored by men. You know those women who, due to their poor previous choices, think all their future men should pay their dues. This is one of women's biggest mistakes in life. She was also not yet spoiled by rich virgins, gifting her expensive products before having sex. It wasn't her type anyway, but there's always the possibility of corruption.

In the same time, even way before meeting Hilde, I was wooing a girl from my university, but who wouldn't give in. She too was in a relationship, with a guy that cheated on her. How I ended up in these situations, breaking up unhappy couples, was a mystery. Probably the abstinence was thrashing my karma. I told her to ditch the bastard and fuck me instead, but she wouldn't. She was sexy as hell, with wild bisexual urges, and that made it terrific. Many times, she was showing me really hot girls that she would have sex with. I was in pain, especially when swimming together naked in the sea. I even promised to paint her naked body on the beach, but even that didn't persuade her. She liked me, but she had principles.

Hilde happened when I was broken as a decomposed puzzle. I asked her out. She refused, but never actually pronounced the no. I was expecting that, and wanted her to play hard to get. You have to pay a lot of attention when courting a woman. If she never says *"no"*, you have something to work with. Same as in sales. I backed off a bit, and for some days, I kept on visiting her shop just creating situations to find out more about her, and to let her know that I'll be around. When seeing her expecting me to ask her out again, I was leaving the store. I've been told by some friends that they like how I'm *ghosting* women in real time, because they deserve it. But don't get fooled by my experience, I was not an expert in seduction. I've lost countless women during my lifetime, for not *acknowledging* them for too long. Timing is everything, if you see them interested, start the game. I usually play by the rule of three: if the first time she refuses, I'm backing off enough to make her think I've given up, just to act again in a different situation or with more passion - even women that don't like you are dying to know why you're not trying anymore after the first time; the third and last time I will try something unique, a symbolic gift, or anything that would trigger her saying, *"fuck it, why not!"*. Hey, I don't know much about expensive gifts before sex, I'm half monkey anyway, right? If that doesn't work either, it's *bye* forever. If she changes her mind after that, she'd have to pursue me like I'm the woman. *"Fuck it, why not!"* If you get to having sex, you then have good reasons to punish her; most of them will ask for punishment during fornication anyway, for their previous audacity to reject you. Nowadays, serenading a woman too much can make her think you're harassing her, or that you're a lunatic with mental issues. In the 21 century the seduction game is shit, and highly risky for a man that actually likes a woman. You can even get a criminal record if you're not paying attention.

One day I found out from her twin sister that Hilde was in the hospital, after falling ill at work. It was nothing serious, but I saw that as an amazing opportunity. I bought a really cute teddy bear, sprayed it with my perfume, Givenchy Play, and passed it to the sister, to give it to her in hospital. I also gave the sister my phone number. That was the last good perfume from Givenchy. I was getting complimented all the time by women, and some men. Even women that I knew for sure they hated me, were falling prey to my vapours. The way that perfume combined with my natural smell was amazing. I knew the bear could not fail. Most women would risk their entire life for a good smelling man, no matter his looks. I had both. I'd say for women good smell is first on their list of priorities, and then beauty. Women took this the extreme. Men are the same, but not as much. I met gorgeous women, so beautiful that you'd drink beer from their pussies - as some men use to say- but who smelled really bad, some emanating a synthetic odour resembling, as I like to call it, sewing machine lubricant. I can still not understand how that is possible. Even so, many men would still fuck them for their looks. Women on the other hand... After a few days she called me to say thank you for the bear, and to ask me if I sprayed it with perfume. I could feel that that worked just as planned. Second time she agreed to go out with me. My rule of three got cut short. I managed to save a bullet. I played three as two. Learn from that.

Our first date took off swiftly, without anything amazing occurring. We kissed as quickly at the end of it, and later she told me, "why did it take you so long to kiss me?". I thought, *"you dick!"*. I was trying to be nice, and you tell me I should've kissed you sooner? I liked her slutty and anxious attitude. *"Let's do this!"* Never be the nice guy.

Our busy schedules were standing in the way, but we could manage it. If I say I was rusty, it would be an overstatement. I invited her to see a movie up in my flat. I had no photos with naked women on my fridge door. What a surprise! She was pretty comfortable, and I was throwing jokes that made me feel sorry for myself. She enjoyed them, so that was ok. I started to take her clothes off before the end of the movie, when, what do you know, she was during *that time of the month...* I was allowed to navigate the top part of her body only, without *parking the car in the garage. "Fuck! Why do women always do this?"* There goes *sex on the first movie...* "I can take care of you, if you want..." Wait, what?! It didn't take her long to grab my legs, like I was the woman in the missionary position. She unbuttoned my trousers, and started working my two hour long erection, like a pro. I was twenty six years old, she was thirty two. It felt weird getting a hand job like that, but it had been a good start. After a while I drove her home. I was living a thug life, having such a horny hottie in my '98 Dacia 1310. I was hard during the whole time. She had loads of BMWs and Audis swaying her way all the time, but I guess I had a more realistic *I don't give a fuck* attitude. I'm pretty sure many of them were planning to break my bones, but being a cop made me more dangerous than they could've ever been, and they knew it. I was their toxic gas.

Next morning I woke up with her smell all around the apartment, and a full-on erection that wouldn't go away. I read somewhere, that if you have an erection for over four hours, you can get lesions on the gland. It must've eased a bit during the night, to let the blood change shifts, because it felt healthy.

There comes a time in every human's life, when the sexual life clicks amazing. With some it starts during high school, and with others later on. My amazing was just beginning. It's not always about the number of women you sleep with, but the quality of them. Most of the ones I know, that had amazing sexual lives during high school or university, are now married with women that don't know how to give an oral, they don't give one altogether, or with men that have erections maybe once a week, if they're lucky. What a sad life, when the amazing happens too early, or when it's gone for good during your prime years. Stay away from people talking bad about the partner they married.

When her period finished, she came by for a movie again, but we never pressed play. I started undressing her from the door, while shoes were flying to the sealing. Fuck it! It wasn't my apartment if something broke. I finally got the chance to uncover her body. I was smelling her skin like I was *Jean-Baptiste Grenouille*, trying to understand how she could smell so good, without wearing any perfume. She was so clean, and with skin so soft, I couldn't believe it. Clumsy at first, I got my head around a woman's body. It's always like that in the beginning. I didn't use a condom, and we decided it was for the best. We tried, but it didn't work. *"Fuck you, Durex!"* We both managed to climax, but I felt something was not quite right; I was rushing too much. *"Slow down cowboy!"* I was sitting on the corner of the bed, and she sat on top of me. I could look into her eyes, while she was taking me inside, fully. Her pupils started dilating, and she leaned her head on my left shoulder. I was squeezing her buttocks, while feeding with her gorgeous breasts, and could feel small earthquakes in her thighs. She grabbed my neck tight, and while being inside of her with all I had, I felt a flow of warm liquid covering me. It was something new. She fell on me slain of powers. "What was that?" She smiled, and looked a bit shy, due to the mess she'd just made. The corner of the bed was all wet. She was a squirter. You never believe these things, until they happen to you. They're like a myth, like a story you listen to, mesmerised. And then it happens. You lucky bastard! I didn't know how to take it; I wasn't planning to make her feel bad about it. After all, I was a fan... I waited for her to come together, and we tried again. She had multiple orgasms, one after another. I was in Heaven, she was in my wet bed. It was a lot to take in. It smelled incredible, and I didn't know if I should taste it or not. I decided to taste it when she wasn't paying attention. She told me she's never done it so many times, and in that quantity. Her sailor barely managed to get her wet, and was accusing her of *anorgasmia.* And that was just our first night. Apparently, money can't make women achieve orgasm. I started studying the female ejaculation, and found out that women have a prostate -against popular culture- called *skene* glands, posted around the urethra, which produce the squirting liquid, filled with the female equivalent type of hormone as the one in a man's prostate liquid. It's the feminine elixir, and it differs in quantity from one woman to another. Quite intriguing, and also good to know if you're a man. Stop acting so weird when she's doing it! If she's not disgusted by your ejaculation, why should you be by her squirt?

That was the beginning of an addiction, that most doctors would have given medical proportions. Like they do with kids with a lot of energy. *"Mam, it's ADHD! Give these pills to your child, and fuck up his future and hormonal explosions..."* In this case, I was a sex addict, we both were. And it felt good. Even my brother was wondering if it's ok to have so much sex. We started seeing each other almost every day, fucking for hours on end. At my place, when my brother was working, in my car, somewhere deep in a seaside forest with wild boars running free, or in secluded areas, on the cliffs next to the sea, places where anyone could have decapitated us, and no one would've found the bodies. "I was so dumb to refuse you, I can't believe I'm finally fucking and showering with you", she told me once, while having a bath. I never asked her what she meant. She tickled my ego, and that made me feel good. The more we made love, the stronger the feelings, and the more we wanted to do it. There wasn't a single day when we fucked less than 3-4 hours, and many times twice a day. Sometimes, when we were doing it in the car, I had to go out to pee, and God, the forest's pungent smell of wild boar was terrifying. She was waiting for me naked and eager, behind the foggy windows. I was surprised my car still had a working suspension. At times I was going to her place, without her parents knowing. I had to cling by the window of her bedroom, and risk being seen by the whole neighbourhood, going in like a burglar. Most of them knew I was a cop, it was a small town. What the hell, this is what cops do in their spare time anyway... Usually, I was at hers at about 9pm-10pm, and leaving at two or three in the morning. It was crazy, like we were in a trance. Sometimes I was spending the whole night. The sleep next to her was the most amazing I've ever had during adulthood. Except the nights when her parents' cuckoo clock kept waking us up every hour. Mental! One time, she went home from town to let me in, and her mother came in to see why she was in bed so early. I was under the duvet, with a massive erection. She was good at disguising me. We fucked in the sea, on the sand in remote areas, with people passing by, we purely did not care. I loved feeling her hot squirt on my thighs in the cold sea water, in the dark, or between flowing sheets. Her smell was even more addictive in the sunshine. I was diving for giant whelks often, and would cook them on a bonfire, then eat them sprinkled with salt. I was feeding my goddess with the best foods the sea had to offer, and she was doing the same to me, at home. No, this isn't an eighties movie about cast away couples on tropical islands!

From the waves, I was watching her bathing in the sun, with her amazing skin and round delicious buttocks, then I would come out of the water like Poseidon, but with the trident between my legs. My wet and cold body would startle her, while penetrating her unannounced. Her outrageous odour was probably attracting all sorts of forest animals, like *paparazzis*, or even wild boars. I could feel it. She knew I wasn't a wild boar. My body wasn't that hairy. Her climax would take her by surprise, and by the time she turned around to hug me, I would run away back into the water, covered by the blinding light of the hot sun. Shortly, she would come into the water looking like an ancient naked *Helena*, wearing only two olive twigs on her temples. She would then grab me, and claim another orgasm. She could take a lot of me. I taught her earlier into our relationship, that she needs to learn how to claim orgasms from her man, when he is tired too often, or not feeling 100% *for sex*. If he can't - *Houston, we have a problem!* In the sea, she was applying that in excess. I was spending more time in the water than her, but when she was coming into the sea, she'd cause tidal waves. The water was dressing us both, united, like when we first started to populate this planet. She'd warm up the sea around me, in an explosion that was sending us to consciousness paradise. She made me lose control spontaneously. I promised an aggressive crab, earlier in the day, that I'd come back with reinforcements, and claim his house. This was our secret beach, that resembled the Caribbean.

Hilde has been the first woman that made me able to pour the same quantity of wine in two glasses, only by listening to its music, while it flows out of the bottle and hits the crystal. It wasn't the first time I was thinking that everything has its own music and frequency, but I had never paid attention to this aspect before, not with so much passion. I have tested this many times after that, and when I finish, the levels of wine in the glasses are equal. Amazing, isn't it? And it's not even that difficult. The same principle applies with women. In a relationship she is the frequency that needs most attention, if you want her to expand freely, and without restraints or compression. When hitting her pitch, she floats like the aurora borealis, giving you what even she didn't know she could offer. As a man, you need to know this – women don't know until you show them.

One evening, after work, I told Hilde that I want us to drink a bottle of wine on the beach. It wasn't the first time we did that, but the wish came to me stirred by a hard day at work, and it seemed the perfect time to do it. Having an amazing woman to go home to is a man's definition of paradise. I've always had the feeling that she had a fetish about having lots of sex in a *real* car, same as *Rebecca De Mornay* on a real train, in *Risky Business*. I was feeling tired but powerful, and we had no time to lose. I picked her up, and she was wearing this red summer dress with white dots. It was a hot summer night, and the moment she stepped into my vintage car, it felt like I was seeing her for the first time. She looked so hot with her blonde hair messed up by the heat, that I wanted to have her, right there and then. Her soft skin allowed my hands to slide freely over her body, in order to cover most of her, until randomly encountering wet patches of evaporating sweat, blended with her amazing pheromones. Those were the moments when the movement of my hands stopped to increase the pressure, also guided by her hand. Each stroke ended with a kiss, and every kiss started a new quest over her body. I wanted her dressed, because her clothes captured the entire beauty of her smell, amplifying my euphoria. I started driving on the empty road, having her exposing in the air current coming inside through the open window. Everything excited her, from the way I was driving, the way I was looking at her, the moon, my desire, to the length of the road. Right after exiting the city and reaching cruising speed, she took my hand and drove it between her thighs, begging me to please her. I suddenly became multidimensional, living on the tips of my fingers. I decided to concentrate more on her than on driving, thinking, *"I don't give a fuck, this is too beautiful!"*. I was feeling her in a way I couldn't before, and while moving her hips in tune with my strokes, she was feeding with the fresh air coming in through her hair and her pores, taking us both in with a never seen before passion. Her breath became fire, and I didn't care about the road. The wine was getting hot, whilst moving with delay from side to side inside the bottle, her image was feeding my insanity, when suddenly she exploded all over my hand, taking me by surprise. Exactly then, a curve happened in the road, but I managed to steer on the right path in a fraction of a second, without letting her know about my lack of judgement. That curve was famous for eating up reckless drivers. She was so hot, that my brain could not conceive what just happened, nor the way it happened. I had to stop on the side of the road to understand what just occurred, and to taste her recovery. We were close to the beach, but we couldn't hold it. The night was still young, and the wine uncorked.

Now that you know about the wild, hot *Dacian* (Romanian) summers, let me tell you about the winters. When no apartment was available, we used to drive on the beach at -20°C, or even lower than that, because of the sea breeze, we would choose a spot, start the heating, and make love for hours. She was getting everything wet, and the number of her orgasms was outrageous. She even had the audacity to skip *counting* some, because they were not powerful enough, although she was squirting on each and every one of them. I started doing some research, and found out that in some cultures, in ancient times, men used to drink their women's squirt, to give them god-like virility. I can confirm! We started eating each other up. I was forever hard. Whenever we were going home, even after five or six hours of continuous fornication, I was in erection mode. I've always been easily excitable, but she was the first woman to have that exaggerated effect on me. And it was getting better and better. I tried to get her as excited as possible just by touching her, without penetration, and one night she managed to squirt without any vaginal or clitoral stimulation. Who knew that was even possible. Our sexual karma was matched in heaven. After just a few months of relationship we were unstoppable, and probably we had more sex that most couples during their whole marriage. A few times, when she was having really explosive orgasms, it seemed that the world was celebrating too, because it coincided with people firing up fireworks for different events. It might've been because we were always fornicating, but why not take credit for the coincidence. We were laughing at the situation, and while I was drinking my wine, she made a habit of dipping my cock into her glass, and taste wine and me in the same time. They were both *au naturel.* The fireworks usually kept lighting up the night sky. It was total depravation, and many times I was clinking with a glass of her squirt. Cheers, baby!

On 15 June 2011 the earth experienced a total eclipse of the Moon. We prepared for that early, with good wine and a charged battery on the car. We went to our favourite spot on the cliffs, point from where you could admire the entire beauty of the sea. It was a clear sky that night, and when the eclipse started, Hilde was already about five squirting orgasms in. I could see the decaying moon in her deep blue eyes. What an energy that night had... She reached about 12-13 orgasms, when we felt like taking a break, not because we could not continue, but because she was going to work the next day. We didn't know when to stop. When does a love making episode stop? It was a total eclipse of the moon alright.

Some nights we saw other couples in cars having sex, but they were driving back hours before us. Other cars were coming and going, we were still there, leaving hand marks on the foggy windows, and deep tracks in the snow. Have you ever peed completely naked at -20°C, at twelve at night, in the strong seaside wind, with a full erection? One second seems like an hour! When driving home we weren't talking much, we left our eyes say it all. And before dropping her off, I would pull the car between some nearby garages, and slide inside of her one more time before bed, surrounded by mountains of snow. She never used to say no to another round, no matter how tired.

Since everything was fantastic, I decided to count her orgasms. She annoyed me when refusing to count the *not so powerful ones*, but what did I care; more for my record. In about one year and a half, she achieved over 1,000 *powerful* orgasms. We've been together about two years.

Eventually the sailor came home, and found her with me. He tried to talk to her at work, but he couldn't. She called me to stay with her, thinking that if he sees me, he'll understand and go away. He didn't believe her. I didn't have to say anything, and he left. I don't usually like seeing my woman's ex, but this didn't disturb me. He looked quite normal and docile. After all, he did leave without saying anything. He didn't fit the category of Gia's boyfriends with weird faces. My university crush was extremely hot, but because of her previous choices, I decided I could not have sex with her. I actually had some feelings for her too, that were beyond the need for carnal pleasures. She was also a bisexual, and that gave me many, many sleepless nights, when I was with Hilde. My girlfriend was different and straight. They were both kinky in different ways, that I liked. She started hating Gia, when she found out that she's my uni friend.

Hilde was always hunted by other men, especially after some rumours came to surface, about our highly frequent sexual life. I never minded that, I actually enjoyed it. If I'm next to a woman, and no man is looking at her, I start asking myself some questions – if I'm with the right woman for me. I am jealous, but within reason, and with a clear head. Hilde was the opposite. I realised that men in general, marry women they think other men don't look at, for *safety*, hoping to cheat on them later on, with women they think other men look at. They don't like women that are depraved only with them, to be their wives. Don't be a retard and ruin a woman's life, marry the woman you and others crave. If you're healthy for each other and matched in Heaven, of course.

I was at Hilde's place one night when she was alone, and around twelve at night we went to the kitchen to have a break, after intense fornication. We were naked in the dark, and outside was raining with lightnings and thunders. She was having some water from the sink, when I started caressing her from behind with a full hard-on. "How are you still hard!", she said. I was kissing her neck, trying to cover her as much as possible with my hands, while sliding my cock between her buttocks. As I looked outside the window, driven by that weird feeling that someone is watching, a lightning allowed me to see a bodily shape in a window, at the top floor of the opposite block, that looked like a man. At times I couldn't help being a cop. I could feel the sweat on both of us increasing and dripping down. It was really hot, and because of the heavy rain, we couldn't open any windows. "Some guy is watching us!". Another lightning struck, and she could see him too. We took it he could as well, and he was still. She had no window curtains to close. We were both looking his way, while I dipped my fingers into her honeypot. "Do you really think he can see us?" She was still extremely wet. It looked like she was constantly horny, and that made me constantly hard. She didn't answer. We kept eyeing his window, while the sharp lights gave us all away. "Make me come right here, in front of him..." After barely finishing her words, I pulled her hips outwards, while she was grabbing the countertop, and entered her hungry and unrestricted. I could feel her pulsating, and hotter inside. Our sweat was trying in vain to cool us down. I started thrusting with power, and she startled. The momentum was slow, but intense. I pulled her blonde hair towards me, while she was struggling to keep her clear blue eyes on that dude's window. I was increasing the rhythm, and she moaned, scared every time I was at the top of her vagina. I wasn't hurting her, she would've told me. I was going faster and faster, and she wanted me to never stop, pulling me with one hand to go deeper and deeper, despite her fears. I could feel her blood pressure increasing at an alarming rate. Her aorta was pushing out on the side of her neck, like it was about to burst. I gripped her to be sure she won't kick me out prematurely. Her chest was all red in the sharp lights of the storm, and her breasts full and pointy. From time to time I could see the shape of the man in the window, changing positions with every lightning. Finally, I could feel her big chemical event building up. I wasn't about to release her. She took her eyes off the window, and turned her head towards me. "Oh my god, don't stop, don't stop, don't stop, don't stop..." Her vagina swelled like the ocean. I could feel her liquids already running down my legs, while enjoying my last thrusts, then she pushed me out with extreme speed, while I was still holding her tight. Her vagina became the *Gates of Troy*. A massive gush took her powers away, and got the floor and my feet all wet. I had to hold her from falling, while trying to keep her in that state as much as possible, by rubbing her whole pulsating pussy. She recovered after quite a few seconds, and when she could stand in the same position as before, her leaning on the countertop, I kneeled in front of her butt cheeks, and started eating and tasting her delicious honey. She was giving herself to me completely. We trusted each other like no one else before. My tongue inside of her was making her purr, and helped rebuild her strength. I felt addicted. She was still pulsating on my lips. I was a god feeding with her, and by feeding me, she knew I would always be firm for her. It is a cycle, you see. She tasted divine, and her curves in the lightning strikes, after orgasm, made her slip on my tongue like warm butter. She kneeled down to make me explode, but I couldn't. She also enjoyed tasting herself on me. I was hard, but numb. She's done that for a few minutes, to please me in front of that shape in the window, while fixating me and him, then we went to bed. The sheets were all wet, but not from our sweat alone. What was happening between us was divine and demonic in the same time. We could not stop craving each other, and we were better at it with every act. Our sexual display was evolving constantly, and could never achieve a limit. The graph of our sex experience was a straight line, pointing half twelve. We had downfalls, but they were rare, and correlated with either work, or our private lives. But even then, we were better than anyone else. At the end, exhausted but never quite finished, she was always like, "Wow baby, what the fuck is wrong with us? Why are we doing it so vigorously?" "Nothing is wrong, this is the new normal", I was telling her, while playing with her hair.

It's weird how God created women. The crazy ones will take your sexual life to unimaginable dimensions, while the most sane, stable women, will have limited to mediocre sex. If you find both in one woman, you can consider yourself the luckiest man alive. It's not about intelligence, I think. I believe the true balance exists - love, sex, intelligence. Although, what do you do when a beautiful crazy woman messes up your standards? Before, I wanted a woman with an interesting job. Now, I want her to kiss my cock every time I'm about to get dressed. Hilde loved that, and if I was to put on my underwear before going to her to kiss my erection, she would turn all mad. Some subject to fight on, wasn't it? Many times she made me unzip, so she could do it, before going to work. You try to walk on the street in tight police uniform, with a hard-on you can't lose. Now, I'm mental!

One night, during dinner with her parents, I got excused to go to the bathroom for a wee. When I was about to go, Hilde opens the door, sticks only her head in, and starts giving me a partial blowjob, while her parents were asking if everything is ok. She stopped, and confirmed we're good. It would've been so easy for them to spot her. She left smiling. I couldn't pee for a while. I was struggling to think at something to put my erection to sleep. I eventually managed to clear my bladder, but it must've took longer than what I was hoping, because her parents sent her back, to check if I was alright. She entered the bathroom, and locked the door. She took her panties off, and invited me to penetrate her from behind. "You're crazy!" She was already extremely wet. I made her orgasm in the palm of my hand, while her cheeks turned burning red. Her body was moving and rubbing against me like a python, behaving after each orgasm, as if it was the beginning of the sexual act. She loved the danger, and I didn't mind. That made me realise a lot of things about me. We were the same. I made sure her leggings were not visibly wet, then we went back to the table. I was ok.

One time we thought to watch a porn movie, to compare ourselves with the professionals of the industry. I let her choose it, and then we began eating each other up. The action turned steamy in no time. After a few minutes we forgot all about the feature. By the time they climaxed once, we were already deep into stage two of our act. We found the movie so boring... And it was a good one, by all standards. She shut the computer down, then jumped on me like in a rodeo.

Gia liked men with weird faces. She once admitted sleeping with a guy that photographed himself doing a partial splits between his two Skodas. *"Oh, God, she fucked a guy with a Skoda!"* He posted that on social media. What a deuce! He fit her pattern perfectly. I didn't want to be in her books of weird looking guys, and plus, also a Skoda club member, and future politician... No sirree! I bet they were running on Diesel too. She was hot though, and eventually single again. She started pursuing me, when I was still in a relationship. My body wanted her, but I couldn't cheat on Hilde. I was thinking often if I could persuade Hilde to accept Gia into our bed, but it was impossible. Hilde would've stabbed me during sleep. *"Look who's in the other boat now!"* I like to be honest and fair with my women. I give them everything they need, they do the same, it's a clean pact. Once the pact is broken, bye! It's harder when the pact is broken and feelings are involved. That's a killer... Otherwise, I'm quite a normal guy, waiting for love with outmost awareness. I had feelings for both, maybe a stronger connection with Gia, but I wasn't willing to give up my sexual paradise for the unknown. Never do it, unless you're truly in love, and it's reciprocal! My stomach was a hurricane. I was telling Gia that I had everything I needed, sexually and some, and that I'm not a cheater. I reminded her that she should have said yes when I was single, and while cheating together during the Commercial Law exam in uni. She was in pain, and wouldn't have it. During a uni friends outing she started crying, confessing that she loved me. I gave her a kiss one night. She thought she was in, but she wasn't. Her image was romantic when seeing me. I still had unfinished business with Hilde, being late for a long and amazing fuck, and dinner cooked by me, made of whelks in red wine and tomato sauce, with loads of dill and garlic. I dived in the sea for them. She might give me a blowjob before, because honestly, we can't wait for that long. We're gonna eat naked, of course, and probably someone will also take photos of us from the flat across the street, with the flash on. Idiot! It was never a quickie with her. Fast would eventually turn into the *devouring of the divine pleasures*. The upstairs neighbours are probably preparing for us as well. The wife is telling Hilde regularly that she envies her, and the husband is spelling *neighbour* when saying *hi*. People living downstairs are old; they've never been my fans. I also have a social media friend request from one of my next door neighbours. He's gay! I show it to Hilde, and she starts laughing. For me it's not funny, because probably my room and his are sharing the same wall. Living in a block of flats is shit. I was scared when she wasn't there. We usually make a lot of noise, and probably he's hoping. I hope he's hoping, and not doing something else... It's flattering, but not funny! He eventually un-friended me. Phew!

We were so good together because we had reconcilable conflicting arguments, on almost anything. They were not serious – this nature was keeping us entertained with each other. 99% of our fights ended up making love, with some continuing even through orgasms. If there is no conflict between a man and a woman, they cannot be happy together. And then, the dangerous ones surfaced. She was overly jealous, and I would not tolerate it. We were yet to find out if we could reconcile all our conflicts. I had no experience with severe jealousy. I could not go anywhere if there were single women involved, colleagues, friends, you name it. There were three absolute options: she had to be there, to keep an eye on the kind of looks I receive from all the single ladies – back home the fight would be imminent; go there alone, if that was a requirement – fight was a must; don't go, and explain why I want to go out with friends, even when she couldn't go – the mother of all fights. She probably thought I was some kind of *Adonis*. The idea that I was a womaniser entered her head from unknown sources. I started being tortured for what previous men have done to her. In the beginning I thought she was unique. In her mind, I was responsible for the best she'd ever lived, and the worst. The latter was wrong, till a certain point in our relationship. The more she was jealous without reason, the worse I behaved. I was new to this jealousy stuff. It taught me the dark side of Julian. Me and *him* could never be friends. She also found out that a teenage neighbour of mine confessed to her friends that she loved me, while crying her head off around the block. Hilde was not jealous during this instance, but thought it was funny when it came out. She could not wait to tell me. *"What the fuck is going on???"*, I was thinking. Probably those were my *Kavorka* years. I was the subject of massive intrigues about which I was the last to know.

Hilde drove me to the point of despair with her cheating fantasies. She had trust issues, and that didn't work for any of us. I don't like it when my woman doesn't trust me. It all starts with trust. I was the only man in her life, that would have not cheated on her. I'm totally devoted, or I leave, and I ask the same. To clarify things once and for all, we drove to a parking lot, and during our argument, I started shouting and hitting the steering wheel. The burst was necessary, but I would've never hit her. She started crying, then we made love. To punish me, she wanted to make love with my toes for a while. She had many fetishes, and this was one of her favourites. She could basically climax using any part of my body. This time, I could've watched a movie with popcorn, because I was not able to reach her body; she had me pinned down. I was trying to reach her like an overweight tomcat. I have this skill with my toes, where I can grab things between the big toe and the *teenager* toe next to it, and throw them away, or pinch very hard. I could also perfectly isolate my big toe for her to enjoy. Hilde loved the way I was taking care of my feet. I'm a strong believer that our overall health starts at our feet. During the act I was a spectator to her marvellous symphony of curves, moans and strings of happiness. Her wet climax over my toe turned me into a super aware beast. She eventually allowed me to enter the equation. We were total when making love, melting into each other. This is a reason why I think we need to keep our bodies clean and healthy, to be total when making love. Many times, I was licking her amazing temple of a body, without lifting my tongue off her skin, before covering the last millimetre. She'd suffer a nurturing apocalypse of intense chemical explosions, throughout my endeavour.

Hilde became obsessed with the idea of me cheating on her with Gia, whom I met before her. We had a couples dinner one night, and she saw how Gia looked at me. Women always know. That was the weirdest dinner I've ever attended. After that, the storm became a hurricane. Hilde was blaming me for how another woman was feeling about me. Men are guilty of that. Next day, I didn't know what was wrong with the car. Driving it seemed weird. After a while, I realised that the steering wheel was bent. The other Julian had to go.

To patch things up I called her to work. It was a hot summer day in July. I was doing a night shift in the marina, and had planned to meet at my office, after the change of shift, when everything was supposed to be pretty quiet. After she finished her shift, she went home for a shower, then rushed towards me. During all that time, I was undressing her in my mind, and time seemed to stretch too much. We were so horny that day, that nothing and no one could stand in the way of our inevitable fornication, not even the fact that I was working, sort of. When she arrived I pulled her inside, locked the door, and started undressing her with rage, not before covering the windows. She didn't oppose, although I was acting with her like a man who's seen a woman for the first time. She loved that rough side of me, and if it ended with torn clothes, even better. She was wearing strong fibre that night, because the latter never happened. The harbour was packed with people, on that torrid day during the weekend. My office was inside a container, transformed to fit the logistics, and look like a functional unit, while the new offices were being built. In seconds I was inside of her, and the intensity was so real, we couldn't believe that it was actually happening. We were struggling to fit on an armchair, while giving our best version to each other, and the air became flames. We were both about to orgasm, when suddenly, someone knocked on the door, on the window, and then on the door again. A few colleagues wanted to check on me. Hearing them she startled, while her vagina clinched around *Major Me*, and I was praying we don't get a *penis captivus*, right there and then. We couldn't believe what was happening, while she was squeezing me with her arms, and moving her hips, hoping to make me explode. I was screaming inside like *Godzilla*, while the bastards were becoming impatient. They started calling me on the mobile phone, and I was one vaginal stroke away from conceiving a baby, when I pulled out, and reached for the phone to switch it on silent. "God damn it! An officer of the law has to pay attention to so many things!" She got scared, seeing how the fun had gone south fast, but unfortunately not her south. We dressed up quickly, and I had no idea about what to do, being able to hear them wanting to call the headquarters, thinking that something was wrong with me. I managed to get to my senses fast, but I still didn't know what to do with the

erection, that couldn't fit my clothes. Somehow I managed to hide the obvious, I told her to stay put, and opened the door, pretending I just woke up. I didn't want them to go inside the office, so I managed to push them away, and locked the door on the outside. "What's up boys?"
"What the fuck, were you sleeping already? It's just the start of the shift…"
"Yeah, well, I had something to do today, and I'm really tired tonight."
"You should be careful, because there's a shift officer checking the people tonight."
"Fuck him, fuck all of them!"
"Ok, we just wanted to see how you are… Sleep tight then!"
"That was it???" I was shouting that in my head. This was the conversation, after they interrupted something out of this world. For that, I felt like hitting them in the forehead with the grip handle of my Glock pistol. I went back inside, and found Hilde's pulse raging, thinking they could go inside the office at any second. Right when we were prepared to go back to business, I received a call through the radio, to go check a yacht. A family wanted to leave the country, and they requested the coast guard officer on duty to do the check. I was on duty alright, having a massive surprise for them. She left undone that night, both forced to postpone our session for the next day.

My dick felt like a marble statue, and I couldn't do anything about it. The walk on the wharf, among all the people who'd come to enjoy the sunset, was like a show off of a trophy. I went to check the yacht and their documents with my zipper in danger. When I got to their vessel I noticed their shocked faces, while I was checking the passports. I could tell they wanted me gone as soon as possible. They were all lined up like never before, while I was telling them to relax. I was looking like a male ballet dancer, my erection being so obvious, you could see it from the crow's nest. I did my best to let them go as quick as possible, despite my stray mind. They could've showed me fake or expired passports, and I couldn't care less. It was amazing how my tension was refusing to dissipate. They were so amiable in order to see me away, and let them sail out of that horror, that no one was saying anything, not even a joke. And I was asking, after clearing my throat, "do you hold any weapons or drugs on board?" They all turned red and answered "no!", in unison. After completing the papers I stepped off their boat, on the pontoon, and finally everyone could breathe again. In my head I offered myself to push their boat with my dick, but they refused, saying the wind was good that night. There was no wind that night. They started their engines and bow thrusters, and left me waving, while showcasing a forced smile. "Bye! I hope you hit sand with the keel!!!" That has been the most awkward border control I have ever done.

During that night I stayed the same, with short phases of semi relaxation. Every time I was peeing, I could feel the smell of her ambrosia, accompanied by ukulele. Her vagina was still on, and till morning, although I was sleepy and in severe pain, I spent my shift watching the old fishermen catching fish under the lantern. My eyes were of a lunatic's, while in the squat position, with the chin in my palms, moving back and forth as a psychopath. She was sleeping in our bed, whilst I was wasted on the wharf, doing a shift I didn't want to do, a night shift.

I realised that if her character wasn't so nuts, I wouldn't have needed anything else, even with true love missing. If you're with the right woman, you wouldn't feel like getting away from her, to go out with the boys excessively, nor would you need to fantasise about other women. You'd want to do things to and with her, constantly. I was waking up in the heat of the night regularly, just to watch her naked body in the wrinkled sheets, while the moonlight was drawing shapes on her round buttocks, thinking how I didn't need anything else, that that's how paradise must feel. The thought that she was mine, and the way she was lying naked next to me, in the dark blue decor of the night, was exhilarating.

Good sex can always patch up a bad argument, but not vice-versa. No matter the perfection of a couple's compatibility, if the sex is not satisfying, the relationship will crumble. With Hilde, her chronic jealousy was a side business that would crumble any relationship. My lack of skill in managing and coping with it wasn't improving things either. The moment you realise the relationship has passed the breaking point signalling breakup is of enormous sadness. Like when the Holy Ghost flies away from things, and leaves behind scorched land. If you've lived amazing moments together, you keep hoping for a big change, that you can still be together, that it's not finished, but you know it is not going to happen. Her behaviour surfaced during our first months, and I wanted to end it. That wouldn't have been the best decision, and she was right. We needed to achieve ripeness. A period of breaking up and coming back together had started. Her parents developed hate towards me, and for good reason. I have caused Hilde a lot of pain close to the end. I was planning to move to London for good, and she found out by mistake. It devastated her. I decided early into the relationship, that I would not take her with me. We were still craving each other, so from time to time, we started making love in secret. I kept going to her place, despite her parents not wanting me there.

Our irreconcilable conflict was not her jealousy though, maybe that had a cure – it was the small and mediocre world she lived in, the lack of creativity. I was thinking big, and she was telling me, "but baby, we need to have a pension!". Small talk and gossip were her thing. She didn't want to become something greater. Her everyday was my poison. I was the inventor of dreaming big, and she couldn't see any chance of independence, of personal utopia.

Another sign that our relationship was not meant for the ages, was the baby lemon tree I gave her at the beginning of our relationship, that didn't grow one inch in two years, while its twin grew over a metre high. My habit of planting stuff has got deep roots into my childhood summers spent at the farm. I didn't give it to her to test the fertility of our relationship, but it shocked me to see it had not grown one bit in such a long time, and that got me thinking. I found it really weird. It was then when I realised the fragility of our connection, that we were meant to go on separate ways. In the end, I drove her in the arms of another man she would've never been with otherwise. She hated the guy, but she wanted to hurt me. In vain I was trying to show my former half-slavic girlfriend that I didn't care, but I did.

I've always had a French connection with Russian women.

The decision to end it was the most difficult I've ever had to take, but it was for the best to go on different paths, than hurt each other indefinitely. What had to be achieved had been achieved. We left behind a broken bed and bathtub. My brother fixed the bathtub with correcting paste, to pass the inspection, and I fixed the bed with a plank, which failed straight after we left.

I flew away to foreign realms with my depression. It never felt worse, it never felt better.

CHAPTER 5

WE NEED TO COOK

Music for this chapter
Wheatus - Teenage Dirtbag
Snoop Dogg - Gin and Juice (feat. Dat Nigga Daz)
Dr. Dre feat Snoop Dogg - Nothin' but A G Thang
Coolio - Gangsta's Paradise

At the age of 25 I was working in the Coast Guard, I had mountains of copies of my first self-published novel taking a lot of space in the flat, had no girlfriend, and no money. What a messed up life to live... My brother and I were living in a rented ground floor flat, when a business idea came to our mind. We needed money really bad. To be a police officer, and not having the financial power to go out when you want, because rent, utilities and food, take up your entire wage, was making me fade away ahead of time. And most people thought, that I should have been happy about having a job, because there are people doing worse. Yup! If you have a fucking job, you're goddamn rich! How can human kind go forward with people thinking like this? You don't see them saying this to politicians' kids, living the life on yachts, in Monaco... I had to get a loan from the bank, to afford my first ever holiday abroad, in Ibiza, at bloody 23! When I came back, all my colleagues were shouting in unison, *"why do you want more money, you don't have enough for Ibiza?"*. If you've ever said this to me, while I was putting my head at stake with the Ministry of Intern, so you and I could live better lives, fuck you! That's why you're reading about me, while being stuck in the same place as twenty years ago. Jobs have to disappear, they're holding people back from achieving full potential.

This time we were ready to make money. We've always had entrepreneurial spirits, it's the future anyway; soon enough it'll be a luxury to have a job (I cannot believe that I was saying this to people before 2020). My life consisted of work, attending some courses at the university, going out for a few drinks every three or four weeks, when the wage came in, and that was just about it. Saying that it was not interesting is an overstatement.

Every summer, there is this passion in *Dacia* (Romania), for making elderflower wine. It's a delicious caprice of June. You pick the flowers when the bush is in full bloom. Use spring water, sugar, quality yeast and lemon juice, et voilá, you've got yourself a refreshing alcoholic drink, that's healthier and tastier, than any white wine you can find on the market. We kept on asking ourselves if the flat was large enough for our project. The balcony was quite accommodating. After a few measurements, we came to the conclusion that it can be done. We asked all our friends if they would buy elderflower wine, if they'd find a source, and most of them acted highly interested. That was our rudimentary market study. You rarely find someone disliking this wine. Although we were living on the seaside, there was an old protected forest nearby, right on the edge of the water, with loads of elderflower. You just had to be willing to climb some fences and trees. The risk of having an encounter with a wild boar was high as well. We drove in the area to see which flowers were accessible, then we bought five 200L barrels.

We loaded them onto our '98 Dacia. That was a weird sight, I'm telling you... I remember driving past a traffic police vehicle, and the guy didn't react. It wasn't legal driving like that, but we took it that the police officer recognised the car, and who we were. Our calculations had to be precise, this was large scale. We filled the barrels with pure water, then added the elderflower bloom. I remember how I was on the phone with Gia one time, planning a drinks outing, when she asked what I was doing. "Oh, well, you see, I'm stirring one tonne of elderflower wine on the balcony..." "What??? You're mad!" The smell in the the apartment was divine. Our production costs were minimal, so by my calculations, we should've made really good profit. Once the fermentation started, we had to keep the windows open 24/7. You don't want to get killed in your sleep, by alcohol vapours and carbon dioxide. Shortly, it started smelling like a cellar in all the rooms. "Bro, do you think we'll be alive in the morning?" No one knew if this had become too big of a project for the small apartment. A tonne of fermenting elderflower must can produce a lot of carbon dioxide and alcohol fumes. We didn't have too many mosquitoes coming into the apartment that June. People have died because they fell asleep in the cellar during fermentation. We turned towards last minute health and safety measures, and sealed the balcony the best we could. "What a beautiful smell! It's turning into wine!" For about two weeks we slept worrying. The fermentation eventually finished, and all looked perfect. We sealed the barrels from oxygen, and left the wine to set. Normally it's 40 days, but we took it off the yeast sooner than that. It tasted amazing, considering the sheer scale of our endeavour. It was probably our best, and for sure, the biggest batch ever. Our flat was packed with elderflower wine 5L bottles. "Wow! What do we do now?" How much do you charge for a litre of elderflower wine, made by two Coast Guard Officers with some skills in organic chemistry, in the balcony of a ground floor flat, in polyethylene barrels? Once we decided the price, we invited everyone to buy. "I'll buy, but bring some samples." Alright, fair enough... We gave more samples of wine than we sold. They were drinking the samples like it was water, but when having to buy, everyone strayed away. "How much?!" It wasn't even expensive, plus the more you bought, the cheaper it got. This is how we found out, that no colleague or friend wants you to make money. Unless they are really good friends, which is a rare thing in this world. When you start a project, never count on anyone else, than yourself and your family. Better keep an eye on some members of the family too. All others will promise they'll be the first ones buying from you, that they'll get the whole batch of anything you sell, even if it's not exceptional, like any new product. Our wine was an example of wine making. The taste was a paragon, even for the big wine producers. No one bought a single litre. They wanted more and more samples, for free. We couldn't take that. The disappointment was so big, we told them, that before giving it all for free, we'd pour it into the sewer. This happened before, with milk, if you know a bit of history.

Our dreams of even offsetting the production costs, were getting shattered. No one was appreciating our efforts, and the scarcity of our product. You cannot buy this type of wine anywhere, and it's highly seasonal. Knowing how to prepare it is paramount. Too much sugar, for the yeast to convert into alcohol, or too much yeast, could spell disaster for the batch. Our wine had almost a perfect balance on the palate, clarity and acidity. When it came to buying, everyone preferred to give their money to someone else, and on lower quality drinks. "Oh, you know, I'm really a beer guy..." "I'm with whiskey myself..." "I'd prefer to buy some vodka..." None kept their word. One litre of our wine cost less than a beer in a pub, yet it was too expensive. It needed to be zero, in any denomination.

The temperature we kept the wine at was wrong. *Dacian* (Romanian) summers are really hot, and we had no adequate conditions to store it. I mean, it was so hot in the flat, I was going about in my underwear, despite all windows being open. We had to get rid of it fast, or risk having to dump it. No one wants to see their work going down the drain like that, especially after the risks we took. The alcohol level was around 12%, which was perfect, so what came to our minds could work. From disappointment, we kept jumping into excitement with every new idea. Our plans were constantly shifting towards the achievement of the same goal, that of making money. What is more expensive than wine? Spirit! We had to act fast, before the wine got spoiled. At 26 degrees, any wine that is not bottled would lose its attributes. It can rapidly become a disgusting vinegary liquid, with faded elderflower impressions. A colleague's parents owned a pretty large copper still pot, that we could use to produce elderflower spirit. They were living in a villa with a fair garden, close to the beach. It didn't take long to set everything up for production. The fire needs to be soft with the still pot, or you could burn the contents, and get smokey spirit. The distillate is basically whiskey before becoming whiskey. You put the spirit in barrels to give it age, colour, depth and flavour, depending on the wood. This one didn't need barrels. The elderflower fragrance was divine. When it started dripping, our joy was massive. The first spirit coming out of the dripping pipe, has a slightly different chemical structure than drinking alcohol, called methanol. Our liver is not capable to synthesise it, so the body gets poisoned.

During the years, people have died after drinking the *forehead* of the still pot, how it's called in popular culture. Usually it has a light blue colour, and depending on the size of the still pot, it can mean you'd have to throw away between one glass and a litre of concoction. At industrial levels, the quantity of this toxic alcohol can be significant. The spirit you want is safe when the proof drops to around 70%-60%, and becomes colourless in the glass. You can compare the two to see the difference. Put them in small clear glasses, and analyse them visually in plain sunlight. Do not drink the *forehead*! Always use a copper or stainless steal still pot. Never use one made from aluminium! It will make you sick, by poisoning your body with a metal as well. During the distillation process, I kept remembering the struggle we've been through to pick the flowers, how I climbed dangerous fences and trees, in a forest with wild boars, and maybe coyotes. At some point we had our mother help us too, and for her it had been ten times harder, because of bad knees. We had to get this right, and turn a profit.

It took us a few days to finish the whole batch, and when we've put the alcohol meter in the spirit, it stopped sinking at 60% proof. Silence suddenly set in the room. We had about 60L of pure delight. We knew for sure, that we were the only ones in the country with that product. We have never heard anyone in the past making it, or if they've ever tasted it. This because of the limited quantities people can make. You make spirit out of something when you have abundance, like from the fermented pulp of the grape, after squeezing the must for wine, or from random fruits you cannot eat for various reasons. But not from elderflower wine, the wine of elves...

We turned to our colleagues again. "Guys, we've got a surprise for you. Have you ever had elderflower spirit before?" When tasting it, they started coughing, and complaining that it's too powerful. "Oh, so you guys do only 40%?" "Oh, man, Julian, that's too strong..." They did admit that the elderflower aroma was really nice. Our price was too high again. It was still cheaper then their usual vodka or whiskey, maybe less than half the price. They were stepping back from this, even more scared. No one wanted to buy from us. We were naive, thinking that selling quality stuff to people is easy. But we weren't going to give it for free. Natural spirits can last forever. We were keeping it in plastic bottles though, and it wasn't good on the long run.

On my following birthday I got so upset about my life and lack of opportunities, that I combined maybe half a litre with cola, and went to the beach with some friends. I was drinking it like water, and at some point, probably when my body said *enough!*, I threw the half empty two litre plastic bottle into the crowd of a live outdoor concert. It probably hit someone in the face. Fuck it! I was destroyed and sick, like you can rarely be from that quantity of alcohol. I'd forgotten it was 60% proof. It was delicious though. Blackout...

You have to understand, that 99% of the people around you don't want you to succeed. Even if they're your friends or not. They might say they do, but they don't. Many psychologists have postulated that bad traits are in the human nature, only to justify most of our actions. Based on the same logic, good traits are in our nature too, so why don't we see an abundance of kind acts? I disagree only with the first one. We have hybridised traits, caused by the idea of money. If money would not exist, we would have totally different opinions about our natural behaviours. We would behave totally different. When being on the same level of fortune as anybody else, you would not manifest envy against someone else. This is why the rich mingle with the rich, and the poor with the poor. Many postulates about natural human behaviour are wrong. Our subconscious is constantly being educated, in the context of our society's rules. You are allowed to blame people, for not being aware of the harm they are causing you. This is a different matter. Being intelligent, sympathetic and compassionate is also a choice, and more in tune with your original nature.

Our last attempt was to go to the local weekly farmers market. We were highly disappointed about everyone. They knew we were struggling with money, and that we had a really good product, but still, they would not pay for it. We woke up really early to go to the market, with a few bottles of different sizes, and single use shots, to offer the tasting experience as well. My brother kept limping, due to the tear of a cruciate ligament in the knee, and was using a walking stick, like Penguin from Batman. This was before the reconstruction surgery. He was wearing a blue suit jacket, jeans, and shiny leather shoes. In the context of a market, he was the accidental odd one alright. I was wearing a hoodie, old jeans and trainers; I was the proper hooligan. Everyone in the market were looking strange at us, while inviting people to taste our spirit. I guessed they thought we were undercover inspectors or something, because their looks were not friendly. They can also tell when someone is a policeman too. You need that skill anyway, when you're not totally legal. During a few hours, we had just a handful of people coming to check our product. They were telling us it could not be from elderflower, that it had to be *fake*. Our blood pressure was increasing, and we were asking each other's approval to slap them. Only one person had the courage to test it. We were overly thrilled. "There you go sir..." "Oh, god! This cannot be natural, it's too strong..." "Sir, we can assure you it's 100% natural. Do you want to buy half a litre? We'll reduce the price a bit for you." "Ok, thanks, I'll have a look around and come back..." He went and bought some spirit from someone that we knew they had poor quality drinks, counterfeit. This is the world we now live in, humans are now scared of quality. The market was closing, and we didn't sell anything. You rarely feel such disappointment. We weren't good at selling, and we had no time, nor money to build a strategy. We weren't allowed to sell it anyway, we had no licence as a company, or self-employed. What we were trying was illegal, but being police officers has its own perks, and that was protecting us somehow.

This had been our biggest endeavour in the city. We had to leave most of the unconsumed batch with our sister and her alcoholic husband, while preparing to leave the country. She promised to fill a 20L oak barrel, and burry it somewhere on her countryside property, for when we come to visit, but that never happened. The elderflower spirit and our efforts have pleased the taste of people we didn't even know, having been offered for free, in my parents' village.

CHAPTER 6

BORDERS ARE CLEAR

Music for this chapter
N.W.A. - Fuck Tha Police
2Pac - Changes feat. Talent
Inner Circle - Bad Boys
Radiohead - Karma Police
Harold Faltermeyer - Axel F
Paul Engemann - Push it to the Limit
Mark Morrison - Return of the Mack

I was a rough unpolished raver when I decided to join the army, in 2004, at 19, with the County Police or how the French love to call it, *Le Jandarmerie*; they're named differently, depending on which country you live in. Their purpose is the same though: to break your bones if you don't listen to the Government. They *care* about your health, but not if you're smart. Wit is not seen as the most important trait of a human, but as a disease. I had to do it, as there was almost no other prospect to get a hold of my life. These specialised troops are filled with some of the most brainwashed people in the *Dacian* (Romanian) armed forces. Most of them would even fuck their mother to apply the law and follow orders, even if the law is bad, and the orders crooked. What's even more sad, is that some of them have studied martial arts for many years. I mean, the main purpose of learning how to fight is to become wiser. The better you are at fighting, the lesser you wish to engage in fighting. Not these guys, which kind of makes them legal terrorists. I wanted out really quick, and by the time I finished my mandatory military service, I joined the Border Police school. Phew! Good riddance! At that school I was chosen by my class, to be a group leader due to my military experience. That brought me more money compared to them, and soon they learned to regret their vote. We couldn't all be chosen leaders anyway. Democracy has great flaws for the many. When they asked us to sign all the admission documents, there was a sheet of paper, through which the Government was committing to provide officers with substantial support for getting a house, and a decent lifestyle. I was baffled and excited. Maybe this country is not so bad after all...

"Bro, I should've been inside the Police Academy, not here", a fellow student was telling me. "What do you mean?" "My uncle is a university professor in my city, and he managed to get me the answers for the exam at the academy. Someone snitched, and the Ministry of Intern sent a team to change the results at the last minute. I knew every answer for all the questions! So many others failed with me... Then he helped me get into this police school." Yes, the system is putrid. Shortly I met many others telling me different stories, while the officers training us were promising that at the end of our two years of training period, we would be way more skilled then the academy folks. It would later confirm. The school was training characters that shouldn't have become police officers, ever. I was probably the dumbest, most normal and naive there. I needed a steady job to become a DJ! Oh, God! The others were sent there by their parents, because they needed some sort of correction, some joined for the bribes, or to be able to mediate personal illegal activities. By the end of our studies, a few students almost got a criminal record for poaching, investigation started by border police officers. They got away due to the intervention of the school. When we started working at the borders, I found out from the news that a former classmate was the main man in an extensive network, selling drugs of high risk. He got arrested on the street by the special forces, and later was freed, after the intervention of his father, former army officer in the Middle East. Other than that, his son was a funny guy, and an idiot when drinking. I felt sorry for him getting caught for that. You don't want the people you've gone to school and drank with to ever get caught, as long as they didn't hurt or kill anyone.

I was sleeping in dormitories that were former stables. During winter the heating was almost non existent. I kept waking up in the morning, to find my bottle of water frozen solid. It was nasty... On TV they were showcasing the facilities, as being to the standards of Harvard university. During classes I felt like being on a law diet. Criminal law, European law, we even debated a comma in a paragraph for endless weeks. A punctuation sign can change the interpretation of the law completely. It is that intricate. Why do you think lawyers forget how to smile naturally. The field activities and physical training were most enjoyable. They allowed us to run on the prairies like native Americans, with AK47s loaded with blanks, trying to catch the other groups, the *bad guys*. Then we would fight each other. The adrenaline rush before the start was painful, yet addictive. Necks were getting trapped, paint would fall off the walls, and after receiving a few punches right in the temple in slow motion, when I was throwing one right in the crack of the other's weak guard, where I wanted, it felt like I was a god. Why I was lying flat on the mat was an enigma. The other threw more accurate punches than me. "See you in next class, bitch!" Then we would go out for drinks. I learned a lot during that period of time about outright conflicts. In the military they don't teach you how to fight someone, in order to have a fight. They train you to take a guy out really quick when the time is right, and you have no chance to talk. When you see police officers fighting criminals like someone's put some rules into the game, that is an untrained officer. There are so many skilled criminals out there, that could take out almost any officer in seconds. If you give them a chance, they will most likely take it, and you could end up dead. That style of fighting was a delight. Finish him quick! At 20 I was too old to become a professional anyway. My performance was poor by any standard, and the time short. I only needed the basics of self-defence. When in an imminent conflict, keep at least one metre and a half distance from the opponent. If that distance is breached, and you see the guy coming close, like wanting to kiss you, hit where it hurts, and put the guy down with minimal contact. A true fighter would never come that close to you, and he would search for mediation. If he's got a weapon, it's better to test your running skills. It's not honourable, but it will keep you alive. Always choose life over honour, when weapons are being used against you. You can't run when you're a police officer though. Luckily, we were armed.

As a police officer you're required not to think, but just to obey orders. If you fail, they do not need you. But you, as an officer, have to understand that you should always protect the good people from the bad, may they be politicians, your bosses or criminals. When you work for the government and think, you realise how you're caught in the middle of a shit game. Full compliance is what they want from you. Like that seagull in Family Guy, when he tells the others that, maybe they should start catching their own fish, instead of scavenging from trawlers. Then he gets called in the boss' office, to explain how thinking works out for him, because they don't have claws or other features to be predators. When you're not wearing a uniform, remember that you will mingle with the people you go against.

You don't know many things about the world when you're being brought up in a normal family. They started teaching us about crowd control psychologies. We would have to do undercover missions in crowds of people, therefore knowing how to control the *mind* of the group, will lead to a turn of events positive for the authorities. *"Excuse me?!"* I was listening with utter disbelief about how we are being controlled, how all protests lead to nothing. The government is layering them with undercover officers, special agents, and spies. Check mate! And this was only introduction literature. At graduation we had all sorts of officials from the ministry assisting the event. If you looked closely at each and every one of them, you could see their corrupt nature. None was *clean*, nor healthy for that matter. Politics kills people and politicians alike. The difference is, a politician might die on a yacht somewhere, whereas a normal person probably in a crappy hospital.

I joined the Coast Guard in my city, and took a position in the south, in a small town close to the border with Bulgaria. Only when you hit the streets, you realise how much crime is around you. I felt like crying during pre-shift briefing, when finding out how many small children are disappearing regularly, and most of them never come back. The numbers are staggering. Where are they going, and how come most are never found? It's easier to find dinosaurs than missing children, or their remains.

Our offices were full of people with impressive forearm muscles, same as Popeye, from carrying a folder with two papers during their entire career. Those were the *bravest* officers, the *matrons* of the house, or the *black widows*. You could not trust them with anything. If you wanted to spread a rumour, they were the most fertile *planters*. We used to call them *tongue in ear*. I joined the unit with the highest grades, and the chief officer wanted to know who I was. He ordered that all newbies get the most difficult missions. Field work it is. I was ready to conduct and lead full investigations, but I had to learn the hard of the job first. I needed to get dirty, literally. On top of that, all newbies are loose ends for a while. They had to make sure I wasn't a spy or a snitch, which could've messed up their border operations. Especially agents with top marks, they're the worst at being honest. I was suspicious to all of my experienced patrol colleagues. I could see it in the way they were trying to get things out from me. I started telling them about my passion for electronic music, and how I would like to DJ. They probably went back to the chief inspector to report, *"Sir, Julian is safe! He's just an idiot in the wrong line of work..."*. I was a raver, attending all parties and festivals I could afford, many times even booking sick leave, if the dates conflicted with work. Upon return, the shift officer was asking me if I found any drug dealers. *"Sir, weirdly enough, it was the cleanest party I've been to, so no, I didn't see any drugs, nor dealers."* They knew I was lying. The hard shifts kept on coming, without being near the passport check point. There was big money involved there, still. My shift officer was a decent guy, and he could see how I did not belong there, despite him naming me as leader of the patrol many times, even when sent with really experienced officers. He knew them better than I did. At one point, he had a second officer straight from the academy, this sexy and voluptuous girl that made me go to work with pleasure. She was very sociable, and liked to mingle with the operatives. About the same age as me, probably she enjoyed our company. We were all hoping but she was into guys with money. One time she was dating this rich dude, that would drive about 200 miles just to take her home, about 30 miles from her work. She must've been really good... Her secondment hadn't been long, she had big dreams.

I started missions that didn't require too much brain power, on the actual border. During summers I had to walk for miles in scorching heat, on the fields or next to the beach, and during winters, through knee deep snow for miles on end. All dressed up as a police officer working in an office. I soon learned I had to bring proper clothes with me. All I was supposed to do was stop people from crossing the border illegally. Seeing footprints heading towards my country was bad. For a while, we had to guard a post sitting in a non functional vehicle, in the blistering cold from the seaside. It was -15°C/-20°C regularly. We were freezing to death for about four hours at a time. This was what I studied for. A few years after, we received brand new vehicles through the European Union programmes. Then we would run out of Diesel, because other officers were stealing it. *"Goddamn it! Shit!! Fuck!!!"* One time we saw some possible drug dealers in a hippie beach resort. A local told us about them. We investigated for too long, and most of the guys split. I told my colleagues to get in straight away, and then ask for backup, but since I was the youngest, they wouldn't listen to me. When my colleague came back with reinforcements, the main dealers disappeared. "Where are the others?" "You fucking idiot, they saw us and left!" My colleagues have also brought the local person, the informer, face to face with the remaining gang that possessed no drugs. "Are these the guys?" Our informer was visibly affected and scared, and I wished to be taken away by seagulls. You never put a source face to face with the presumed criminal! Back at the station my two colleagues became legends. I was just caught in the middle. I grew up in a tough seaside town, with drug dealers, pimps and other criminals, so it was in my instinct how to act in situations like that. The girl I was smooching with, when we were about three years old, lost her virginity probably when she was nine or ten, and she started going with pimps, while I was still playing with toys. My team was mostly made up of normal, inexperienced and naive guys, striving too much to be in the grace of the Inspector. Life was hard for everyone, there was no need to make it difficult for the public we swore to protect with our lives.

The few things I did have in common with most of my colleagues was pussyfooting around and drinking. Not at 8am though... I come from a whole bloodline of drunkards, but alcohol before 12pm is poison for me. We were in this horrendous pub after one night shift, still wearing our uniforms, drinking beers and spirits. My beer was foaming every time I was taking a sip from the bottle. Guys, I know how to drink a beer, but not at this time in the morning. They were all making fun of me. The other people there were sitting at the next table, and they were two local gypsies that looked like the gym was their bedroom. They were part of gangs that used to procure prostitutes for the chiefs of police. When their clans were fighting with swords in plain street, only our superiors could calm them down. They had a close connection. At a certain point one of them sniffs something white off the table, and one of us sees him. He turns around and goes, "the nerve on you, to sniff that in front of police officers!" My head went, "oh, shit!". "Dude calm down..." "Julian, don't, I'm gonna deal with these guys!" "Man, we're police officers in uniform, drinking in a bar at 8am, we'll catch them later!" The guy stood up from the table, and shadowed my incompetent buddy. "Oh, yeah? What are you going to do?" People like that know when an officer is in a situation he shouldn't be in. My colleague was already feeling the heat, we all were. The others were saying something to tackle the guy, when I had to intervene due to flashes in front of my eyes. None of those images were good for us, because we didn't have our guns. There was no guarantee we could tackle them. The only skills we had were *Vodkaikido, Beer Kune Do* and *Whiskeyrate.* "Listen, buddy, forgive my colleague, we're just having some drinks after work, and he doesn't know what he's saying... You are free to do whatever you want, it's a free country. If I wasn't wearing the uniform, I would've joined you, because it looked good quality!" "See???" He started pointing at me. "See? You should listen to your colleague, he's more experienced than you are! Thank you, my friend!" He shook my hand, then he sat back down looking angry. The others turned all quiet, with some whispering swearings from time to time. I took a sip of beer, and it was still foaming. It was probably the most disgusting beer I've ever had. "Motherfuckers, doing that in front of us, what are we?" "Drop it man, I want to go home alive!" After that I promised I would never go out with them straight after a night shift, because they were acting like retards. They knew those gypsies were part of a local gang always at ease with the District Attorney. No matter the result of that, it would've been really bad for us, not them. I just wanted to go to sleep without broken ribs or purple eyes. To this day, I can't figure out if I've been a coward, or saved the day. All I knew was that in case of a fight, I could not count on any of them.

At one point in time my parents were living at our farm with vineyard, in a small village on the Danube river. My father went into a conflict with some officials, and after my first year in the Coast Guard, I received a report that I have attacked someone with an axe. "Wow! Really?" Even my mother didn't know what actually happened, as she was not present during the alleged assault. All my higher officers were on top of me. "But I don't know these people! I haven't even been to the farm in months!" When a police officer receives such a severe complaint it's bad, because no one knows if you actually did it or not, and this enigma is forcing them to look at me with different eyes. No one even checked if I was working the day they said it happened. The fire started burning down from the highest levels, but without a specific date. They're not telling the officer anything but "you must be guilty!". The officials in the village wanted to hurt my parents, by hitting me and my brother. They knew me better because I've done my first four years of school in that village, so they decided to target only me. Little did they know I was indestructible. I didn't give a damn about what people thought about me. Most of my colleagues were laughing at the news, and my shift officer offered full support. He was the only one, that wholeheartedly told the investigators I was innocent. They wanted me to write a statement. It contained one sentence: *"I have nothing to declare"*. This, right here, is prosecution's worst nightmare. They had to prove my case, and that meant a lot of wasted time. My mother came to the city to speak with the chief inspector of the entire Coast Guard, despite my requests to stay calm. I couldn't stop her, so we went to see him. He didn't listen too much of what she had to say. We left his office, and while on the bus home, I get a call from him on my personal number. "Sir?" "When did you finish school?" "A year ago, sir..." "Listen to me, little punk, I'll take your rank for what you did! Aren't you ashamed, to assault someone with an axe!" Then he hung up. He had no proof of anything, but when you're in a really high position, you can treat anyone the way you want. He had been totally unprofessional, and disregarded any benefit of the doubt. Remembering what I've been through during police school, the sweat I had to put in to catch a position in my city, I flipped. My face turned all red, and probably I was really close to a stroke. I felt like crying, but I couldn't. Have you ever been in a state like that? My mother looked scared, and started crying. I was expanding to unimaginable limits. My flow of energy could affect someone on the other side of the planet. I have never hated someone so much in my entire life. I could not take that from a corrupt officer with a crooked past. My entire body was tense, while concentrating to calm down. I was praying no one in the bus does anything to annoy me, because probably I had never been so dangerous. I was so ready to fight, that I wanted to fight anyone, especially the inspector. The rush I was experiencing felt like unlimited hate and destruction power. That was another level of madness. All caused by one person. I wanted to break his bones, literally. I was innocent. It took me a while to calm down. I was exhausted at the end of the day.

The investigation continued, and all calmed down really quick, like nothing had happened. I had to check whether they found out if I was guilty or not. No one was rushing to give a verdict. They made fools of themselves, and they knew it. The inspector never apologised. Towards the end of my career in the force, he'd been downgraded to inspector of my unit. Now we were working together, but he was leaning on the walls when walking. He was really sick, and telling us stories about how he fucked a famous reporter on a boat, when she came to the seaside for an interview. I could just push him, and he would've fallen over like a leaf. I felt sorry for him.

During the 2008 financial crisis, the Government wanted to save money, and how else could they do it, than by cutting down the police officers' wages with 25%, overnight. It was tragic! The whole world was conspiring against my wellbeing. Many officers were renting their home, and to recover some of the loses, they deregistered their rent contracts with the local council, to stop paying council tax, and to get a higher band of the rent money coming with the wage. It wasn't legal, but also not sufficient to cover the overnight wage cut. Everyone was looking to get more money by any means. With a yearly wage of around £5,000, I could barely afford half a '98 Dacia. Soon the scam got out, and the ministry found out about the trick. They stopped paying the rent money to the ones renting, until proving that during certain years the tenants had legal contracts registered with the council. The legal stuff was more complicated to fully explain. What is important to mention, is that they could not prove people wrong. This is because tenants and landlord alike could deregister the contract. Most officers agreed that with the landlords, for a higher rent in hand for example. In my unit, everyone concerned sent the proper documentation to get verified. A commission inside the inspectorate was formed, and the investigations started. Weirdly enough, some colleagues re-registered their contracts just in time, and after talking to the investigators, they received money in their accounts pretty quick. But not me and my brother. They called us specifically to testify in front of the commission. We suspected someone close snitched on us. In their opinion we were getting too much money from this scam. All in all, we could barely survive. One year, our mother was working in Italy, with her health degrading fast, and kept on sending us euros to be able to cover the costs of living. My brother and I had to appear in front of the commission, one at a time.

I've put my tablet on the desk, turned off. "Officer, please, no electronic devices are to be present!" "Oh, sorry, but I'll leave it here, switched off." "Ok, fine." Little did they know, that I had a sneaky app on the tablet, recording everything even turned off. "Mr Stan, you do know that what you have done can get you fired and prosecuted?" "I haven't done anything!" "You know that by getting more money than you should, makes it impossible for others to get it, that actually need it?" "I don't know what you're talking about. I did not deregistered the contract with the council." "Then who did?" "It could've been the landlord, how should I know... And please don't tell me I'm guilty, do you have any consistent proof against me?" "We will gather more, and we'll sent it to the ministry, you'll have to appear in front of them too." "Ok, send it then." One of the Officers was trying to soften my heart. "Do you know that I have a mortgage, and not getting any money from the Government to cover for it? And I have a wife and kids... Many people have mortgages and don't get anything, while you get rent money!" "Excuse me, but you chose to be married with kids, it's not my problem, and you don't want to know my opinion about people with mortgages..." The guy didn't like my attitude. I was pissed off. He had a mortgage and renting the house, and living with rent to get the money, same as I was. He was a bigger scammer than most of us, preaching from a power position. I felt like slapping his glasses off. The meeting ended there, and soon our files were sent to the Ministry of Intern. The guy took it so bad, that he started an investigation on me, accusing me of insubordination, swearing at a superior, and cursing at the coats of arms representing the Coast Guard and *Dacia* (Romania). He went all in. This last one came against me after deleting the recording on the tablet. What I've done was illegal as well. When the accusations were brought to my attention, I had confirmation that the guy was mental. All happened between me and two officers. I had no chance of escaping, but I knew it wasn't true. For that you get a criminal record, even prison if all goes well behind closed doors. Being a police officer and doing that, means also aggravating circumstances. In a few days, a guy from the investigation office came to talk with me, another corrupt officer, carrying a pre-written paper of about 500 words. "Mr Stan, please read this, and then sign at the bottom." Basically he wanted me to admit everything, by signing a text that also had no punctuation marks, not even a comma. With that paper they wanted to flush me down the toilet. I could feel my face burning when looking at him, and he noticed it. "But this is admitting to what I'm accused of, and you didn't even use any commas throughout the text..." The union representative intervened, "Julian, I'll take it from here", feeling that I was about to snap. "Mr Stan will not sign this. Who wrote it?" "I did." "Excuse me, I have to go back to work. I will not sign it, please continue the investigation." And I left the room, with the investigator visibly irritated. "Have a good day!" It wasn't too much about what that document was accusing me of, but about how it was edited. It told me that he probably payed to pass all his exams during high school, academy, university, you name it. How can you not use commas in a text of half a thousand words! I am disgusted by poor grammar, especially coming from presumed highly educated people. By asking me to sign such a document he was totally disrespectful. It's all about respect, and that cleared my thinking. The next day I told my unit's inspector that, if they continue with the harassment, I will drag all of them to a civil court, and destroy their careers and house of cards. I knew they were all crooked, and I could prove it, if I was to dig really deep. I promised that the same would happen with my unit, if I had no local support. I was totally covered by my clean file and good performance. My words moved up to the highest levels, because the result of the investigation was not late to come in. What should've got me probably a criminal record, finished with a verbal warning, which meant nothing for my file. It couldn't have ended without something, and their change of hearts proved my case. They wouldn't have given the case away, if all those things they said I've done were true. They never lose, unless the accused officer is also a secret agent, or has strong connections. Most officers from the Coast Guard headquarters started to hate the Stan brothers.

After a few years of freezing and burning in the hot sun, they decided to take me to passport control, in a border check point congested almost every day. Joining the European Union allowed exponentially more traffic between countries, and probably also decreased the volume and reasons for bribe. I got scared when I saw some of my colleagues in the check point with hands full of money, in different currencies. That was a serious danger to my situation, because if one falls, everyone could fall. Getting a criminal record for a few euros? I don't think so... Give me a million euros to allow you to smuggle something, and you'll find me somewhere in the Caribbean, doing shots with the locals, I used to tell people trying to get me dirty. Now, they wanted me to check thousands of passports a night, after I've forgotten almost everything I learned during police school. I said no to their offer. My shift officers didn't like that, but could not force anyone. I accepted only jobs where the privileged of the shift were getting posted, in the chic marina or the commercial harbour, where if you had to check 20 passports, and to issue a visa, was a very busy shift. I also didn't mind the incidental carton of cigarettes and the occasional bottles of Uzo. At first, some of the veterans on the shift were like, "but you don't smoke, why do you want to share them?" "Don't worry man, I'll turn them into money in no time." We had to keep an eye on each other all the time. The temptation to not share was high. There is a custom around the world, that the captain of the ship gives something to the Coast Guard Officers coming to do the check, may it be bottles of alcohol, cartons of cigarettes or food. In some countries, the police officers snatch whatever they like, without asking anyone. From the border checkpoint the money was going up the ladder, to really high levels, MPs and ministers. By the time I left the force, bribe wrecked families and ruined careers. I never believed in a police officer career anyway, because it's not possible; you'd have to change into some nasty human being, and agree to many humiliating things, to achieve high levels and stay there.

Following the wage cut of 2008, many police officers took it to the streets. I didn't participate, as I'm a strong believer that human gatherings in large numbers are useless, no matter the cause. Inside the crowds there were police officers no one knew... They went to the presidential residency shouting *"come on out, you dirty dog!!!"*, and then many threw their caps into the courtyard behind the gates. The *Jandarmerie* beat up some police officers that did not play by the rules of the protest. We had a lot of cooperation missions with them in the 30km border zone, but orders had to be followed... Governments turn brothers against brothers. Gradual repercussions were not late to arrive. The Ministry of Intern asked for lists with the ones that participated. Weirdly enough, the situation of the economy became worse. The Government was *exhausted*, and needed to save more money. As punishment, they announced that many police officers had to be scrapped, so they invented a police knowledge test in order to keep your position. It was totally illegal, but when you come up with a new, instant law, actions that were illegal yesterday are perfectly legal today. That was exactly what happened. My brother scored high, I barely passed the test. I didn't care anymore, as we had plans to leave the country anyway. Many lost their jobs, especially experienced officers with no *support*. Some woke up with diabetes the next day, and their hair went unusually white. From police officer with a solid plinth, to bum with a family to feed. The president knew what he was doing, a man suspected of being former KGB aficionado, and who was directly responsible of terminating *Dacia*'s (Romania) sea defence capabilities, leaving the country at the mercy of the US, Russia and China. There are two types of countries in this world: countries that lead, and countries that serve. Digging deeper, I managed to find out that *Dacia*'s (Romania) president has a US general in his council. It is not a reciprocal practice!

My officers wanted me and my brother gone, but we passed the exam. They got used to me always refusing increased responsibilities in the main border checkpoint, which meant finishing the shift looking ten years older, and risking to get a criminal record for the money others were dealing in the offices. I wanted nothing to do with it. Sometimes there were unannounced checks and trials from the corruption bureau, and I still remember a video with a colleague getting caught with money in his hand, then being grounded by undercover officers. People up there were making sure we knew when integrity checks were being done, but sometimes people needed to be caught, to wash the business by going in the media, and showing that things are under control, fair and the officers clean.

The uselessness of some of my colleagues and higher officers became apparent during a conflict with a Ukrainian, waiting in the queue to cross to Bulgaria. He wanted us to move faster with the documents, because they were getting dehydrated. There wasn't much we could do, and he was stepping on our nerves. You should never be aggressive with calm and decent officers. The border point chief came out without any badge or uniform to talk to him. The guy's wife stepped in, and the redneck officer pushed her away before introducing himself. The Ukrainian grabbed him with lightning speed, pulled the T-shirt over his head, and started drawing blood with his punches. The chief came back all torn, and with blood running on his face. We all went outside to see what happened, but no one was doing anything, while the guy kept on swearing in poor English, and advancing towards the entrance in the building. I then jumped on him, and blocked his neck and backbone, in a grip that could cause severe damage if done wrong. I didn't know what else to do, I had the guy locked. With no free hands, I desperately needed help from someone to cuff him. My team leader was standing in the doorway doing nothing, while I was shouting at him to bring me handcuffs, or help me. The Ukrainian was struggling to get out but he couldn't. My pulse was raging when I realised that I was on my own. I received no help from my colleagues. It never felt more disappointing. I released the guy from the grip, and pushed him away to avoid being hit. When I jumped on him I didn't know exactly what happened, except that he beat the chief. Later I was told about the mistakes of the border point commander. With all his experience, he didn't know how to talk to people, and had broken the simplest protocol. The Ukrainian didn't know he was an officer, and he reacted when his wife got pushed away. But not helping your colleague when fighting a supposed attacker? Later they profiled the person, and we found out that he was an active military in the Ukrainian special forces. I was shocked at the news, as he probably could've snapped my bones in half in direct confrontation. He did *work* the officer with skill. Following the events I told everyone in my team not to count on me with anything. You never look at your colleague fighting someone without helping! That was a code I could not live by.

During one of my last night shifts, when preparing to go to sleep, not caring about the job anymore, we got a call from the officer controlling the infrared camera, that two people were crossing the border illegally. We went from zero to hero in seconds. Guided through the dark by our colleagues, we were driving the jeep like blindfolded, as we couldn't give away our position by using the headlights. They could still hear the engine revving, but in the night the direction of the sound can trick you. Vision plays a huge role in hearing. We nailed the illegals, two Iraqis with no documents. Luckily for us, they were unarmed. In the border point everyone wanted to shut their phones down. "No! Dude, look into their messages!" I could not believe how dumb they all were. We checked them, and found loads of messages from a local phone number. Their guide was desperately trying to reach them. *"Are you close?" "Did you manage to cross??" My* patrol colleague went, "what do you say Julian, should we go find the guy?" "Fuck yeah!" It was around 2am. We drove towards the town, and exactly at the entrance, on the main road, a Turkish guy was waiting in his car. "Good evening, sir! Why are you waiting here?" I could see him stuttering. He didn't do much to answer the question. We checked his documents, and my colleague gave them back. "Ok, Julian you go with him in the car, and tell him to drive to the border checkpoint." "Are you mad? YOU go in the same car with the suspect, with him driving!" Police officers are not as smart as you'd think; that is why they work for the Government. In the past, a police officer caught a guy stealing from the harbour, then he jumped in his car towards the police station. The suspect was driving. Knowing that he's going to jail, he turned suicidal, and almost drove off a bridge. The officer on the passenger's seat barely pulled the handbrake to avoid the disaster. "You go with him!" "I can't, I'm the driver of the jeep!" "Ok then, I'll hold his ID and vehicle documents, and ask him to drive in front towards the border point. In case he runs away, we'll catch him later." My colleague wanted me to get hurt. What's the point of having a gun with you, if the criminal is holding the steering wheel. We proceeded how I said, and scored one of the biggest captures in years. He was the guide of the Iraqis. We never got anything for that from the Coast Guard, not even a thank you from the upper echelon. If I wouldn't have intervened to read their phones, most probably the guide would have escaped.

It was time to go in front of the commission from the ministry. Together with my brother, we decided to write our own case papers. We were good at that, and they could not believe the quality of our defence. In the meantime, we discovered that the union was rotten too, its chief being more crooked than the word itself. Unions are there to keep you under leash. They usually say, "Oh, you want to take legal action against your company? Why don't you organise yourselves into one group and start one case; it's easier, and since the cause is the same..." Unions don't want individual court cases, because the big boys know this would cripple the system and the defendant. This is how you destroy a company or a wealthy person, by starting endless court cases, individually. The defence lawyers would have to charge the court fees for each separate trial. We agreed to have a representative during the meeting, but because he had no paper with our consent, they threw him out of the room. Our verbal representation was flawless. We agreed on what to say, then lies probably seemed like pure truth, even to the most experienced psychologist. Instead of trying to catch us, they were praising us for standing our ground so well. Our case was nothing compared to what was happening on a larger scale, and they knew it. We won the case, and they had to pay us money from arrears. Back at the Coast Guard headquarters, most people could not believe it. The accountancy department asked us to come and sign some documents as a final procedure, and told us not to be sad, because some people up there were talking good things about us, despite the general feel.

Our career was ending when we asked for one year unpaid holiday, and got rejected. We then booked a meeting with the general inspector of border police. There, we found higher officers that acted all cool and tough with us on the coast, crying at doors to change positions inside the ministry. It was hard for everyone, but they were people I couldn't feel sorry for. With them it was karma. "Look at this idiot, crying and asking for help! You're not so cool now, are you? Where's your whip?" Look at us, two operative officers, relaxed in front of the same doors, no matter the result. They saw us, and were trying to hide. The chief inspector, with sneaky blue eyes, didn't even shake our hands when rejecting our request. "I wish you best of luck in your careers!" "Same to you, sir!" We left smiling and radiating, knowing it would soon be over.

When the wage cut happened, we asked to see our complete file from the archives. I remembered the Government's written commitment. That stirred things up a lot, and the ministry only allowed us to see 75% of our files. Other documents, although they were our personal records, could not be accessed. The only way was to go through a court of law, but that would've taken years, and many closed door arguments and shuffles. The most important agreements signed by the Government were not part of the accessible percentage. Governments have to disappear!

We booked our entire holiday, and boarded the flight to London, each with a suitcase and less than £2,000 in our pockets, altogether. We landed in Marylebone, then took a bus to Hempstead Heath, where we started knocking on doors to see who's got rooms to rent. Little we knew that it is one of the most expensive boroughs in London. Maybe we'll own houses there one day... I mean, even living in the sewers would still cost you £1,000 in this city. A sweet and compassionate British lady told us which magazine would suit our purpose. God bless her! I sent my resignation on December 23rd 2013 through fax. It contained only one sentence, sharp as a samurai's blade. One of my best Christmas presents ever!

CHAPTER 7

IT'S BLOOD!

Music for this chapter
Charlie Steinmann - It's Such a Good Night (Scoobidoo Love)
Aaron Neville - Like Bird on a Wire
Gnarls Barkley - Who's Gonna Save My Soul
Tame Impala - The Less I Know The Better
Tears For Fears - Everybody Wants To Rule The World
London Grammar - Wasting My Young Years
Tourist x The Range - Last
Viggo Dyst - A Few Thoughts Combined
O'Flynn - Talia
Joseph Ray - Lose My Mind
Tor - Lens

Welcome to London! Oh yeah, baby! I arrived in one of the most famous cities in the world in late 2013, at 28 years old, carrying a huge load of knowledge about how this world works. Yet, I had many things left to learn about everything, including myself. I was in a challenging depression, but not because of having to leave my country and a toxic relationship, that was the best decision I have ever made, but due to why I had to leave. I was upset with almost all the people I knew, with the country I left behind, and especially with me. For the first time, I was overly upset with myself for being so delayed. Why did it have to take me 28 years to understand what is going on in the world! Thinking that some people fail to open their eyes till the end of life was of no comfort to me. Always compare yourself with the best people you know. I found a job relatively quick, through a workforce agency. My ego has never been high when having to work. I was willing to do almost anything, even to become a male escort for rich ladies. I was telling my brother that we had to build our bodies first, but we didn't really have money to go to the gym. We were struggling financially, eating £1 frozen pizzas cooked in the microwave, with double cream. I've looked into that seriously. There is a huge demand of men among London's high end liberal ladies. Chelsea, here we come! Despite my intentions, I started in a warehouse run by Indians. From Coast Guard Officer, with years of experience under my belt, and an expert in travel documents, to packing helicopters in one of Wembley's shitholes. It was a disgusting job, but I've never seen it as being too low for my level. It was all leading to my adjustment in a highly different country. I also had to face, that all this unidirectional racism in developed countries is a way to control people and create conflict, because racism goes both ways, brown/black against white too, but somehow no one talks about it. Accusing current generations for something caused by people that are long dead, is not a sign of evolution, nor intelligence. Human attitude and lack of self-education create all these conflicts. You can not accuse your parents or school education after becoming an adult. I learned to live with the situation till the end of the shift, when walking home soaked. I was going to work completely wet as well. Thinking about it, probably that winter England had seen the most rain. Talking about life making it miserable for you... After two and a half months, somewhere during early March, we woke up with a beautiful sun punching through the dirty curtains of our disgusting rotten room, straight into our faces. It was a divine revelation. I suddenly told my brother, "bro, I don't want to work there anymore." He approved me straight away. "Fuck their warehouse!" We left the managers with loads of packing to finish. We told them to call us if they really want us back, with a consistent wage increase proposal. "What kind of increase were you thinking about, could you give us a number?" "Oh, you don't want to know how much we would ask... You decide, and then call us." They never did. "Adios, Patels!"

We switched to survival mode for a couple of months, until we've been sent by the agency to work for Kodak. "Wow, so exciting!" During the induction they told us they're one of the most environmentally friendly companies. It was the opposite, but our trainer had to present it that way. We learned how to pack photographic paper, loads of it, and for the first time, I've seen automated robots carrying the massive paper rolls to the cutting room. "Cool!" We've also been introduced to the cutting box, containing blades so sharp, they could cut the air, and then the air would cut you. This was happening if you'd stare at the knives for too long. Even the Kevlar gloves used to load the paper in the machine were crying. The chemicals they were using in that factory could cause any type of cancer you can think of. When they were *baking*, you'd feel this smell of sauerkraut in the morning, coming from a furnace that was steaming shy, kind of like *Thomas the Tank Engine*. This reminds me of the times when I was a kid in my small seaside town, living not far from a sulphuric acid factory. When they were processing, the night sky would turn all orange, and a pungent smell would invade our houses (similar with the burning clutch smell). "Wow! It's so beautiful!", while mum was scolding me to go inside, and close the balcony door. You can guess what happened with most of the people that worked there. It was quite like in *The Simpsons*. The job soon became a 12h nightmare, when we started packing Ektacolor paper in complete darkness. It's amazing how your eyes can adjust in 10-15 minutes. Soon you'd be able to distinguish the others' faces. Coming out into normal light was painful. It didn't take long till my hands started looking like they were decomposing, from all the dry paper bags, the chemicals on the paper and on the protective gloves. Kodak was falling apart, while the naive employees kept on hoping that the good days will come back. They used to be paid so well, that they had their own bank branch inside the factory, to manage their finances. From an example in business, the company had been mulled by the managers till collapse. Eastman was probably turning in his grave. Now it's being taught as a negative management example in economics schools all over the world. The tragedy lies in them inventing the digital camera, but not investing in it! It wasn't poor management, they knew what they were doing. Kodak was so good with their employees that, at the end of the factory in the UK, before what was left of it got sent to Germany, the employees would get support towards new well-paid jobs. Before this, they asked who'd want to willingly leave with a fat redundancy pay-check. Some said yes, and moved to the Caribbean, others hoped for the best, and got scraps at the end. How many companies in the UK would do that for their workers? I've always thought that the US are masters of marketing and running companies. Kodak UK belonged to a British pension fund, but it kept the American approach on how to treat employees. During the factory's last months, I tried to escape that carcinogenic environment, and got a job in this professional sales company looking for outstanding salesmen. Considering my sales skills, I knew I'll be crap at it but hey, why not give it a try. After all, they were the ones sending me an invitation to apply, after seeing my CV online. I never understood how a company can actually consider my

CV as being exceptional. It's all over the place. If you'd have a look at it, you would think the owner is a mad man, and start asking why I'm not rich, living in a hilltop villa in Monaco. I attended this company's interview, and got the job. "Wow! What did I do well?" They liked the fact that I knew how to start and finish things. It was also a multicultural company, a must in a colourful city like London. The more diversity, the higher the number of contracts. A British can close British businesses quicker, an Indian, corner shops, and a Dacian, Dacian businesses and the rest. At first, I had to learn a four pages pitch, the bread and butter of sales. It took me a while, but I got there in the end. I knew each and every word by heart. They liked that. Acting the pitch like it's natural conversation was a totally different experience. I was proper rubbish at it, and felt like an idiot when going into a shop, and starting to read it from the retina, like Arnold in *Terminator*. They put me in the custody of this really smart and beautiful Bulgarian girl, who was amazing at closing businesses. We were selling British Telecommunications contracts, the Microsoft of the internet and landlines. Everyone knew they were crap, so it wasn't an easy job. A while back, this company used to sell contracts for BT's competition. Now, we were trying to switch them back. Crazy! I was thinking, *"oh, man, why have I gotten into this!"*. For the first two weeks I got trained. By the end of it I had enough courage to pitch businesses on my own. I still looked like a jackass when doing it, but I passed the trials. Then I got my own area, somewhere in Stoke Newington. The next two weeks I've done really good, actually exceeding expectations. At the office we would practice with each other till perfection. It was proper acting, and nothing else. We had answers for any objection the business owners would throw at us. We aimed for a smile, then a first *yes*, then the second, third, closed! “Yes, another contract!” Then the issues with the broadband would arise. “Ok, I will stay away from that shop for a while...” I was elegant throughout that experience.

When I arrived in London, I wished I’d have the chance to live the white collars’ life for a while. Suits, suitcases, shiny shoes, great hair due, well in my case sexy shinny skull and perfect eyebrows, and pub at the end. Little did I know how sad and meaningless their lives are, with money but no time to live. I was looking like a businessman when doing sales, rushing through the underground with my coffee to catch the right train, then reading the financial column from a leftover newspaper. This time I was heading the same way as the rush hour people. First hour in the morning I was in the office with broken eyes, practicing the pitch, and telling everyone the difficulties I encountered the day before. Then again in the train with the businessmen, towards my own area of the map. I would enter a business I had visited ten times before, and trying again. “Sir, you need this internet, let’s talk business!” I was definitely the shittiest salesman in the office, and among the oldest, but I could definitely see myself progressing. The feeling was amazing. There was a lot of career progression at stake, but the more I was doing it, the more I doubted that I’d have my own office one day. I was in this Catalan guy’s team, helping him reach the next level. The better I did, the higher the chances he’d move to the next level, being able to choose the city of his office, almost anywhere in the world. It was a far fetched dream, a nirvana. I stopped performing after four weeks and a bit. I was exhausted. Waking up at 5am to be in the office at 8am, and went home at 11pm-12pm, then waking up again at 5am, five days a week, even weekends sometimes. Most of my colleagues were in their early twenties, a perfect age span to do sales, but I was 31, and bored to death of hard work. At the end of every work day we would meet in a pub or club, and drank the evening away, close to midnight or even later than that. How can you wake up fresh the next day... It was brilliant though, and socialising like that in the amazing pubs and restaurants of central London was idyllic. In that company I have worked with the nicest and most professional people I have ever met. They were really young, hard working, and brilliant at doing sales. It was short but intense. In little over one month I've accumulated years of experience. This way I discovered how many businesses with zero clients are being kept open for money laundering. The team made me feel like I had super skills, when in my opinion it was the opposite. We were having drinks on the side of the Thames, cheering like one big family. "Cheers!"

The last two weeks I got a very different and difficult area, Canary Wharf. I go into this restaurant, and start pitching the manger. "Oh, mate, you have to talk to Gordon Ramsay if you want to change the phone lines..." Yes, it was the restaurant of the famous chef. I felt exhausted, because most businesses there are big companies. *"Fuck me, you're disgusting! Bring me a fucking cappuccino then, and step on it, you dumbass!"* I enjoyed it on the edge of the water, thinking at what to do next. After a month and a half I decided I could not do it anymore. I don't know if I managed to close someone in the last weeks. The company kept on paying me, but I had to make sales. I have disappointed a lot of friends with my decision, but I explained my situation. I was in my thirties, and needed money bad. Only the fixed wage was not cutting it, I needed the commission really bad. Before I left we had our last dinner somewhere in Vauxhall, and everyone kept expressing their regrets for my departure. They could see me becoming a successful salesman. Seeing them like that made me sad, but it had to happen. They made me feel important for once, and saw in me what I couldn't. After I left, a few others left too. When I heard that I started feeling even worse. "You leaving opened my eyes!" "Oh God, please don't say you're leaving because I'm doing it, you're 100 times better than me at this, I wish I was this good when I was your age..." The last unexpected payment I got a few months later was £2. By my calculations they didn't owe me anything. The company was quite fair.

I started a part time job in the famous KOKO club, in Camden, while still working for Kodak. That was intense! I would not recommend having ice with your drinks in that location. Please don't ask around why, just don't have ice... Working there was a nightmare. Cleaning the club was a version of hell. It's a nice location to have fun, if the gig is matching your taste, but never work there as a bar staff, unless you're a qualified bartender. One of the biggest joys for some lucky ones, was when they were finding money, wallets or smartphones. Despite doing hours under a questionable contract, the managers did not miss a payment, even if I let them down, resigning without giving too much of a notice. Respect! I took the decision one night, "fuck it, I'm outta here!". My brain couldn't have it anymore. Working where people are having fun is degrading.

During my beginnings in London I was planning to change my life completely. I started applying to all sorts of castings for movie extras. One time I played in this medieval documentary for the BBC (no, it's not what you think, you sick pervert), about the wars between the Scotts and the Anglo-Saxons. It was filmed on this famous battlefield close to Bournemouth. I mean, how often do you get to wear an authentic Scottish outfit, and a whole goats skin. I paid for the train ticket almost the entire money I made for the day.

The second movie was a feature called *Set the Thames on fire*, about a dystopian flooded London, in which the survivors were fighting for food and dominance. We filmed somewhere in central London. I was one of the security officers team, patrolling the streets. I had to wear full customised outfit, including a gas mask. During a break, the director offered us lunch on the set. After having a blueberry muffin, one of the extras, that knew more about the producers, told us that the director's boyfriend cooked the food. The Director was a man. "Pardon? His boyfriend?" "Yes, he's a chef in this high end restaurant." The idiot couldn't keep it to himself. I instantly felt like someone punched me in the throat. I was imagining digesting the muffin in reverse. I wished I didn't know that information. You don't want to find out that your man chef is playing with another man's *brown whole* and *dingy*, and then preparing your food. That information spoiled all the fun. After about two years the movie came out, premiering in Europe on the Southbank, in London, during the BFI movie festival. Before that, it was played during the Palms Springs movie festival. I was super ecstatic that my image reached the US too. We booked tickets to see it, and before the screening, my mother kept on bragging at the bar, that her son is playing in the movie. "Mom, calm down, it's just for a few seconds, and my face is not showing." We did understand her excitement though. I could not wait to see myself too. I read the description of the movie before going, and something sounded a bit fishy. They pressed play, and there I was, walking in front of the camera. Woohoo! The happiness didn't last for long, as after just about ten minutes into the action, I was apologising to my mother for the excruciating experience. My brother expressed his intension to punch me in the face at the end. The whole action was centred around gays, inspired by the director's student years in Shoreditch. It wasn't graphic, but still quite intense, with disgusting Noel Fielding lasciviously smelling the chair, after a man sat on it, acting all horny and ready to fuck the guy. It was horrible but, we had to stay till the end. It was my first movie... My mother was hurting, and many times covering her eyes in disgrace. She was also scheduled to have her first total knee replacement surgery the next morning. I was disgusted and disappointed. *"I've been duped! D'oh!"* Do not watch that movie if you're straight! Even gay people are probably considering it a disgrace.

I knew I've adapted to London's lifestyle, when I found myself in a private hire car, next to this gorgeous British woman with a really sexy and educated accent. She was skeptical about getting a hire car, being used to book only black cabs. I thought, *"am I dating someone like that?"*. When I see their sour faces, I always think at the *Fake Taxi* dude, *"where to, love?"*. Maybe I'm watching the wrong *tube*. We were heading to her place, after having dinner in Shoreditch, both drunk. Cosy in the warmth of the car, we started kissing like crazy, while I was slipping my hand inside her panties, making it very difficult for the driver to concentrate. She kept on telling me to wait till we got home, but I continued on being nasty. She loved it. This is how I got my one star rating, and was probably very close to being banned from the platform, after my first ever booking. I felt sorry for the guy, Arab by the looks, most probably totally against PDA, especially in the back of his car. I would do it all over again, because she was really hot. In the morning, accompanied by coffee and warm bagels, with butter and yeast extract, we were both amusing at the night before. Yes, we were both lovers, not haters!

After leaving the sales company, Kodak ended production as well. Towards the end everyone found out how the pension fund already sold the land to developers, that would turn it into houses. Now it's called Eastman Village, after the founder of the company. Unanimously, all Kodak technicians were saying that they would never buy a house built on that contaminated land. They were expressing worries for the ones that would live there, having their children playing on those grounds. To give you an idea of the types of chemicals used to coat the photographic paper, I can say that they were using tanks of liquid silver (mercury). The developer of the village is Barratt, one of the biggest construction companies in the UK. I can bet on anything, that they haven't done an analysis of the soil before starting construction. And if they did, and came back clean, it couldn't be true. Shortly after Kodak finished, at least two of my colleagues died of different forms of cancer, and at least one had his prostate removed. They were all happy to get good money, but for a high price.

Soon I got a job as sales advisor for Three phone network, where I was earning less than when I used to work in the warehouse. After three years in the UK, I was going backwards. *"What is this shit?"* Upper level managers were visiting us, trying to explain the company's vision, "you know, not many people have this opportunity to grow in a young network..." "Mate, I need good money, what's all this £1,300 a month?" At the end of the first month I was sweating, because I had bills I needed to cover. This is a job for students that want to develop some skills in sales. I was doing quite good for my level, but that wasn't the point. I've worked there for about two months, until an agency worker and friend from Kodak, told my brother about the secret company all Kodak staff were getting jobs in. The agency staff was not supposed to know about this move, because they knew we were better workers, smoother through interviews, better weed appreciators, and with higher studies. When we found out, most of them were pissed off about us showing up at interviews, during which some line managers from Kodak would fail, and agency workers would get full time jobs.

When I left Three I saddened some people once more, especially this super sexy Indian girl, that didn't really like me at first. She looked like almost crying. I never thought that people could see me as a good friend and colleague, in such a short time. I left the network straight after passing the interview with the secret company, a human plasma processing lab called Bio Products Laboratory. I got a position as Technician 3 in Large Scale Fractionation of human blood plasma. In my mind I turned into a doctor overnight. And I wasn't that far from the truth, because I was extracting the antibodies from the human plasma, the yellowish liquid coming out through the skin when you get a scratch, right before the red blood cells start gushing out. They both form the blood together with the serum. Most doctors don't know anything about how vaccines are made, or what the Orange Guide and Pharmacovigilance Practices are all about. I was definitely better than most British GPs, that go on search engines to see what the treatment might be.

During the tour of the lab, our guide was telling us that there wasn't a better time to join the company. They were planning to expand the process. Finally, for once I wasn't getting, *"you're late Julian, this company used to be so good, you're too late, too late..."*. All my previous jobs had been like that, to the point that I started thinking that when I was born, the doctor told the newborn me, *"you're too late Julian, it used to be so good living on this planet..."*.

This probably actually happened, since I was born during communism. I was now in a company with good and recognised perspective. During the induction, I found out that I would probably struggle with the gowning procedures. "You wash hands with antibacterial soap and plenty of water, you disinfect, you change into the clean boots, you take the overall out of the sealed bag with minimal contact, while avoiding it touching the floor, get in it slowly, you put the head cover on, you disinfect, you put the mask on when inside the department, and lastly, put on the cotton gloves and then the surgical gloves. In the production area you must use protection goggles at all times." Some people did not accept the job due to these procedures. It wasn't easy having to comply with it, and working at between -5°C-0°C. A lot of Kodak staff got really good jobs in this company, with no previous experience for the positions offered. There was this guy I used to bag paper with on the production line, and now he was taking interviews of people applying for jobs in this pharmaceutical company. Yes, their union and Kodak took really good care of them. This was the first sign, that the new company was not on top of its own business. Naming a team leader with no previous experience, who doesn't know the process, to manage people with over 10-15 years experience in producing medicine?! *"What the heck is going on!"* I learned really quick, that it was that type of company promoting the weakest, while whipping the skilled to exhaustion. "See it this way: you're too good to be promoted, or to lose you from the department..."

Here I was, working for Bio Products Laboratory as a lab technician, doing titrations, and adding cancer inducing chemicals to the human plasma, or that could pierce through your skin, in order to isolate the proteins (immunoglobulins). People from NASA had nothing on me, they were splitting opinions, I was fractioning the plasma by controlling its pH. At the first stage of extraction they were called Gamma Globulins, and they represented about 35% of the paste we collected. They were telling us that in China the yield is better. We all know why... Good immunity is based on exposure. An unexposed human cannot be healthy. If my high school chemistry teacher would've seen me, probably she would have done everything in her power to stop the production, and kick me out of the lab. Or maybe she wasn't good at making me like chemistry?! Hmmm... Well, this time I was really good at it. It was nothing more than following a recipe. When deviations would happen, meaning unexpected events in the process, man or non-man made, then the experience and skill would come in handy. After one year, the duration of training, I had both. During my three years in the company, I had no major event that could have endangered the batch of plasma, coming from about 7,500 donors, whose market value was estimated at about £6.5 million. I alone could've ruined it at any stage of the process. The fact that we were actually saving peoples' lives was quite a drive for me to be good. Never before had I had a life saving job. They've all been the opposite. The lab is producing coagulation factors, immunoglobulins, albumin, and specific vaccines like tetanus, rabies, anti-D (for mothers with rhesus negative or Rh- blood type) and zoster (shingles). Reading through the process documentation, and then actually doing it, fascinated me for the first year. I was also lucky to get a job in that department, without any prior experience. That has propelled my experience into an industry that is really difficult to access without prior studies or experience, and I have to thank them for that. This is the beauty of developed countries like the UK, they don't care about your studies that much, but about how capable you are to pick up something new, and be good at it. The problem of this particular company was that they didn't want to pay consistent wages, to people specialised in biotechnology. You can't say their approach was completely flawed. I mean, look at 2020, and what qualified scientists did with the science they should have protected. Biologists are now telling you that you have no immunity, and that a safe vaccine can be developed in 6 months, instead of ten years... Would you want these schooled scientists to be your saviours?

When getting the job I was promised a flourishing career, personal development, and access to higher levels based on my performance. I've been grateful for the opportunity but I never promised I would give them my life. Soon everyone started telling me that I joined the company too late, again! "It used to be so good before, man, when we were in the NHS..." "Oh, no, not again!" The production manager was this Indian fella, let's call him *Samantha*, who knew nothing about managing people or production. I gave him a woman's name, because a lot of men under his level liked kissing his ass, hence me assuming that other men found him delicious, including my team leader, who was shit scared of him. He enjoyed playing the submissive character in almost any situation that included *Samantha*, the technicians' number one felon. You basically had to beg for a promotion, no matter how good you were, whereas if you were friends with him, you'd get the next level way ahead of time, without even being trained. Word went around, that he didn't care about people one bit. He brought his *cousin* in the company, and created a special position for her, called *training facilitator*. After speaking with other managers, I learned that everyone thought she was actually his sister. Cousin probably sounded less conspicuous. She didn't know what we were doing, but had the power to tell us what to do and how to train, annoying everyone around her. She was getting the middle finger from all when leaving the office. It was becoming more and more clear, that the company's promises during the induction week would not keep. After six months I was already training other technicians, although I shouldn't have done it without being taken to the next level, that of Technician 2. In the beginning they promised that, if I do good, I will become a Technician 2 somewhere between six months to one year. I'm a man of honour, if you promised me something and you don't deliver, you're fucked. If I promise I always deliver. I delivered, and now I was training others. After six months I didn't say anything, willing to learn, and become even better during another set of six months, despite the fact that others got their promotion in as little as four months. *Samantha* probably had the shiniest brown butt... It was fine! After one year my attitude changed, as I was more trained than the requirements. "Where is my promotion?" "I sent your file to *Samantha*, now it's up to him...", I was assured by my incompetent team leader. When speaking with other managers, I learned that no one talked with them about my promotion. They were all playing me, it wasn't just my team leader lying to me, they all were.

At some point a team leader position became available in my department, so I applied. Everybody knew who will get the job, it was no secret, but I wanted to experience that type of interview. They had to make it a competition, because it wasn't an in-role promotion. You were changing the wage band too. During the interview day I've done mistakes that I was aware of, with questions even my team leader could not answer, and during the group project I've been the best there, aspect that attracted the attention of our assessors. I failed the contest, and the guy we all knew will get the position, got it. He was a good hardworking guy that had worked there for ages; he deserved it. He was also one of my first trainers. After a few days I've been called by this Arab manufacturing shift manager, impressed by how I had performed during the group project. Let's call this guy *Camel*. He was known as *Mr Useless*, because he wasn't helping anyone, despite making daft promises. In his office he was explaining me how he'll talk with my team leader, in order to put me on the path to become a Technician 2. He was promising that I will learn what I already knew after six months. He had no idea that I was actually fit for Technician 1. He's been the most boring person I talked to in that company. Needless to say, he never had any meeting about me with my team leader. His wife worked in the same area as us, and she was the only employee allowed to wear bacteria trap sneakers, instead of protective boots.

I was becoming very impatient. In the meantime, the company was hiring people constantly, with different contracts for the same positions. The turnover was scary. I had a young guy on my shift with a Masters in organic chemistry, and who was being paid £3,000/year less than me. When debating this aspect, they told us that they also considered our previous experience in pharmaceuticals. Neither had any, and if someone should have been paid less, it was me. Due to his lack of experience with employers, my colleague was too vocal for his own good, and didn't know how to fix it legally. Compared to him, I had many surprises for them. Eventually, around April 2019, after two years and three months, I forced my team leader to get in touch with Human Resources to see what is going on. The answer was that I got the promotion to Technician 2. "Aren't you happy?" I was fuming, because I was training Technicians 2 when I was a Technician 3, all while the British boyfriend of

Samantha's cousin got promoted to Technician 1, without being as prepared as I was. He was going through promotions in record time. That was the tipping point. Plus, everyone hated the guy, as he was a known snitch, and that he was avoiding helping his colleagues when struggling. Is your work rubbish? Let's get you promoted!

In the lab everything was more than 30 years old. The method we were using to separate the proteins from the liquid was centrifugation, with huge centrifuges that would spin a 300kg steel bowl, at over 5,000 rotations per minute. Beforehand we would treat the plasma with different chemicals, like 99% acetic acid, ethanol and caustic, to control the pH under low temperature. Because he knew not the process, we would lie to the team leader many times, about the severity of some situations when close to causing a deviation. "Is the temperature alright?" "Oh, yes, it should be like that at this stage..." And maybe we were sweating, and running about trying to fix it. "How's the pH?" "All good!" The process would start with receiving the plasma, treating it with silica to isolate the impurities, then filter it through massive presses. Some filters could even catch the viruses. No wonder that down the process they would cost about £15,000 each, or more! Then we'd add chemicals to change the pH (potential hydrogen) during the precipitation stage, and after a certain time of maturation, it would all come down from massive Cohn vessels, through the installation, right into the bowls that would be spun by heavy duty centrifuges. After hours of centrifugation, the coagulated proteins in the treated plasma would stick to the sides of the steel bowls, while the liquid was taking another route upstairs, into another collection vessel. Harvesting the paste from the bowls was always hectic. "Go-go-go! Open that centrifuge! Prepare for battle!" "Julian, how's the *specifics*?"

"All good!" "Oh, fuck, the centrifuge went off again!" "Restart it, and leave it to go in production!" "Guys, the other fraction is off, we need to start preparing the other room!" "I'll paste!", someone would shout, hoping to avoid scrubbing the room during harvesting, and after. Two of us would be the harvesters, so they'd get equipped with the second overall and a second set of aseptic gloves. Due to the need for fresh air and oxygen, all of us would have the mask off. It would've been almost impossible to get out of that conundrum with the mask on. Plus, we all felt knackered at the end of the shift. All that PPE to protect the product was draining the strength out of us, and especially the mask, was hated by everyone for restricting our breathing. The first paste would get weighed and stored in -40°C freezers for further processing, towards the third and second fraction, while the liquid would be processed straight away for the fourth and fifth fractions, the latter being the albumin (not immunoglobulin - helps the body to produce blood if you've lost a lot). The second fraction was the immunoglobulin, and a 20kg box would be worth around £500,000. No wonder, one immunoglobulin shot was about £5,000 on the shelf. This is also paying for the fat managerial bonuses, for doing a good job with saving money with the wages of the people producing the medicine... We were getting about four boxes of immunoglobulin paste per 6,000 litres batch of human plasma. When I first started working there I found it extremely disgusting, but I got used with it eventually. Still, you didn't want to be splashed in the eyes with plasma from over 7,000 people. The raw material was coming only from the USA, because weirdly enough, they didn't have any cases of mad cow disease. Science says that the disease can stay inactive in the brain for up to twenty years, so the Americans didn't want to risk getting it from Europeans... They were the biggest buyers of the medicine too. Plasma centres are constantly opening on that belt close to Mexico, where the rednecks live. Our products were approved by the FDA (Food and Drug Administration) in the States, and by the MHRA (Medicines and Healthcare products Regulatory Agency) in the United Kingdom. Because of this, many other smaller countries would find it easy to buy the products, being vetted by such powerful bodies.

We were the most hard-working shift, in the most difficult, and physically challenging department. We'd always be ahead with production but get a bonus once in a blue moon. The wage was crap for the risks and dangers, and when we did get a bonus, they were throwing at us reasons why it couldn't be higher. They were always making sure that we got less money than more. If other departments were behind schedule, we'd get no bonus, so basically we could have died trying to keep up with their demands, but because others downstream could not cope with the flow, we didn't deserve any incentive either. Their logic was totally screwed, but well planned. When they eventually gave me the Technician 2 promotion, they've done it in April, so I didn't qualify for the promotion, and the yearly 2% 5% wage increase as well. Every time, they were looking to cut your access to better money, although others have been promoted and got the yearly increase too, but not from my shift. Soon I found out that the company was also promoting people, with different money for the same positions. That lab was, and I believe it still is, managed by idiots. What they didn't realise, is that practices as these were totally against the Orange Guide, which sets a clear guidance on how employees should be treated in GMP (Good Manufacturing Practice) companies, especially pharmaceuticals. By mistreating employees, you put the lives of your patients in danger. I couldn't find a happy technician in my department, except probably my team leader. He was oblivious to what was happening with us, and him. One of the biggest problems we had was numbers. They were refusing to hire the right number of people for the size of the tasks, causing our exhaustion. When having a few days off it felt like paradise. If people were getting sick, the pressure would've been even higher. Many times we were coming to work with flu, colds, aches and pains, you name it. There were not enough people. Sometimes there were openings for overtime, but you'd have to go work on a shift that would let you do everything by yourself. All others wanted to do overtime on our shift, because they knew how good we were. One time, *Samantha* proposed that they split our shift, to go fix the issues on all other shifts, and this crossed the line with the elders of my shift. "No fucking way! If he does that, we'll change departments!" It never happened. The lab was constantly bleeding really good and skilled people, leaving for better companies and higher pay.

Bio Products Laboratory used to be called Lister Institute of Preventive Medicine, after Dr Joseph Lister, a pioneer in medical science. Until roughly 2013, the company was part of the NHS (National Health Service), producing blood plasma derived life-saving medicine. They were a non-for-profit company, that offered really good contracts to their employees, and a chunky pension. I never believed in pension, thinking it's a trap for the naive and financially-uneducated, but within these terms, it means above average. In 2013, someone in the government decided to sell the business to a US based equity firm, Bain Capital, for £200 million. By contract, they promised to invest many millions, in order to take the lab to really high standards. Keep in mind that when the NHS owned it, the price of the medicines was really accessible for patients and hospitals. Now, the health service and the patients are paying a premium price for it. After about a year, the American firm probably thought the lab isn't worth the effort, and decided to sell it again, this time to a Chinese investment fund called CREAT, for a whopping £820 million. That's more than four times the price it got sold for by the UK Government, without any improvements being made! CREAT have invested massively in the pharmaceutical industry. They also own the German company Biotest, to which we were sending one of the fractions. So now, the Chinese own a strategic UK company already approved by the FDA and MHRA. When I hear British people saying that the UK is different, and that the politicians in power know what they are doing, that they are protecting the NHS, I laugh. No, mate, the destruction of your health service started long time ago, one company at a time, as in any other country with a similar system. Everything needs to be privatised, so you pay money for the smallest medical service. Otherwise, why would the government allow a foreign investment fund to take control of your vital medicine? Someone up there, in Westminster, got a lot of money for the transaction. And if you didn't know, investment funds use these companies to launder *many monies*. As an example for those who don't know economics, if you'd have £100 million dirty money, would you prefer to lose it all, and risk going to jail too, or wash them through a company or companies, lose £60 million, but get to keep £40 million of *clean* money? If it's an offshore company that's saving lives even better. When the business became private, what they've done to the NHS employees is humiliating. If they chose to keep their current contract, therefore still getting the chunky percentage in the pension pot paid by the company, and receive the yearly wage increase and the sporadic bonuses, no matter their work performance during the year, they had to say goodbye to promotions. They would stay in the current position indefinitely. If they would apply for a different one and get it, the new contract would come into force, therefore lose their NHS benefits.

A lot of questions came to our minds, when the management discovered a massive fault with the filters during the yearly shutdown. Each pharmaceutical company is forced by the regulators to shut down production for four weeks every year, to fix issues, improve and then at the end, to have a deep cleaning of the production areas. In 2018, the technicians have discovered that the HEPA filters failed in all production areas, and they didn't know when they failed, putting many already processed batches at risk. Instead of hiring specialists from HEPA to come and test the filters regularly, the company decided to use its own unskilled people. These filters make sure that the air in the lab is as clean as possible. They had to stop production for four months to investigate, totalling a loss of about £35 million. I'd say it was more than that, but this is the number they advanced. Bye-bye sporadic bonus! During a town hall meeting, the CEO was telling us how the investors were fully supporting the company during the hard times. Although there was someone responsible for the flop, no one got fired. Those four months have been a great time to work there! I could also practice my Julian shots on the pool table. Everyone was scared of my unpredictable game moves. All I could hear from the guys was, *"fuck you, Julian, and your lucky shots!"* How could the company function properly, if even the CEO, a slim Canadian guy in his fifties, didn't know what he was saying. During all meetings with the staff, whenever someone was asking him a question, he would pass it to one of the top managers. I remember when *Camel*'s wife asked him a question for about two minutes, in the most broken Indian-English I have ever heard. Then he went, "I think I know what you're trying to say, so I'll pass it to *Frank*, who's got the right answer..." That time I didn't blame him for not being able to answer that specific, vast, and vague question. I was surprised how during important meetings with the CEO, no one in that company was asking about the work conditions, pay, and bonuses. It seemed like we were there as sacrifice for the god of vaccines. People got word that CREAT is investing massively in the German company Biotest, and way less in BPL, raising concerns about the safety of the job. It wouldn't have been the first British company taken to Germany. Another rumour was that they were planning to shut it down, and clear the natural park it sits on. When asked about all that, the CEO answered that he does not have information about why the investors are placing way more money in Germany. An amazing and comforting answer from the head of the company. At the end of the meeting I wanted to clarify something, so I asked him in person if it is possible to buy shares in the company. He replied, "you cannot, because it's a private company", and then he left swiftly. It was then, when I realised that I was talking with the dumbest pharmaceuticals CEO. That was the first paradoxical answer I have ever received from someone. Soon he got replaced by a Chinese CEO. He took his millions and left.

The production management was so poor, that sometimes we had to discard whole batches for different reasons that could've been avoided, or because they expired before the next department could process it. This translated into hospitals and patients not getting vital medicine. The cherry on the cake was our health and safety. My chemist colleague got fed up with it all, and filed a grievance, after discovering loads of missing risk assessments of the procedures with the chemicals. For example, we were weighing Celpure (silica) like flour, instead of having a machine to do it for us. Then we'd carry the bags to the upstairs Cohn vessel, and add it to the plasma by hand, increasing the risk of inhaling cancerous particles tenfold. We shouldn't have had direct contact with it. After building a new processing facility, for a fraction we used to send away, they've installed a Celpure machine that would eliminate the human exposure. But not for the large scale fractionation. We would only wear a mask with a ventilated and expired filter, that had silica all over it. There was no procedure in place to change that filter. My colleague had a meeting with the new health and safety manager, who inherited big problems he did not create. He was a decent guy, and in the grievance outcome he admitted that the risk assessments were missing, and that it wasn't right. With a paper like that, you'd crush the company in a court of law. The chemist was put in charge of sorting the papers out, but he was already leaving the company. Another important asset lost. I was a trained risk assessor, but the situation was so bad, that you didn't know where to start. If I was to stop people from using cleaning products and other chemicals, until doing a proper risk assessment, it would have disrupted the entire production in the department, against *Samantha*'s objectives. After the issues with the room filters, I heard him whispering to a contractor he knew, "if there's another issue in this lab, I think I'll have to find another job..." We all wished he'd do that by his own volition. Another worrying fact was that, some employees didn't want him to go! "And what, having another manager that could be worse? I like it as it is, I have a mortgage, I'm comfortable", and so on. In a society, you live how you live because people accept it. But if you'd live in utopia, you wouldn't want that to change either, would you, so it's all about getting used to something, about your level of acceptance and servitude. Don't get used with the cancer in your life, it's being forced on you, so you think it's normal. When things can be improved but you're opposing, because *it is what it is* or *this will do*, you're actually going against the good people that want things to be better, which makes you a bad character; you're the one against a common language, because you're caught in a trap by your own stupidity and recklessness; nothing is for sure. In 2019, we had some inspectors from the German regulatory body, coming to check the laboratory. They fried *Samantha*, and we all loved it. Once in our office, one of the inspectors opened a cabinet, and started checking the documents. "Why iz ze pizza menu with ze GMP documents?! Iz zis proper GMP Mr *Zamantha*?" We almost burst into laughing. Because I was the first one in his visual range, *Samantha* gave me a look, like he wanted to kill me. *"Go on, bitch! I'll slap you silly!"*

The problem we had with some of the cleaning products was serious. There was no risk assessment for Peroxide. When using it to disinfect the production areas, we'd get irritated eyes and lungs, we'd lose our smell and taste, and no one was doing anything about that. By the new standards, we all had *covid.* If we were to take them to court, they'd now be shut. A colleague stumbled upon an old article online, from around 2008, when the lab was still in the NHS. They were describing the business, as producing vital medicine in improper conditions. Everything there was very much happening still. "Oh, man, this place didn't change a bit!" Because they weren't ever fixing the issues for good, it couldn't have been a proper aseptic environment. Pipes leaking, centrifuges with rust and spilling out oil, bad floors with cracks, and many others. After every shutdown, almost nothing changed. *Samantha* was taking care of everything. No one responsible was getting fired, only technicians. They were willing to lose experienced technicians, like they were nothing. Considering that in the pharmaceutical industry the human resource is like gold, because it takes a great amount of time to train someone, the company should've begged us to stay. Almost every technician was trying to fix the issues, but without any support. I had my own projects to simplify and improve the way we work, they sent me to Six Sigma training, but all for nothing. There was no one on the other side. They were binning all our projects. I remember one day, seeing a really fine stream gushing out through a connection between two pipes, during the cleaning process. You could barely se it. The problem was that during the cleaning, there was a caustic stage, and if that gets in your eye or on the skin, you're in big trouble, because it burns right through. It took weeks for it to be repaired, like it wasn't important. Keeping in mind that we were dealing with multiple tasks at any time, it would've been extremely easy to forget about the caustic spray, and get it into our eyes.

During the yearly month-long shutdown, the lab would organise a patient day, inviting random patients to expose their struggles, and how our medicine is improving their lives. In 2017, they invited this mother with her daughter from the United States. It was then when I have assisted to the biggest case of parental cruelty and selfishness. The kid was about 12, and had been born with this very rare condition, where you have no immunity. She had this valve attached to her throat, through which she'd get our immunoglobulin shot. Because she's had all her veins punctured, getting injections the normal way was no longer an option. It was a case I have never seen before, and it made my legs a bit shaky hearing her talk. What infuriated me was the story behind her condition, and her heartless and immoral parents. Before bringing her into this world, the mother kept on having miscarriages. At one point, she decided with her husband to go and have proper checks done. After extensive medical investigations, they found out that they were not genetically compatible. This meant that, if one of their babies would be born alive, it would have severe health issues. Even after knowing this, they kept on trying to have a baby, just because they wanted a child of their own, no matter the consequences. Eventually, the girl we had in front of us was born, but without immunity. She could never go outside to play as normal kids do, she needed medicine continuously, and constant care. Poor kid! Her mother was telling the story as if her wish to have a child was supposed to melt our hearts. Some of my colleagues were crying, while I was thinking that someone should put her and the husband next to each other, and hit them in the face with a wooden chair. What kind of humans are you, wanting to have your own baby, even when you know close to 100% that it's going to live a life of hell?

After getting my promotion with one year and three months delay, I started my plan. They messed up with the wrong guy. My team leader was asking me, "aren't you happy, Julian? Isn't this what you wanted?". *"No! You fucking passive-good-for-nothing-Indian-ass-licking-dick-head!"* Because of your incompetence I've lost important days of my life, hoping, and have been disadvantaged through nepotism. This is what you get when you give a team leader position to an individual with no previous experience with people, or in leading positions. We were a good team with or without him, and if it was to vote him out, it would've been unanimous. He was blessed with the best people in LSF, and he was taking a piss at us. A while back I started doing private hire driving in London, as a side gig, so I had all the backup I needed to confront anyone in BPL. I was such a good driver, that after more than 8,000 rides, my driver rating was 4.99 out of five stars. I was ok. Previously, the team leader kept on telling us, that he was not allowed to put all qualifying people forward for promotion at the same time. He didn't want to tell us who the manager was, but we knew. "Oh, yeah, it's Samantha, that fucking prick... He never cares about anyone...", the seniors in the department used to say. I also went to speak with my shift's MSM about the delay in promotion. He went, "Julian, you're a really good Technician, I don't have an answer to why you've been promoted so late..." Without any second thought I filed a grievance, asking for clarification about my delayed promotion and the amount they owed me, taking as reference the day I turned one year in the company. The text in the grievance was extensive. "You will get a lot of people upset with this. I don't think this is the way to go forward, if in the future you want to get what you want...", my team leader went. He was always talking about diplomacy, about which he knew nothing. I've been diplomatic, and it failed. When that happens, it's full on conflict. In a diplomatic act both parties have to compromise, and if one side is to blame for a particular situation, they need to be held responsible, and pay for compensation. His understanding of diplomacy meant turning against the team you are supposed to lead. I couldn't blame him though, he did vote for Brexit... "Those fucking unelected politicians from Brussels!" He didn't realise that he was unelected too, and that if voting from hate, you should not be allowed to vote in the first place. He also didn't know his country's history, that without Europe, England would've looked way different and poorer, that France first vetoed the UK joining the Union, as they knew they will eventually do what they actually did, running with the money by voting for exit. He was oblivious about many things.

When acknowledging my grievance, the HR business partner promised me an enquiry into the facts brought forward, and that she would give me a decision within two weeks. It took two months to get the decision, and a lot of chasing up, then I found out she didn't talk to anyone named in my grievance. She had a face matching her soul. Her opinion was that nothing I've brought forward was true, and that no harm was done. She also explained to me, that in order to become a Technician 1, the position had to become available. She didn't know anything, as that was an in-role promotion. She was either stupid or playing stupid. I presumed it was both, so I appealed the decision. Before the grievance I started acting all depressed, frustrated and confused, to make my way through the procedures, and through what I was planning to do. I booked a few days sick, then came back to work. I was going to get the money they owed me, one way or another. No one does this to me without repercussions; call it karma. I was thinking often if I should interfere to create a coup against my team leader, but I wasn't that bad of a person. It was his luck. If the company wanted him there, it wasn't my right to interfere, although he did play with me fulfilling my destiny in the company. In situations like this it's best if you let time deal with everyone. Better yet, did I really want to continue working in a company that doesn't care about their best employees?

After receiving the decision of my grievance, the plan was in full swing. I filed for an appeal with the site manager. Straight away I went to my doctor, and explained the situation with my work. I met him after a few early morning hours of private hire driving. When I entered the clinic I was, and looked exhausted, while wearing a black T-shirt and black jeans. Everything was planned to the smallest detail. My situation wasn't new for the doctor, as he explained that more and more people have these issues with their employers. "Take your time to recover! I'm gonna give you three months off. If nothing is fixed, and you don't feel fit, we can extend it." I hit BPL with a three months medical certificate of sick leave, accusing depression, anxiety and exhaustion. These appeared in the grievance too. For comfort, always choose something that it's very difficult for them to check. Because I was working two jobs, I looked exhausted and depressed all the time anyway. Working 12 hours shifts, then driving for 12 hours in my spare time was no joke, and it often took its toll on me. During the years, I have built my library with what happened inside BPL, just in case they were stupid enough to go against me; I would've closed their lab. Now it was full-on silent war. Nowadays you have to act smart and sharp. Passive non-conforming will truly change our world. You can no longer take control through fighting, indoors or outdoors. During my stray moments, I was thinking how it would go, if I'd take them to court. I would've done everything to lose at first, and then hit them with everything at the appeal stage. Appeals are fun! But that was a far fetched dream, as I had no money to start the procedures. I had bigger plans with my money. Now I was self-employed full time, and getting my normal wage from BPL. Because I had worked there for over two years, I was entitled to four months full pay, and four months half pay during sickness. It was brilliant. I was going to cash in more money than they owed me. My medical certificate hit them in the face, especially the team leader. *"Manage this, you prick!"* I felt sorry for my team, but I didn't cause the conflict. They knew I was right. When a company mistreats you, be merciless, hit them back smart, and with everything you've got. I kept on telling the managers, that I didn't move to the UK to spoil the workforce market, by accepting to work for scraps or to be disrespected. For the risks we were taking, our wages should have exceeded £5,000 easily, not a third of that, with the prospect of getting less. In the meantime, the site manager, this complacent and crooked man in his fifties, arranged a meeting for my appeal sometime during my sick leave. At the appeal he kept on telling me that no issues were found, that there is no quota for Technician 2, and that in any case, my team leader will be retrained about how promotions work. He also wanted me to name all the technicians that I knew they got promoted in record time. He had all that data himself, or at least it was really easy to find, he just had to check the records. His comments about my promotion were, that my team leader decided when I was ready for the next level (a guy who didn't know the process), and that my file got lost on the way to human resources, when he eventually sent it. For that reason, he was willing to give me three months of Technician 2 pay, for January 2019 til April of the same year. Another colleague got promoted in the same time with me, but he never got money for those months. His file didn't get lost in the mail. Now, I was asking the site manager for a Technician 1 position, same as the unskilled guy that had received it without deserving it, move that shocked the entire department. I kept telling him about the processes I was skilled in, and he motivated, "yeah, but how often do we get to process *specifics* (tetanus, rabies, factor-D, zoster)...". That was not even a requirement for Technician 2. The site manager was more of a redneck than George Bush Jr.. I promised I will speak with the CEO about everything, as I had all the transcripts. When they heard that, I started getting emails from HR, asking why I wanted to contact him, because the CEO does not deal with issues in production, but only with the state of the business. His PA rerouted my emails back to HR. He would have never read my complaint. The CEO has to know about everything that happens in the company. If I was in his place, and found out that they're stopping employees from contacting me about unresolved issues, I would've scrapped all the managers in the middle, on the spot. You rarely hear about a more disrespectful company. They were the best at mistreating employees, and their competition got word of that. Eventually, they called me to see how I was, after more than three months, when I got the second sickness certificate for another three months. I was living a brilliant life, working full time as private hire, getting money for being sick, and for a few months, earning three times the BPL wage. I had many reasons to spend my money on all sorts of fancy dinners with my girlfriend, and on holidays. During the meeting with the HR partner, to see if I'm recovering well, all turned against my team leader. He was standing there, with his usual dumb grinning on his face, disproving everything that happened. I wasn't right with anything, even my good work had never happened. It was total disappointment, and I felt like punching them both. I changed my mind about talking with the CEO, after doing a bit of research about him. He was an active director in four different pharmaceutical companies, and had full white hair. A Chinese man with white hair? He looked like he was working for the triads. It's also highly difficult to find photos with him on the internet. Very, very suspicious!

In the light of recent events, BPL are saying on their website that their plasma is *Covid-19* free. Everybody is taking a chance at benefiting from the damaging stupidity we are living in. They should say the plasma is full of *Covid-19* specific IgGs. This would make their medicine seem more encompassing for people depending on their vaccine, the *Gammaplex* for example. Another clue about how unskilled the managers of that laboratory are. If the USA are passing law to force all Americans to take the potentially deadly mRNA vaccine, BPL will experience a huge drop in the quality of their most important IgG vaccine, the *Gammaplex*. It's because most of the human plasma comes from the US, and a lot of it from the Texas area. With the new vaccine, the immunity of healthy people will suffer, as the mRNA one is creating an autoimmune disease, and poor quality IgG. I hope this gives you an idea of what can happen if you mess up the immunity of healthy people donating plasma to save the highly vulnerable, that have no immunity altogether. There aren't other alternatives for them, so their lives will probably get cut short. IgG is very difficult to reproduce in a lab. I know the chemistry of *Gammaplex*, so I can bet that its quality and efficacy will drop, once all people are inoculated in the US.

Recently I came across this study conducted by German scientists, about the source of BPL Plasma (the US branch of BPL Group for collecting the raw material - plasma). Much of that plasma is being processed by Biotest, a biotech company producing plasma derived medicine, same as BPL. Both companies can process about the same quantity of plasma, around 1.5 million litres per year, each. Biotest is owned by the same Chinese investment group, CREAT. The researchers have found out, that the BPL Plasma centre in El Paso area, close to the border with Mexico, is collecting plasma mainly from Mexicans. In the UK, we were being told that plasma is coming only from Americans with solid and tracked medical records. We were regularly discarding bottles of plasma suspected of HIV, from people with gaps in their medical records, with tattoos, etc.. In the US there is this law, banning doctors from rejecting a patient that wants to donate; they cannot discriminate. That only applies to citizens or residents with no ties to Europe, not to Mexicans, or any other tourists, who should not be able to donate in the first place. Apparently, what technicians are being told is not quite accurate and misleading. From what I could find, Mexico is a country that banned blood plasma collections from its citizens in 1987, due to an explosion in HIV cases. Today, Mexicans with B1/B2 visas (travel visas) are crossing the border, specifically to donate blood plasma, for about US$400 a month. The FDA, run by people named by the Big Pharma, have called safe a maximum of 108 plasma donations per year from one individual, whereas the European Union does not allow more than 33 plasma donations per year, for each individual. This huge disparity in judgement between two powerful regulators is something to look at. Who is right? Find out we shall. If, as European, you travel to the US under B1 visa, you will not be allowed to donate plasma, because your visa could get cancelled, and because you come from Europe, continent with a previous *situation* of mad cow disease. It's been a while since that happened, but the US still consider that a threat to human health. What a laugh, the US teaching the world medicine. On the other hand, they do like closing a blind eye to the fact that, people from another country are crossing the border to donate plasma excessively, for money. They also know about the previous HIV situation in Mexico. If you look into history, all major contaminations with HIV happened in the early '80s-mid '80s, no mater the countries concerned. During the same years, there was mercury (Hg) in vaccines. So, why is the FDA allowing this? For money, of course. Plasma is liquid gold. The German scientists went further with their undercover research, and tested a few of the

Mexican regular donors. They discovered that their levels of IgG and IgM were similar to a person with acquired immunodeficiency. The results hit in the lower range of the approved limits for a healthy individual. It means that that Mexican is at high risk of developing an immune disease, getting a powerful infection or dying. Think of Enterprise starship being fired at with the magnetic shield off. Due to this behaviour of plasma donors, there are huge implications for the medicine produced by BPL. People that donate this frequently cannot rebuild their antibodies fast enough, to constantly provide quality IgG in their plasma. You build antibodies during, and after being infected with something. The probability of infecting a patient with a virus is really low, even if HIV would be present, due to the chemical processes the plasma goes through in the lab, but that does not mean that the potency of the immunoglobulin cannot enter a downtrend, nor it completely eliminates the risk of infecting a patient with something. Who is receiving the shot will probably feel it in time. The price of *Gammaplex* will probably stay the same, or maybe increase with demand. The following aspect of this situation is quite concerning. BPL Group's business is so big, that it is willing to sacrifice the lives of millions, just to save thousands. It takes roughly 1,300 donations to keep a patient alive, for a year. Do you still think Big Pharma cares about human lives? Take the money out of the equation, and no one would be willing to do it. I'm not saying they should stop, but to protect the donors too. The fact that they allow people from another country to donate illegally is a criminal act altogether. It's fine if the FDA is in charge. Truth is, if poor people would not donate, no one would. The richer you are, the more likely it is that you'll say pass to such a burden, because it is a huge shock for your body. Not as big as when donating full blood, but still, the impact of such donating practices is massive, even for the healthiest of bodies. In order to donate twice a week, the donor needs to have a strict diet, otherwise it would make him/her unfit to donate, maybe due to too much sugar in the blood, increased fat, etc.. Good immunity derives over 90% from what and how you eat, so by not eating properly and healthy, and donating constantly on the limit of legality and biologically possible, trouble will come sooner than later. No doctor is advising these donors. Who is actually monitoring the ones that stop donating? No one cares about them, if they're dead due to aggressive donating, or in a condition that requires the medicine they used to donate plasma for. If you think deeper, it's quite smart how the Big Pharma works. By allowing donors to overdo it, they're also increasing the demand for plasma derived products, which in return requires more irresponsible donors, all under the umbrella of merciless regulators. The German and British regulators are allowing such practices, because the US is the main buyer of the final product. For smooth operations, a lot of money is going into politics as donations. The benefactors will then be able to influence regulatory policies and laws. Now, try to imagine China's power in all of this. They own BPL and most companies in the human plasma business. You don't hear about them, but they surely own you.

At the beginning of 2020 I booked the days of holiday I was entitled to for two months of work, then I went back, close to the end of January. They all thought I've quenched my thirst for revenge. The team leader was setting me up for retraining, while a manager wanted me to be in charge of keeping an eye on the yields, and draw these fancy charts. They didn't know I had handed my resignation notice to HR. It hit them in the head after a few days. "Julian, you could've told us, so we don't plan for you anymore!" I just wanted to work with my team for one last time, trying to make up for the months they didn't have me. I knew how difficult it must have been for them. I had the leaving drinks at the end, and although the team leader promised he'll attend, he never did. He was a complete resentful idiot. People from other shifts have attended. If you've had vital medicine produced by BPL between 2017 and 2020, I might have worked on the batch. I wish I could've done more; it was an honour to be part of your wellbeing.

CHAPTER 8

JUST ANOTHER GERMAN *KETCHUP* COMPANY

Music for this chapter
Hans Zimmer - Wheel of Fortune
Rob Dougan - Clubbed to Death
Propellerheads - Spybreak
Jaydee - Plastic Dreams 2003
Darude - Feel the Beat

Moving to a really big city is similar to when you start dancing in a club. The second time you look at the clock, it's six in the morning. What?! Where did the time fly? Londoners know this really well. Once here, your life slips away really fast, if you don't have a proper escape plan. Large cities put chains on your life. They're traps for submission, and total compliance. You get caught in the loop career-fun-survival-repeat, and without realising it, you're sixty, homeless, sick, friendless, and depressed. This is why, my brother and I planned to open our own company as soon as possible. Time is passing by anyway. At first we didn't really know what to sell, but after a few months of brainstorming, we started to flood all business meetings we had access to. Soon we found ourselves in Southwark, attending business seminars next to other established entrepreneurs and lawyers, from some of the biggest law firms in the UK. Mostly we were spectators without any questions, indulging with the free booze and food. By the end of the meetings we felt quite tipsy and stuffed, like the homeless thief under the bridge, in *Dennis the Menace*. Before that, we'd find out that the UK is investing massively in startups, but not getting much back. Hmmm... It didn't make any sense. So the government is giving free money, to businesses with no prospect. To me it sounds like pocketing the money through friends. Some lawyers were asking the right questions, while we got crammed at the 25th floor, and admired London's skyline through the glass walls. We hoped we'd get free money through one of those public programmes, to build our notes mobile app. We created a structure of our app idea, and went to pitch it to the mobile development companies. It didn't take us long to present it to one of the biggest programming companies in the city. "Are you Polish?" "No, we are from *Dacia* (Romania)..." "Oh, you looked Polish." This couldn't have worked. We crossed it off our list, then went to the next. Their account manager met us in this spacious conference room, where we pitched our idea. "Ok, I'll send you the quote through email, after discussing it with our engineers." In a couple of days, we found out that they were charging somewhere around £50,000 for the completed project, and on top of that, the cost for bug fixes and constant updates. I sent them a very obscene reply, in which I was telling them that the quote was outrageous and unfair, for a small company like ours, among other things. I wasn't right in the head to compose such a reply, but we had a lot of *cohones*. My brother proofed the email before sending it. We felt tired of working our asses off for scrap wages, and then pay everything to hungry programming companies.

In the meantime, we took our chance to improve our inherited chocolate recipe, thus managing to create new products. Chocolate seemed the most viable business idea for us. When we were little, our mother used to work in the kids seaside summer camp, where one of the desserts was in-house made chocolate. She was an expert in that. We've tweaked her recipe to look good in a package, and by doing so, we managed to create our first amazing truffles. Every good business needs branding though. During the years, we learned how to clear our minds when brainstorming, in order to produce amazing ideas. On a holiday in Ibiza, whilst in a very quiet and inspiring part of the island, I came up with the name *Eden Chocolat.* Back in London, my brother added *Chocstanza* to the equation, and in the end we decided to call the brand, *Eden Chocolat be more chocstanza.* When you have a really good idea, it is wise to get it branded the legal way, if you want to avoid it being stolen or copied. To prevent this, we went online and applied for a trademark, with the Intellectual Property Office (IPO). After the initial checks were done, our trademark got published in the public register, for the required amount of time. The logo also included a hummingbird in a round circle, with five stars on top, sign that I designed just with a mini iPad, and a stylus. If anyone that already owned a registered trademark thought that our new addition would infringe their rights, they'd have to take action against our sign's registration by filing an opposition. We were confident that something like this would never happen. Our ideas are too cool to be similar with someone else's. In the meantime, we thought that having a story of our chocolate, to print it on the chocolate bags, would be ideal. So I conceived a short story that goes like this:

In the 1800s, the whole of Europe was in the dark. The night was covering every nook, and all the people had only the stars and the candles to guide them. Quite often, even the stars were hiding beyond the blanket of clouds. When the night came, Europe went into complete darkness. From above, you could see nothing. By the end of the century, the brave and loveable people in a town of a far away country, a place of scented flowers and magic, thought it was enough. Their streets were ink blue, and all they could hear was the wolves howling. So, they started using the waters of the river flowing through the city, to create electricity. Then, they chopped a fir tree from the nearby forest, they carved it into a wonderful pillar, and placed it with care in the modest square of their little town. Using very old and dusted manuals, the craftsmen also built their first light emitting capsule, which they named "lamp". They installed wires between the pillar and the nearby electricity lodge on the river, and placed the lamp on top. As protection, the glass masters have created a crystal globe to protect the lamp, which had an opening at the top for ventilation. The sky was full of stars that night, and it looked as if the gods in heaven were celebrating. The entire population of the town rushed to see the new light emitting device in action. The mayor was there, and he was handed the switch. He pressed it, and suddenly they had light. The joy was immense, as they finally had their street lit up for the first time. From above the continent, you could see the dimmed little dot of light, in a sea of pitch black. In heaven, the reveller Dionysos was partying hard, when his attention was suddenly caught by the earthly street light, while indulging with ambrosial chocolate. Being amazed by the ingenious idea, he dropped a piece towards the little European town. Scared that the God of the Sun might find out about his recklessness, he quickly sent a hummingbird to bring back the piece of chocolate, before getting into the hands of humans. The chocolate was falling like a shooting star towards the light, when it landed straight into the crystal globe, but without damaging the lamp. The hummingbird went in with lightning speed to recover it, and when preparing to fly back, it noticed that all the eyes of the people were watching the action. In that instant moment, the hummingbird got frozen in the globe forever, as it wasn't supposed to be seen by humans. Since then, those people have kept the chocolate recipe a secret, and called the bird in the crystal, Eden. That secret recipe lives on today, with Eden Chocolat be more chocstanza.

The period of initial publication of our mark finished, so we started celebrating. "Yes, we've got our first trademark in the UK!" We started designing the packaging, when we received an email from the Intellectual Property Office, informing us that someone has filed for opposition against our visual trademark. "What? No! No!! No!!!" But we paid for an initial assessment, and the IPO said it was good for registration. We figured it's another way for the office to make more money. Obviously, they are not doing a good job in assessing new trademark applications. "Who is it?" I was reading through the email attachment, that was describing briefly the reasons for opposition, as filed by Heirler Cenovis GmbH. "What, GmbH?! Isn't this a German company?" It was a German company owning a group of brands, that produced sauces and other foods you can find in usual supermarkets. "Bro, they're a ketchup company! Hahaha!" We discovered that they also have their own supermarket, in the north of England. Among all these things, they also have the word *Eden*, registered as word trademark. "Oh, come on! Our trademark is way more complex than theirs. How can anyone confuse the two?" We went on the IPO website to make sure the email was not a scam, despite it looking legitimate. Next to our trademark it said *opposed*. Our fangs were showing, while growling like a pack of wolves, ready to attack. "You're going down, Heirler!" "But wait, they opposed past the legal term..." "Oh, wait, no they didn't, they filed in the last day, the email was delayed." "Damn it, man! What do we do?" During that time we worked for Kodak, so our funds were limited, and not assured every week. We loved going into a litigation in our country, but this was something else. It had to be done in English, and under a different legal settlement. "Wait a minute! Intellectual Property Law is uniform, England is in the European Union..." Previously I registered a trademark in *Dacia* (Romania), therefore we knew something about the specific legislation. Our years of criminal and commercial law could definitely be of help. We had a lot of skill when writing documents in our own language. This time, it could only improve our English substantially. "Fuck it, bro, let's do it!" It took us five minutes to decide to stand tall against all opposition. They were the ones that should've been afraid, because we could not lose anything, no matter the final decision. We saw this as a unique chance to create great personal history in British IPO litigation. These big words would scare even experienced trademark lawyers around the world. The good side was that it's one, kind of uniform, Intellectual Property Law in all countries, and the downside, that it is really complex in interpretation. The latter was on our side the most. In general, in law this is what you want, *open to interpretation*. This is why, many times, the one with the best lawyer wins, and why many criminals escape prison or get highly reduced sentences, despite the severity of their actions. Intellectual Property Law is the most fluid in this sense. The opposition was based on the fact that the word *Eden* from our trademark, would be the only word emphasised by the average viewer (customer), creating confusion, and assimilating our brand with theirs, *Eden*. The older trademark was registered on the class of products containing chocolate, our main product, and different types of confectionery, among other products. They didn't want *Eden Chocolat be more chocstanza*, plus the visual drawing, to be registered on the same class. "Excuse me? The brand is telling the viewer how to pronounce the trademark, not the other way around!" The owner of *Sofa King Amazing* educated you to spell the whole structure, not just *Sofa* or *King* or *Amazing*. You would go to buy a fucking amazing sofa from *Sofa-King-Amazing*. The opponent was clearly in the wrong. Plus, how can you register a word from the international vocabulary as your own trademark, and then ban all others to use it when forming other trademarks. "Outrageous!" During conflicts like this, you realise the mess the lawmakers have made of the Intellectual Property Law, by allowing companies with a lot of money and influence, to get protection for words in use at a large scale. When a newly formed word that is also a trademark, like *zap*, for example, goes into our daily use, it loses its attribute as trademark. If everyone is saying *I'm zap-ing this and that*, the trademark *zap* is no longer a trademark. Replace *zap* with the name of a famous online search engine, to understand where I'm coming from. So in our case, we couldn't understand how an entity can own the word *Eden* as trademark, when it's a widespread and highly used word from the vocabulary. If a new word entering the vocabulary cannot be a trademark, isn't the opposite a fail in the assessment of a trademark's fitness for registration? The more we read the law, the more dense it got.

The opposition papers were signed by this fancy lawyer, from one of the biggest law firms in the UK, Squire

Patton Boggs. "Holy crap, dude, we're going against giants! It's gonna be beautiful!" Their office building in central London is almost as big as the MI5's. The more we studied them, the bigger our giggles got. The representative lawyer was full of honours on the law firm's website, and one of his personal quotes included his opinion that, it is highly difficult to litigate in the UK in Intellectual Property, because the law is clear, transparent, and precedented. "Look at this guy, let's see how difficult it is to litigate in the UK then..." The IPO asked us to reply, if we wanted to go forward or withdraw our trademark from registration, without any further action. "No way, we paid £200 for that! It means two 12 hours shifts in Kodak..." We sent the paper containing our stance, basically dismissing everything the opponent had said. It was ON. Now, the Opposition had to compile the Skeleton Argument, in support of their case. "Man, look at these guys, they're affiliated with that satanic sect *Skull & Bones*! Skeleton Arguments, pfff..." We both acted quite childish about the whole thing. Why take the *fun* out of *fundamental*? In the end it was our company, and what can be more beautiful, than two Directors defending their intellectual property in a Tribunal. The only impediment was our constant exhaustion due to constant work, that could have made it difficult to have the papers ready in time.

The Opponent had to supply the Skeleton Arguments by a certain date. When we thought they'd forgotten about everything, in the evening of the last day, we received them from the law firm, with a carbon copy sent to the IPO. "Damn it, again!" "So this is how they want to play, sending the documents during the last legal hours, toying with us..." They weren't playing *pick-a-boo* with us, it's how lawyers work, to give you false hopes, and if possible, less time to write your own documents properly; maybe, at any point during the procedures, you'll make a mistake because of the short time. Just think this way: if your opposition has two weeks to submit, and they send in a week's time, and you'd have the same amount of time to submit yours, they'd then give you an extra week, three weeks in total, during which you can sharpen your reply. If they send their case right at the end of the two weeks term, you've got only two full weeks to write yours. Why give the other side the advantage of more time? "Bastards!" Learning fast is key in law, so we did the same. "It's 23:58! Send now! Tick-tock-tick-tock... Mwahahaha!" Our interpretation of their arguments was as professional as it can get. We started researching the law, browsing different cases they named in support of their opposition, and new ones in support of our application. Research and precedent is vital to winning. Our main pillar was, a word from the vocabulary cannot be a stand-alone trademark. Even more, we found loads of other older trademarks registered as *Eden -something-*, on the same class of products, and before the registration of our opponent's trademark. "How is that possible?" We discovered that it's all about someone opposing against the registration of your trademark. The law allows it, as long as the trademarks are not identical, or fraudulently similar; in this case your trademark won't pass IPO's initial assessment. If the new mark is just similar in a way, it could get registered. It's twisted, I know. But how did the word *Eden* get registered as trademark, when previous trademarks on the same class of products, and identical products, contain the same word in their composition? In a fair review, our opponent was in the wrong, for having received the right to registration. With registrations like this, the lawmakers and judges have proven their lack of capacity, skill, and backbone in front of big companies' lobbying. Every institution is corrupt in one way or another. They call it an imperfect system. Isn't it perfect, to be imperfect on big money? Who cares about that, when you've got money, and can register any trademark you want. The more we discovered, the more outrageous and obvious it got. They didn't want our trademark to get registered, period. We knew that we had a great advantage against them. When they saw the documents signed by us two, they probably realised we were not Polish, and that we had no professional representation. You know what they say about the people representing themselves... They were going to underestimate us, big time. Even in their first arguments, we picked up on a subjective interpretation in the text of the German bred representative of the opponent, a definite no-no when debating a case for a client. We went against it straight away, pointing it out using twisted interpretation. For us it was personal, while struggling to keep our objectiveness. Together in a litigation, we are probably the best non-professional attorneys you can find. Fuck Harvard and Oxford, say hello to life experience, and international law aficionados! Underestimating us will most probably lose you the case.

Before setting a date for the hearing, the Intellectual Property Office asked us if we'd like to go to Newport, in Wales, for the meeting, or do it from London, through video conference. We felt like inflicting the highest financial damage on the ketchup company, but we couldn't do it, despite having some money. It would've been beautiful, forcing their attorney to travel all that way. Our situation turned dire, when discovering that they had set the hearing, right after one of our night shifts. "Bro, we're going to be knackered!" We couldn't book it off either, as the workforce agency didn't have that many shifts to give us. The only way was to push ourselves to do it. Because I was better at

English, I would plea for our case, while being handed the documents, in logical and strategic order, by my brother. We also prepared a bullet point summary, with the main topics we should debate. During that morning, we were so tired after bagging photographic paper in the dark, that we could barely keep our eyes open. At 7am we finished the shift, and at 10am we arrived somewhere behind the Houses of Parliament and London Abbey, at the Intellectual Property Office. We got there first, formally dressed, and ready to charge. Because of our tiredness, the joy of what we were doing could not be present. The Opponent's representative was this senior partner in the law firm, with loads of experience in intellectual property litigation. Upon arrival, she didn't even say good morning, or anything else for that matter. "What kind of professionalism is that!" I was asking my brother if I should wink at her in the elevator, but he disagreed. Looking like a zombie is not compatible with flirting in a professional situation. She was this British lady, whose years of experience in law and representations have only made her apathetic, and unpleasant to have around. I'm good at reading women, even when exhausted, and she wasn't a good read. We took our seats in the room, in front of this massive television screen. The appointed QC, acting as a judge, was an experienced attorney in intellectual property. He talked to us from Wales. The opposition went first with the presentation of their case. Considering the experience she's put on the law firm's website, we branded her representation as average. Multiple times, it seemed like it was her first hearing, while having difficulties with her words. We both expected impressiveness from her. What had to be proven by our side, was the use of our mark under the shape as in the application for trademark, and that the average customer will spell the word part of the visual trademark as we tell them to, *Eden Chocolat be more* chocstanza, and not just *Eden*, no matter the visual representation. We already had a website and invoices for chocolate sales, whereas for how the mark will be spelt, there was precedent aplenty. My brother kept passing me documents to talk about, making sure nothing gets left behind. The tiredness was king, and soon I could barely concentrate, while losing my train of thought often. I was also struggling with finding my way through professional English, and no one could help me, as my brother was in the same situation. We fought for our cause the best we could, but the feeling that we were going to lose crept in. The QC was in total agreement with the opposition, without considering any proof or precedent. For them it was a matter of ego as well. They could not allow untrained representatives to step on years of law school and court experience. We could understand that, but it was unacceptable. The case had to be judged exhaustively and objectively. Seeing almost all our proof and arguments dismissed, I could feel my face burning. The whole situation woke us up a bit, but it wasn't enough. The opposition was winning, without too much effort. At the end, we asked the tribunal for the date when we'll have the decision. After being told that it will take about two months, we rushed home sleeping on the underground, while holding the files really tight. It would've been better to present our case a bit drunk, than do it with chronic tiredness. Time went by quick, and after the two months, we started calling the IPO about the decision. "Oh, right, the QC is on paternal leave, he'll write the decision when back in office." "Pardon? He's on paternal leave?! So, only one person is writing the decisions? There's no one else to hold his spot?" "Mr Stan, there's nothing we can do right now, you have to wait until he's back. You'll receive the decision in a timely manner." These are the ways of the British Intellectual Property Office. If an attorney goes on holiday, the applicants have to wait indefinitely to have a decision. The files keep piling up, and when back at work, the singular QC's office is full of case files, up to the ceiling. We kept on calling every month, only to get irrational answers. An institution making millions, is using only a few attorneys for hundreds, maybe thousands of cases. Where is all that money going? I doubt there aren't enough skilled people to work in intellectual property. The decision was issued after about six months, with massive errors of judgement, but which favoured the opposition to win. The opponent was also given a £600 compensation, towards court and representation fees. That was no surprise, and it actually made us think clearer. We picked up on the errors with the outmost professionalism. It was clear, that the QC got emotional with his decision and interpretation of the law. Have you ever seen a judge's decision issued in haste? It's hilarious! His colleagues probably told him about our impatience. We've done nothing wrong. He was the one who said two months to issue a decision. Not many attorneys have a backbone... By delaying it so much, and to a certain degree intentionally, he abused his powers. You'll find many judges or attorneys doing it, since they cannot be held responsible without their consent.

Going forward, we had a better base with the flawed decision, so we filed for an appeal that drew us back another £200. The case was becoming an addiction, and by knowing how everything looks like during the hearing, we could be more prepared. We had a lot of time to find even more proof in support of our mark, and to set traps for the opposition. When you decide to appeal, you have to make it all about unleashing your full potential. Don't fixate on the final result, but on being the best you can. Probably Squire Patton Boggs were thinking, *"who the fuck are these guys?"*. Our appeal was quite lengthy, and it tackled each and every point of the decision, to exhaustion. Despite having limited time to build the case, we've put together an amazing ensemble of precedent and case studies. When the opposition sent their response, we noticed that our comments caused some outrage among the case workers in the law firm. The German bred attorney ditched the case, and passed it to this inexperienced **part-time associate**, who made gross mistakes when writing the appeal response. *"Oh, man, just hire us as partners if you lack skill"*, we started thinking.

This time, the date of the appeal did not fall after our night shift. We also planned to be perfectly rested, and in full capacity. No more alcohol the night before, maybe a little bit, just a few shots... The consistent documentation had to be presented flawlessly. The appeal was chaired by a QC from London, no more video conferencing. In the meantime, we managed to place our chocolate truffles in two shops in London. When it all started, we've been given the right to present our case before the opposition. We began by debating all the erroneous points from the decision, and for the first time, the QC was agreeing with us in some measure. It seemed like taking forever, and the more we were debating, the more ideas were coming to us. We were on fire! Even my English was almost error free. Eventually, we asked the permission to play a little trademark recognition game with the opposition, and the QC allowed it. "Ok, this isn't a rule during these procedures, but go on." I could not wait to unleash the heavy artillery on the opposition. My brother was passing me all these figurative, verbal, and easily recognisable trademarks, warming up Ms attorney. When building the case, we had this epiphany about how to demonstrate that the creator of the trademark is educating the customers on how to spell the trademark, and that they have no power of spelling it by random choice. The opposition was even pronouncing *chocstanza* as *COCKstanza*... You don't read *chocstix* as *COCKstix*, do you? We instantly realised what she was missing in her life. It was sad... All the trademarks we were showing had a premeditated order, down to the last sheet of paper. I was so glad to see the latter. On it, we had the word *SEAT* written with capital letters. "Ms attorney, can you please read this word for us?" "Mr Stan, we cannot keep it up like this, you have to conclude you appeal...", the QC intervened. "Apologies, I promise this is the last one." "Could you please read the word, Ms?" "Of course, it's *SEAT*!" She pronounced it like the Spanish car maker, SEAT. She fell in our trap like a rookie. "Why did you pronounce it like the car maker, SEAT, when it's the English word *SEAT*, as in stool or car seat?" The QC intervened, "Mr Stan, let's not make Ms attorney here feel uncomfortable, she's just representing her client..." He started smiling at our breakthrough, while the opposition's attorney turned all red. We could see her boiling after falling out of grace. "Mr QC, considering the proof brought forward and the latter demonstration, we strongly believe that our sign meets the criteria, and is fit for registration as trademark." The opposition's comments have been visibly affected by the previous flop, as she could barely find her words. We could see that the QC started to like us a bit, and he even threw us a bone, by suggesting that we could add more products from the same class of products, as in the Nice classification, that the opponent had or didn't have. We jumped on the offering as hawks, and even tried to add the cocoa as *beans*. He didn't allow it, but we had to at least try. We've broken through the barriers with SEAT. They landed with the case straight in the bog. From *the new mark will be confused with the older trademark, and therefore it cannot be registered*, the situation turned into splitting the products from the same class, and even sharing existing ones. We wanted to add cocoa to our product list but we realised that once registered, no one will check if we're putting the trademark on our chocolates or not. Plus, we could use only the word truffles on the package, and cocoa in the small print among the ingredients. From a win for the opposition, it was turning into a win situation for us, an unexpected turn of events. How can you not love a good appeal! By the end of it we were bursting. We could not wait to get out of the building to celebrate. When leaving, we saw the QC and the attorney staying behind, and chatting like old friends. Outside, with the Houses of Parliament in the background, we jumped for joy, while congratulating each other for the unexpectedly good representation in a tribunal. We managed to tick all topics we planned to present, which is rare in a court of law, and impressive for rookies. The QC promised us the final decision in about two weeks, and we believed him blindly. Straight after, we hit a pub to get wasted. A lot more than two weeks had passed, without a decision. We called the IPO to see what was going on, being anxious to know the result. Confirmation was needed. It took about six months from the appeal hearing to get the decision, and about two years from the start of the procedures. The wait eventually paid off, because we won the registration of our trademark, on the same class of products as the opponent's. Success felt amazing, and it had to be accompanied by good champagne. We managed to litigate in the United Kingdom, without the help of an expensive attorney. We showed the big law firm how to not underestimate the underdog, but I'm pretty sure we were the only ones learning from it all. We felt sorry for Ms attorney a bit, because probably she pulled the short straw, having to represent against two non-professionals, of a nationality known in the UK's politics and media, mainly for working in construction, or in the crime industry, also in her native language. It must've been way worse than *pro bono* work, for a senior partner with years of experience. In this specific case it wasn't *pro bono* though. If you are ever in a situation like this with your trademark application, don't settle just for the products in the Nice classification, you can add way more from the same class, and throw it at the opponent in court. If you have a great idea of a new word trademark, register it as word trademark only. You can design it as you please after registration, and no one will ever be able to copy you, or use your word in their trademark. We got what we wanted, but in the light of the events, we decided to simplify our brand, and call our amazing chocolate truffles only *Chocstanza*.

After the win, we wanted to see the law firm's headquarters. We pondered on the idea of applying for an attorney job with them, just to give them something to talk about. They needed new talent badly. Considering how good we look in suits, we could've entered their building without being asked for ID passes, with the security probably saying, *"good morning Sirs, go win some cases!"*.

CHAPTER 9

THE COW EXPERIMENT

Music for this chapter
Italian Mafia - Sicilian Heart
Bomfunk MC's - Freestyler
AC/DC - Who Made Who

You live your life in a context. That context is almost totally out of your control. You may try to change it during your lifetime, in a bigger or smaller part, but there is a great chance that you'll be overwhelmed by the task. It requires a lot of mental and physical strength. The entire context is too big for any human to change completely and irreversibly. This is due to the sheer number of people supporting it. By not trying to change anything in your life, you're actually hurting many people that want to change things for the better. Non-conforming is in our nature. How can it not be, when even if you're the kindest person alive, someone will eventually poke at you, willing to take you on. Even if you're still not engaged in supporting the current context, it does not mean that you're not hurting anyone. In a context, you cannot be on the sidelines and innocent, in the same time. You have to chose a side. Remember that only one side needs your help. The bigger context needs you to do nothing or actively support it, if you want to, i.e. politicians, conformists, etc..

Conflict runs deep in our daily life. I dream of living in a world, where no one is trying to fuck your life up for personal gain. You've been trained to live like this, and now you don't want it to change. We're charging with everything we've got and merciless, against anyone smart enough to point out the truth, who's probably trying to swap our current existence, for a better future. *"Sit down, you fucking antisocial prick, and listen to the prime minister speaking!"*

This is what happened in 2008. My family chose a side, when the great context changed, and wanted us to do nothing, even after severe intrusions in our daily lives. That was the last important year of our farm, before the inevitable divorce of my parents. A *zoonotic bovine leukosis* pandemic appeared out of nowhere. One case was discovered somewhere in a remote village, and the authorities started panicking. The vets were told to test all the cows in the country. They were just taking blood from the animal, then sending it to be tested by the Veterinary Health Directorate (DSV) of the district you belonged to. Everything was quite sudden, and panic engulfed the entire country. Farmers had been switched, to wish they got rid of the infected cows, just to limit the spread, and start afresh. *"Where did the virus come from?"*, everyone was asking. The health authorities were unanimously telling us that an infected cow grazed on a pasture, had put the virus on grass, then another cow came and grazed with the infected grass, and so forth. They couldn't explain which one was *cow-patient-zero* though. It was bad, from a medical point of view. In my parents' village cows started testing positive, and tens of them were being taken away by force, without any compensation from the government, as if the owners were to blame. Apparently, we were living with that virus without knowing. If one cow tested positive, then it had to be isolated at once, and put to sleep. There was almost no cow that tested negative. Some villagers were so poor, that almost their entire lives were depending on the animal. Some had amazing specimens from rare breeds. What made it interesting, and questionable in the same measure, was that only the most beautiful and healthy looking cows were testing positive. Never bovines with underlying conditions, even with tuberculosis. The latter were still allowed to join the village's daily herd (two paid cowboys were taking them to the fields). "Our cow tested positive, they're gonna come and take it away..." Our mother called us to ask for advice. The vet in the village was a known drunkard and a crook. No one trusted him. A family tried to stand their ground. They didn't want to give the cow away, as she didn't have any of the disease's symptoms. They were being helped by their daughter, who worked for one of these labs, that kept on getting positive results for almost every healthy looking cow in the village. They soon had to stand down, when their daughter received threats that she would lose her job, if she helped them keep the animal. My brother and I started browsing the studies about this disease that appeared from nowhere. It smelled fishy. We had enough experience in the police force, to be able to spot criminal acts from great distance. We told our parents to refuse access to anyone trying to get our cow. They listened to us and then, the vet and people from the council, started giving threats with issuing costly fines. We booked time off, just to go to the farm and check if any symptoms were present. Our mother was crying. She didn't want to lose a healthy animal with good genes. The vet kept telling them that trouble was around the corner, if they didn't comply. The orders to collect the cows came from the highest levels in the ministry of agriculture. After a close inspection, we could not see any signs of the aforementioned disease. Our beautiful cow was healthy as ever. We went back to the city, and told our parents not to agree with anything. We would take care of the situation. They also banned our animal to mingle with the village's herd, which now was formed of what was left in the village, mostly weak and old cows, and some truly ill, with contagious diseases. The most beautiful ones had gone to the incinerator. Before long, the vet came to my parents with people from the Veterinary Health Directorate (DSV), to convince them to give away the cow. They moved quickly to intimidation. The discussions got tense, and while my mother went inside to get some papers, my father grabbed an axe, and started issuing threats towards the officials. They left shortly after that. We heard that something might have happened, only when they started investigating our father. He was the only one that knew what he'd done. He received a fine for that, and my mother told him to deal with it himself. We told him not to do anything excessive. Being diplomatic in situations as this, can make you highly poisonous for the aggressors. It's hard to think that authorities that should care about you can be the criminals, but this is what it has come to. Meanwhile, we sent a request for a retesting of the cow's blood, with us being present. Initially, the

Veterinary Health Directorate (DSV) agreed, but then they suddenly changed their minds, without giving us any reasons. The conflict was growing fast, and creating a precedent. They knew we worked as police officers, so being too aggressive was kind of dangerous. People from the village started seeing the vet coming out of really expensive cars with tinted windows. For a village that size, and a person as the vet, that was unprecedented too. That's the sign that they're trying to profile you, and that they didn't like what they found. People in suits started visiting our farm, trying to speak with our parents. My mother knew not to talk with anyone she didn't know. We started contacting private labs for unbiased retesting, but they all refused to do it, for any amount of money. That was a clear sign, that something was definitely wrong with the whole testing campaign. The Veterinary Health Directorate (DSV) in the district we lived and worked, refused to do the testing, without even hearing what we had to say. "If the test was positive with our other branch, we cannot do another test. It means the cow needs to be sacrificed." Basically, the only way to have a second test was to send blood to a lab outside the country, and that would've been really expensive. Weirdly enough, the whole pandemic happened shortly after a campaign of vaccinating all the cows against a certain virus. My parents were not told what the vaccine was for. "There's a virus running around, so they sent us these vaccines for all the cows...", the vet told my mother. It took us a while to put the puzzle together. You're not dealing with situations as this every day. There were great forces behind the project of getting rid of the cows. To increase our fire power, and to dig out more evidence for ourselves, we wrote to this weekly tv show debating countryside life, hosted by the national television station, the equivalent of the BBC, both as corrupt. A reporter made her way to interview our parents at the farm, then they went to speak with the Veterinary Health Directorate (DSV) of the district, that deals with the entire area of the Danube Delta. The village was under their authority. When the reporter came back to give a resolution to my mother, their vehicle was filled with expensive and rare fish. She said that they will do the show, but that nothing will be solved. This was due to the forces involved in the whole campaign, leading up to the then acting president of *Dacia* (Romania), a former snitch for the commies, spy, traitor, wife beater, etc.. The general message was, that we should comply with giving the cow away. Between words, she was telling my mother that someone might get hurt in the process. We said no. After the show aired, they stopped taking any more cows from the village, without asking the owners first. If the cow tested positive, they'd ban it from mingling with the others; self-isolation forever. Somehow the virus slowly disappeared, after throwing many families in extreme poverty. There were other *pandemics* in the past, like bird or swine flu, that destroyed whole livelihoods in Eastern Europe. We never gave our animals to be sacrificed despite the pressures, as they were healthy. Yes, we've seen the 2020 scenario before...

A bit later, an undercover reporter found a staggering number of confiscated cows, grazing peacefully on this private land, owned by people with political connections. They've never been incinerated. Probably they got sold to the big burger restaurant chains. After things calmed down, villagers started thanking our mother for taking action and saving their animals. If we complied, the campaign probably would've continued. The damage was immense anyway. A cow is an important animal in the farm. Ours never developed any symptoms, she was healthy as an ox.

Eventually, after many hours of drinking in the village's bars, an upset drunk redneck strapped a belt around the vet's throat, strangled him, then dragged his body through the dusty streets, horrifying children and adults alike. That murder shocked the entire community. Some idiots, including his family, were silently accusing my mother of casting spells that got him killed. We never wished him to die, nor to get hurt in any way, despite his actions causing tremendous pain to many people. That was definitely karma. Never hurt people, especially your own!

It's crazy, but it makes sense now, in 2021, that we are intentionally pushed towards the edge of survival, and off the cliff, with the mRNA vaccine. After working, and being in direct conflict with the Government, I'm comparing it with the super-hyped Young George sheepdog, in *Far from the madding crowds*. Watch that movie to understand why.

That was a scam, to substantially reduce the cattle across the world, for the sudden gain of the powerful, and the accelerated weakening of the normal folk. Can you see beef sold by Eastern Europe to the US? Or *Dacian* (Romanian) wagyu to Japan? It's weird how, for millions of years, we didn't have one autoimmune disease, and in the modern world, there's a new one emerging every ten years or less. Even in animals that are essential to humans, and only in certain countries. A biologist told me recently, that it takes a virus around 800 years to modify so much, to be able to infect a new species. The chances of that mutation to happen when two viruses meet the same animal, are one in a few trillion. I tend to believe the guy. Firstly, because he's honest and it matches what we know about immunity, and because most scientists don't believe in God, but they do believe in dangerous mutations happening very often, even if the chances of it happening are extremely low, and not having any clear data to actually confirm it. They never believe that it can *escape* from a private biotech lab, which implies high risks of actually happening. It's the same as believing in fairies. They're talking more and more about getting rid of the cows, and eating more artificial meat. What were the odds that this plan coincides with an array of cattle diseases, imaginary or man made. Before this incident, there have been swine flu epidemics, and people from the same village lost thousands of pigs without compensation. That coincided with a peak in pork meat production, and all specimens had been vaccinated beforehand. It's conspicuous that Europe has all of these dangerous diseases, while the US, the country with the most cattle, didn't even have one single case of mad cow disease. Did they ever have swine flu?

CHAPTER 10

THE PANDEMIC DEBATE

Music for this chapter

Hans Zimmer - Time
Hans Zimmer - We Built Our Own World
Stephen McKeon - Bing Abi
Ramin Djawadi - Westworld
Peter Joseph - Zeitgeist Film Series (05 Pesante)
Howard Shore Bulletin Board (Music From "The Silence of the Lambs")
Mike Oldfield - Tubular Bells Pt. 1
Thomas Newman - Whisper of a Thrill
James Horner - Words Through the Sky
Hans Zimmer - Idyll's End
Depayk Solo - Follow the Light (Borneo Remix)
Franky Rizardo - No Judgement
Jayden Klight - Rejuvenated Cell Party
Marcelo Paladini - Drifting Birds
Franky Wah - Green & Gold
Franky Wah - Not in Love feat. LOWES
Bonobo - Nightlite feat. Bajka
Bonobo - Animals
Above & Beyond - Can't Sleep
Pathologic -Main Menu
Johannes Kobike, Robert Williamson - Meeting the Interns (Pathology OST)
Aphex Twin - Heliosphan
Aphex Twin - Polynomial C
Jeigo - Far Away
Ephemera - Drop Shots Blunted
Human Movement - Reframed
Leon Vynehall - Dumbo
Fantastic Man - Time Apprentice
Rage Against the Machine - Wake Up
Tourist - Last

"Hell is empty, and all the devils are here."

WILLIAM SHAKESPEARE

What can hurt more, than when you find out that what you used to believe in is not real, or than what you hoped that would not happen, does happen? These are two different situations, in which pain is the same. The first situation expresses the naive, and the second the fool. In both cases the result is identical, an inevitable future that will occur no matter what. If there would be a saviour opportunity, neither would take it because nothing happened yet. And so, the end of humanity as we know it starts to unfold. We are causing the end of human kind!

Got coronavirus symptoms? Get tested. High temperature or new continuous cough or loss of taste or smell? No one in your household should leave home if any one person has symptoms. Find out how to get a test, and how long to isolate, at nhs.uk/coronavirus. *Stay alert, control the virus, save lives. Hands-face-space.*

This advert talks about symptomatic people, so why are they testing everyone?

Whenever a species reproduces in really high numbers, beyond any predator's ability to control it, nature will develop a way to test the most genetically fit by releasing a bug. Unfortunately for the weakest, they don't have medicine. Humans do. We also have classes, fear, intelligence, power, systems, and conspiracy. The latter is like a slug, leaving traces of slime. Some people can see the traces, but they never get to see the slug. The others think the slime is a natural occurrence, and oppose the few for trying to discover the snail. The third category is trying to take advantage of any crisis.

Terrorism

-the unlawful use of violence and intimidation, especially against civilians, in the pursuit of political aims.

I would like to add that the above definition is incomplete. Law can be a way of terrorism too. Issuing new law overnight that restricts natural freedoms, all in the name of a synthetic or non-existent danger, is terrorism. No one should have the power to issue new law overnight. Martial Law or State of Emergency powers should be eliminated. The Government should act as a fair and sustainable guidance, and not as an aggressive parent for adults.

Crimes against humanity

-crimes against humanity refer to specific crimes committed in the context of a large-scale attack targeting civilians, regardless of their nationality.

Genocide

-the deliberate killing of a large number of people from a particular nation or ethnic group, with the aim of destroying that nation or group.

These are three powerful definitions of acts happening on our planet as I write this. Sadly, this *pandemic* is all three combined. Evidently, lawful use of violence is an accepted concept. Fight with the government, and you will have your bones broken in an instant. 2020, what a fucking mess! Many think that terrorism can be caused by a certain nationality, a person or a group of people. Few think that it can hide behind the law we're all trying to protect, laws that civilians have no control of. After becoming a police officer I started thinking deeper and deeper, about what I've gotten myself into, willingly. In early school years they are brainwashing us that we live in this perfect world, that we'll work in a perfect environment where no one is corrupt, and that everything is fair. We choose our careers, I join the police school, where they start a deeper process of trying to corrupt my system of beliefs. I will enforce the law to protect the good citizens of my country, in a perfectly balanced environment. In the meantime I learn how to control crowds of people, if the good citizens ever try to oppose the imposed system. As I start my career I can see an increased protection of criminals, bribe going up the ladder to the top levels, in an archaic pattern that seemed to have been here long time before my arrival. I started wondering where the corruption stops, who is the last person on this planet deciding all this. In my country, I managed to see that by following the money, you get to the highest possible levels of a state. Then you understand that the president used to be a special agent, trained both by the USA and Russia, with the acknowledgment of all other major powers. Ok, by now I understood that it was no longer about the money. Let's discuss power. So presidents are being trained from their cradle, and helped by other presidents of the biggest powers in this world. Beyond this you have got agencies that control the development of almost everything, in the same pack with the richest of this world that are making everything private, testing different ways of how we should live, creating conflict, monopolies, cartels, the top ten richest men, the laws that govern us, and plagues. But the ladder doesn't end there for me, there's more to be discovered. Why? Because death cannot scare all people in politics. Some other force is corrupting in this perfect manner. When something big is happening, all politicians in all countries agree on everything, as if they'd sleep in the same bed, like they're married and cannot tell on each other. If by any chance one tries to oppose, the next day he's in with the gang like they gave him a potion. The media flows in the same direction too, and all other organisations that were supposed to keep an open eye, are being blinded by the darkness. Even the people that would die anyway don't say anything on their deathbeds, they're taking all the secrets with them on the other side. The church everyone confuses with God is useless as well. Even when people are being killed at a global scale, they are still not telling about what is going on. The only difference between the government and the church is that one is doing it, and the others are accepting it. They know there is life after death, but still refuse to die with honour. Hence my belief that the global corruption surrounding our planet, and poisoning the entire human kind, cannot be of human origin! It is too big of a secret to be so. The *person* at the top cannot be human, a spitting image of the light that created us. I'm reserving the right to be wrong about this, if it isn't true. Call me a fool. I wish we invent an independent AI to pull every human being out of the ghettos, to count us, and round us up on a single patch of land. 7.8 billion people, one next to each other, and then search if there is anyone else left. I would like to meet each and every one of you, shake your hand, and see who is disturbed by my presence. I bet I'd be able to point out all the bad seeds, just by exhaling in your direction. That's right, bitches, I'm eating a lot of organic garlic as preventive measure, and when I feel bad. If with all of us out in the open there would still be movement in the sky, and in or on the ground, we would then know what this planet is up against.

Coronavirus

A type of common virus that infects humans, typically leading to an upper respiratory infection (URI). Seven different types of human coronavirus have been identified, and hundreds of strains, and counting. Most people will be infected with at least one type of coronavirus in their lifetime. The viruses are spread through the air by coughing and sneezing, close personal contact, touching an object or surface contaminated with the virus and rarely, by faecal contamination. You can spread a coronavirus whether you're infected or not, with or without symptoms, although the chances of being infectious while asymptomatic are really low due to your strong immunity. The illness caused by most coronaviruses usually lasts a short time, and is characterised by runny nose, sore throat, feeling unwell, cough, and fever.

But this is not all. There are hundreds of strains of all these coronaviruses attacking us daily. Each one of these can get us sick or killed. You go to the other side of the planet from where you live, and most probably you'll get infected with a local coronavirus strain that is not found home. When I moved to the UK, in 2013, I caught a cold and cough that lasted for one month. Obviously I had encountered a new strain of coronavirus, not found in *Dacia* (Romania).

How does a new strain appear?

When a coronavirus infects a person it captures one cell, and then it starts replicating by creating copies of itself, and spreading to other healthy cells. The hijacking occurs via a protein on the outer layer of the virus that can attach itself to, and penetrate the human cell. During the replication process, for whatever reason, a mutation can occur, that is slightly different than the original coronavirus. That is a new strain of the virus, which can infect a person that already had the original coronavirus. This does not mean that the symptoms will be as severe as the first time the person had the original coronavirus. Our bodies are trained, and already have the memory to produce specific antibodies to tackle the new strain relatively quick. Whenever you get sick with a coronavirus, you either get a new coronavirus you've never had before, or a new strain of an old coronavirus that had visited you in the past, situation when you'd have mild symptoms, compared with the first encounter with the completely new bug. No one knows how many strains of coronavirus are around the world, because they keep mutating constantly from one person to another. It can also stay the same without mutating for longer periods of time. This is extremely difficult to monitor, measure, and keep under control.

The Wuhan Coronavirus

SARS-Cov-2 is the latest coronavirus released by nature, or modified in a lab to be able to infect humans. I tend to believe it was modified by humans, because we have laboratories around the world that are developing and testing new viruses. When you play like this, it's fairly easy for one to escape and spread. There is no doubt about it. To be clear, once a virus is in nature, you can only protect yourself from it if you live in a bubble costume, with an oxygen feed pipe connected to a wall. Exactly in the same way how the scientists are dressed when testing viruses in the labs. This is a coronavirus though, and our bodies are trained to deal with this family of viruses. To get rid of it, our bodies will start to produce specific IgGs to deactivate the infectious virus cells.

Until that happens, the coronavirus will try, and probably will succeed in inflicting a considerable damage to a high number of healthy cells. This does not mean that you will die. Because of this, the reconstruction stage will take longer than the infectious stage, which is proven by science to be around five days, depending on your body's ability to fight. The healthier and younger you are the sooner the virus will be deactivated, and you can no longer infect someone else. This is old science, but in 2020 it seems that everything has been forgotten for some reason. Or it's being kept secret intentionally. I'm saying this because all measures taken are heading us with amazing speed towards a totalitarian state. What you are reading here might be older than your grandparents. With a coronavirus you cannot infect anyone else from the sixth day. It would be a rare occurrence if that was to happen. Even if you still feel sick, it's only your body trying to rebuild. If you still have a high temperature, it means that you have a secondary infection that your body is struggling to shrug off, and therefore you need some sort of medication or medical attention. You should seek help straight away if you've had the fever for MORE THAN ONE DAY! High temperature is a sign that your body is struggling to win the fight. After the fifth day from infection your body begins its reconstruction, and to discard the inactive virus cells. They can appear even in your faeces for up to 43 days. This has been proven by science, but I am not going to reference everything here because you need to do your own studies. You will never learn how to develop an analytical attitude towards what is happening with your life, if you always receive information on a silver platter. You have to be engaged in finding the truth!

What does *symptoms* mean?

This is where people get confused all the time. In common belief symptoms have to be severe. Wrong! Any change that takes you from your ideal state of wellbeing to some sort of discomfort is a symptom. It means that something is wrong with your body, and it does not imply that it has to be a virus. It can also be bacteria. If you feel a slight discomfort in your throat or nose, maybe runny nose or multiple sneezing episodes, all these are symptoms of *something*. No matter how healthy you are, if you're contracting a completely new virus, it is impossible to have absolutely no symptoms. So, you don't have antibodies for the coronavirus (which is attacking the respiratory system) but you're immune?! That is impossible. How the authorities have described the symptoms of SARS-Cov-2 is wrong. Most people testing *positive* have no symptoms. That's because the testing method is wrongly interpreted, inaccurate and incomplete.

My personal experience with the Wuhan coronavirus

A coronavirus is producing cough, sneezing and inflammation of the synovial mucosa and of the lungs, to favour the spread to other hosts. It's how it works. Without a high viral load, i.e. inflammation/irritation, the chances of you passing on the virus is highly unlikely. You cannot spread a coronavirus without inflammation/symptoms. Even if it's in your throat, the tonsils will deactivate it maybe in a few hours or even minutes from contact. This is why they are there. Most viruses in your mouth are deactivated cells. What you feel when you contract the new coronavirus can be slightly different from one individual to another. The first symptoms are a sore/dry throat and lungs. This is how you'll wake up on the first day of infection. You will start coughing often, and your voice will become low pitched and somehow robotic. It is not a productive cough, meaning there will be no phlegm coming out. You will just cough, and feel pain in the lungs and throat. The change in speech is significant. When pulling air in you'll feel an increased discomfort. During the first two days you will not have a runny nose or wet eyes. Loss of smell and taste is common to all coronaviruses and influenza. With this coronavirus it is not relevant. Your body will ask for copious amounts of water, and you should cave in. Hydrate yourself accordingly, and keep your body satisfied. This means WATER! It is really important. I was waking up during the night to drink around one litre of water in one go. It was weird, but it felt good and the right thing to do. With all coronaviruses you get dehydrated, but this was something else. You should not drink cold water, it needs to be at room temperature. Once you have water you should feel a release. From the third day your ears and nose will get blocked. You might develop high temperature, but only if your body is weak. High temperature is not a must with the new coronavirus, but it can happen even to a healthy individual. My mother developed fever on the second day of infection, but there were other factors that contributed to her weakness. She started drinking water like crazy as well. A couple of days before she began fasting for Easter, and had only water with a bit of bread. When I brought the new virus in the house she had been an easy victim. Her body was already weak, topped with her missing some important organs, and also having a blood pressure issue. Viruses love weak bodies. This is why we get sick in the first place. Our immune system is not constant, it fluctuates based on multiple factors: overall state, food, exposure, strain, age, etc.. On my third day of infection, and my mother's second day of infection we called the ambulance, as her temperature was increasing. They came in about 5-10 minutes. "That was quick, thank you!" "You're lucky, we were in the area." The paramedics advised us to set an appointment with the GP the next day, to give her some antibiotics. I could control my cough a bit already, from day three. They refused to test us, and recommended to take care of each other because we were doing the *right thing*. We did as they said, and my mother's temperature dropped to normal limits after one day of antibiotics. She took them for about five days. Her cough lasted for about one more week. Although she was 64 years old, the paramedics told us we should not take her to the hospital, despite doing an overall assessment of the situation. This happened at the beginning of March 2020. My brother had only a discomfort in his throat for about two days, and that was it. I had it between 29 February 2020 and 06 March 2020. Currently I'm working as a private hire driver in London. Throughout the lockdowns I haven't stopped working. Since I've had the new virus I'm therefore immune, and cannot pass it on to other people if I ever get it in my system again. Most of my riders during 2020 have been thousands of people from the hospitals, staff working directly with *Covid-19* patients, and even people going home from hospitals with presumed *Covid-19*. I am writing this chapter at the beginning of December 2020, and I have never had any symptoms of cold or flu from March. Therefore, as far as I'm concerned, you develop immunity to this new virus for at least nine months, and counting. This includes my mother and brother because we live together. Whatever virus I get, they will get it too. If any scientist is telling you that you're not developing immunity he is lying to you, and we are standing proof. One year immunity is normal for a coronavirus.

The Media

This is the real injection right here. The perfect vaccine for the brain. We all know that the entire media is controlled, but we decide to do nothing. We still agree to watch and read it, and we keep on paying our tv licences, like blind people. We basically pay to get stupid. From 2020 the media has to be restructured completely. They are always creating wars and conflicts among people. The owners are sponsoring campaigns and parties without any consequence. Science and the media are at opposite ends. They are never with the people that actually support them. Same as the church, the media is an incredible tool to control people by polarising them. To continue under this form the whole media should be owned by the people, with full access to all documents and activities for each individual. Adios, Media, you're done on this planet!

The Church

Father? Hello! Is anybody there? Are you still investigating the paedophile gay priests, or they've been forgiven, and further allowed to satisfy their carnal pleasures, in the name of a *Lord* that has nothing to do with the Divine Light? In 2020, the Church has never been more silent. After a bit of digging, I managed to find out that theology students are being taught how to never oppose the government. Gone are the days when the church were giving shelter to Robin Hoods. How can the keepers of real faith go along with the measures taken? In my opinion, the Church as an institution lost its right to exist anymore. It should get banned by the people. The Church needs to be taken down as an institution, together with all governments. They are one and the same, and this year stands as proof. This should be the new beginning, one faith in the context of Creation - God, zero religions, zero secret cults. I come from a culture where priests and the Church are part of a human's daily existence, but this year they have betrayed the faith they promised to protect. They cannot guide us towards the light anymore, we'll go alone on the bright side from now on, guided only by true believers, the real priests. The Church as an institution is null as of 2020. The level of praying for the good of the world done by these priests, can be seen in the advance of the satanic plan during the last 12 months. The Church is another millennia old lying institution, created just to control you. Despite its appearance, it is another instrument of the evil, disguised as God. It never fought for your freedom, it never will. Go to church and prey to God, but obey your corrupt government! This statement here cannot be the right way we should live.

The Government

The Government is more liable to make mistakes when lying, than when telling the truth. This is why they messed up the numbers, nothing makes sense, and they have to revise the erroneous charts previously presented to the public. Besides the scientists you see having speeches on television, there are hundreds of other highly skilled people, putting together all sorts of accurate studies, sharp as knives. They can tell the population's every move, before you even think of doing something. They know you will go out in the streets trying to overturn their decisions, and they also know with pinpoint accuracy how many people will die, based on any decision they will make. Do you know that even one month of economical shutdown, will kill more people that any coronavirus probably will in more than a year? And these are healthy people, that would have no problem with getting rid of the virus from their system. They will never tell you this, because it will make them look bad. If they take the *wrong* decisions, they will back it to the end of the world. This is politics! You cannot know they have done the *wrong* thing. Plus, political correctness implies taking full responsibility for any decision. Politicians know they will be fine no matter what, they're rich anyway. The opposition will come to power, and take it from there, towards the same crooked plan. Take brexit as example - all British prime ministers, after the vote, have declared that they will get brexit done. None debated that half of the country voted for staying in the European Union. Or about the omnipresent negative marketing towards the Union during the vote, which was conspicuous and clearly biased. The fact that it was allowed should have started at least an emergency enquiry into the promoters. This is political correctness - choosing something and backing it fully, disregarding any other details, even if they are more important than the choice made. This is how in only four years, the UK lost more money than what they paid to the EU during their entire membership of 47 years, adjusted with inflation. This is what is happening with the forced pandemic of 2020 - by trying to save one person with any coronavirus or flu, they are willing to kill 10-20 other healthy people by shutting the economies. If this makes sense to you, I am afraid you are a highly troubled individual, that should not take part in society. During this whole time, the opposition in the UK's Parliament was an even worse enemy of the people than the party in power. When they were talking about local lockdowns, the opposition was pushing for another six months of full, and stricter lockdown than the previous one. Instead of explaining the testing method, and take the veil off the secrecy about what is truly happening to patients in hospitals, they were promoting measures to kill more healthy people by burying the economy even deeper. To end the lockdowns, they're turning to you again, by forcing you to have a vaccine that you don't need. So they concocted a communistic plan against the people, then they ask you to compromise your life for something they created. How does that work? This is another proof that, no matter who is coming to power, they will only continue the same biased plan, without asking the people if they accept it. Right wing, left wing, they're the same wing! Today, hospitals are refusing to treat your condition without a useless coronavirus test, motivating it that they don't know which ward they should put you in. Outrageous and criminal!

Someone online was making a good point during recent months. There are so many implications to what is happening now, that it is almost impossible to fully conceive all of them on your own. The following one is easy to comprehend. This guy was saying how rich countries have a responsibility towards poor countries, which is undeniable. During normal times, they are handing out billions of foreign aid. In 2020 all economies have been intentionally crashed, therefore even the richest countries have put foreign aid at the back of the list, or have scrapped it altogether. I'll let you figure out how many healthy people will die due to these cuts, since no one is taking responsibility anymore for the poor countries already in trouble.

The Good Vaccine Approach

Bringing out a vaccine for a coronavirus is madness!

Let's assume that we do want to accelerate the immunity. The best approach to immunise the population, currently, is by creating an immunoglobulin jab, not a vaccine with purified virus RNA. I have promoted this since the beginning of the planned pandemic, because it is an old and most effective treatment. And this is why. If a person has underlying conditions or an autoimmune disease, or both, putting three-four strains of the purified virus in them won't do much to help them, plus they have to do it every year. If they live in the UK, and travel to Serbia, they will get another strain of the flu that is not in circulation in the UK, even if they had the flu vaccine. The spectrum of virus strains is very wide, and almost impossible to put in a single vaccine. Plus, the costs to make new vaccines every year is immense, and vaccinating all ages is a huge mistake, and scientifically it makes no sense. If you have a condition, or a weak immune system you need already produced specific immunoglobulins, same as IgG rabies jab for example. And if a person has a weak immune system, why would you put the virus in the person in the first place? They cannot produce proper immunity, and if they do, it's short lived and probably insufficient! There are people still dying with flu, even if they had the jab. No doctor will tell you this. It's never caused by a vaccine...

After working in a lab producing immunoglobulins, I now understand how a campaign against a virus should work. People with health conditions need specific antibodies injections, and then maybe to be exposed to the virus. Not intentionally of course, but through normal living, then monitored to see how long they keep it, and if they've encountered the virus. This can be easily done through a high performance specific IgG test for use at home or in a lab. This approach would be infinitely less costly than inventing, and producing a totally new vaccine. It would also have no severe side effects, like putting your life in danger, as it would only contain naturally produced human proteins and non toxic suspension. They can even be administered through IV solutions. This way the healthy can develop strong immune responses, and then be used to protect the weak, by donating IgG-rich plasma that can be processed to create IgG jabs. The process is really expensive, but compared with the one of developing and producing new RNA vaccines it means nothing. Also, there are plenty of biotech labs doing it, and the levels of production would be really low, because you would need to vaccinate only the weak with the IgG shot. Most people don't need immunisation for flu, coronaviruses, and many others. Our bodies are full of specific antibodies at any moment. I have done it with my own hands, and no PhD or bio-scientist can tell me different. They have probably never extracted antibodies from human plasma; maybe they read in books about what I was doing.

What is happening now will irreversibly tarnish people's trust in medical science and doctors. PhD means nothing anymore. If a person with the highest level of medical studies, can say that asymptomatic people are getting others sick, that GMOs and their byproducts are good, when they produce inflammation in the body, that even immune people need the mRNA vaccine, that the mRNA vaccine is *good*, and that's it, that masks work, that this is a real pandemic, their knowledge, or lack of it, is killing healthy and ill people alike. Probably my GP has a PhD too, but after talking with her about the vaccine, I realised that she knows nothing, even about the basics of immunity. I spoke with nurses assisting surgeons in the operating theatre, that didn't know how immunity actually works. They wanted me to give them more information, when they found out that I used to work in human plasma processing. Healthcare professionals of all levels told me that they're still learning about how to combat this virus... A coronavirus! We have thousands of strains attacking us daily, and they are still learning. But they are not questioning one bit why patients with flu are being treated as *Covid-19*. How can we trust doctors anymore, when normal people know more about the human body through personal study. In 2020 the PhD title is equal to zero, at least for me and my family. I feel sorry for the doctors that are really trying to raise the alarm, but no one is paying attention to them, or they're being threatened by higher levels.

These are respiratory diseases. Some doctors are trying to tell people that you cannot infect anyone if you're asymptomatic, and other highly skilled practitioners, neurologists, etc., that are confused by the low mortality rate from Covid-19, and the empty hospital wards dealing with respiratory conditions. Why aren't these people listened to, and even supported to raise the alarm? Why aren't you allowed in the hospital, even if you've had the actual new virus?

If you're a medic, can you understand how scary it is for me, to see doctors conforming to what the government is telling us? Wearing the mask everywhere, thinking that it works outside an aseptic environment, opening the window fully when in my car, for ventilation, even at zero degrees, and on motorway, saying that all these numbers in the media are real, and that the PCR is right... So, you don't get pneumonia anymore, from driving a convertible during winter? Don't be a pawn playing the game blindly. You're a fucking doctor! You should always speak the truth about science, not eat up what an MP is saying, nor an office scientist that most likely works for the secret services too.

Does this mean that you didn't know what you were doing before 2020? Seeing a doctor not applying the science correctly is hell! How can anyone trust you anymore, when you act like an employee in a corporation, without applying what you studied in medical school. *"I do what I'm being told."* As a doctor, with this crooked mentality, you are killing people, and bringing hell into the mainstream.

If it's a real pandemic, then why is the entire world spending billions on developing new technologies to vaccinate, instead of forcing the pharmaceutical companies to produce effective solutions with existing technologies, that are already proven to work hundreds of times better than an RNA vaccine. It would cost hundreds of millions, or less. And now we are talking about highly damaging, and also not tested properly, *genetic* vaccines. With the method I am promoting here we are currently keeping alive people with NO fucking immune system. There are people living right now, because I was extracting a whole array of IgGs from human plasma. You don't need a flu jab, nor a coronavirus jab. The Governments and all the real scientists know that these technologies are here, and that they work just perfect. The reason why you cannot have an antibody test done at home right now, is because you'd find out the real numbers that had the new virus already. Hospitals and labs know that they are using the wrong testing methods, or at least incomplete. As long as you keep on testing, this pandemic will never end. We are being confronted with secrecy with a purpose. In a real pandemic, pharmaceutical companies should be forced to give up profits for saving lives, if that was the real goal. The IgG shots would still cost a lot of money, but given that most people don't need it, it would mean a residual cost for the health services worldwide, and with a really high survival rate and efficiency. The current pandemic is all about changing the way we live, to a high degree, and offloading as many people as possible, ill or healthy. What you should do is conducting your own research, then sending a letter to your government asking for explanations. If millions would do it, they would have to change their tone and approach towards proven science. The world and solutions are in your hand. Anyone who has developed immunity to this new virus should not take any vaccine. It is scientifically wrong. Even more than this, if you have antibodies for the new coronavirus, and also have the vaccine, it'll be worse for you than for people that don't have the immunity, because your body's immune system will start conflicting with the vaccine. *If I've produced antibodies for this in the past, why are the healthy cells producing this spike protein?*

They want to make your body vaccine dependant, and if one year you decide not to have it, your body will have counted on you having it regularly, so the chances of you dying will increase tenfold. This also because your immune system is drained every time you have a vaccine. When death will happen, they will have a bigger tool to scare the others. *"Look, he died because he didn't have the vaccine!"*, which will have a bigger impact in convincing people to have it regularly. We are just guinea pigs in an artificial loop of fear and despair. From fear you do irrational things, and from despair you make it a habit.

What happens in the hospitals stays in the hospitals

What happens in hospitals around the world in 2020, is the biggest premeditated malpractice campaign in the history of human kind. The level of coverup just to keep one's job is unprecedented. I'm 100% certain that the level of intimidation from upper levels is unprecedented too. If a serious and fair investigation would start to look into what happened with the patients that died of *Covid-19*, would lose us probably over 90% of doctors and nurses. The health services worldwide would collapse, with medical staff getting permanent criminal records, banned from practicing medicine ever again, or going to prison for many years. Even the shortages of staff they're talking about are due to some testing positive, and having to self-isolate. This is an easy way to cripple a health service, isn't it? In the last months I had to confront so much resistance from people, when telling them that the treatment the patients are receiving in hospitals might be wrong, and their condition most probably is getting worse as result, that I might just be inhumane in the eyes of everyone. I keep on telling people that the hospitals don't know exactly which virus is making them sick only from the PCR testing. They might not even have any active virus in them, the PCR could give a fake positive if by any chance the patient is discarding any old virus. And they receive treatment for coronavirus, although they might not need it. Why do you think they don't allow others in the hospital. This virus is clearly less deadly than flu or previous coronaviruses because over 99% of the nurses working in *Covid-19* wings didn't get it. Which increases the chances that most patients are ill due to flu or previous coronaviruses, for which nurses already have antibodies. Don't put their protection on the PPE because that would not help to protect them. They use aprons their entire shift without cleaning them, reusing masks, gloves, etc., and going from *Covid-19* wards to other non *Covid-19* wards. Aprons cannot protect against viruses, visors neither, nor masks. They are not protected against any virus with the PPE, and how they use it. There are strict procedures on how you should use the PPE to increase the chances of protection, but all those have been broken; it couldn't have been any other way, as PPE is still scarce. I have been told that even in the lab I used to work, technicians have to reuse single use masks, practice that before could've gotten you fired on the spot. This year, the standard levels of aseptic dropped significantly everywhere, including medicine making and testing. 2020 is synonymous with huge intentional decay in human care and practice.

How admissions work nowadays, as confirmed by hospital staff, is crucial to further understanding this so-called pandemic. Once you present yourself to the hospital for admission, you'd be put into the *Covid-19* wards until the PCR test result comes in, probably after two or three days. If the result is negative, then they would send you to the right ward. By then you could have been infected with a virus contracted from the ill patients, now spreading it to other non-infected wards. All the nurses I talked to said this is completely wrong. And it's obvious why. If you test positive, then you stay in that infectious ward even if you don't have any symptoms. During all this time your condition could get worse, because the staff's main goal is to determine if you've got *Covid-19*, not if you need immediate medical care for the specific issue that brought you to the hospital in the first place. *"Excuse me, I've got some pains in my abdomen, I think it might be the appendicitis..." "Oh, wait we need to see if you've got Covid-19, your presumed appendicitis can wait."* You have no idea how many patients have told me that they had to shout at medical staff, to focus their attention on the actual physical condition. Some have reported that doctors didn't want to operate appendicitis close to bursting. This is routine surgery nowadays but if it bursts, there's more than 80% chances that you'll die from the infection.

Nowadays in hospitals *Covid-19* is the main killer. Nothing else matters. You know what's really the most known killer in hospitals around the world? *Staphylococcus Aureus*, or other secondary bacterial infection. They're not banning people from entering the hospital based on this, nor on any other coronavirus or flu, so why would they do it now, if not to stop people from seeing what is actually happening with the patients, and to block the health services everywhere by forcing people to use private healthcare.

In November 2020, I had a nurse in my vehicle who told me that she'd take the vaccine, no matter if she's immune or not because if you are to die you'd die anyway. And she is taking care of patients... Shouldn't the reverse be valid as well? Why take the vaccine, if you're to die you'd die anyway... These stupid people are taking care of you!

If you look at the evolution of ventilators you will notice that after spring, everyone stopped talking about running out of them. And their numbers of infected people have gone way higher, compared to the months when there were not enough ventilators. They will tell you that they learned more about this virus, and that not all patients need one now. This means that they did kill people in hospitals, by ventilating the shit out of patients with dry lungs caused by the new virus, and with other viruses like SARS-Covid-1, MERS, Influenza, etc. Look at April's numbers in the UK. They stopped talking about ventilators during that time, maybe May. Then they discovered the Ozone therapy, which was known to regenerate lung tissue, years in advance. Even so, they're not using it largely in the UK. It's early 2021, and I'm still being told by doctors and nurses that they ventilate people, and also inject them with an RNA inhibitor, called *Remdesivir*, approved by MHRA and the FDA as an emergency. Like they don't know about this medicine, called

Ivermectin, that won the Nobel Prize for fighting viral infections. All this information was known years in advance, since Satoshi Omura got the Nobel Prize for its discovery in 2015. Why did they have to approve a new, poorly tested *Remdesivir*?

Now they are promoting plasma treatment like it's a new technology. Plasma treatment was used in the First World War by doctors and sanitary corps on the battle fields. This confirms what I kept telling people all around me. I have worked in the IgG vaccines industry, and I strongly think this should've been the strategy from the beginning, giving IgG shots to the vulnerable only, not RNA or mRNA vaccines. The infrastructure, the processes, and the data are there already! But this side of the industry is mostly owned by the Chinese, who want to make profit from the existing processes, and most probably monopolise the sector to prevent the world from having access to reliable and proven treatments, that also work for different illnesses. I have asked many doctors and nurses, in person or online, about why they want to vaccinate the immune as well, and they either chose to be silent - mostly online, or they told me that you can get reinfected, so that's why you need the vaccine. Of course you can get reinfected, but because you had it once, you might not feel anything due to the potency of your immunity. But you always infect, and get infected with everything that's around you, this is why your plasma is always loaded with antibodies at any time. There is nothing you can do about getting reinfected or passing the virus to someone else, IT IS CALLED NATURE! Once you die you stop spreading diseases around you. Although by being healthy, the chances of you spreading coronaviruses are close to null.

There is a big issue with taking plasma with *Covid-19* IgGs from immune people, and putting it into the vulnerable.

That plasma needs extensive testing because you can pass way worse things to the receiver, if the donor's health hasn't been monitored properly during the years. HIV is one of the main viruses that can be passed on through raw plasma, because it's a virus that can be seen months later after infection. There have been cases in the past when patients got HIV from blood transfusions. It's not something new, and I'm pretty sure that if the NHS cannot treat a person with a coronavirus with existing treatments, they will most likely fuck up with the plasma treatment. I'm willing to bet on it!

With every respiratory disease your level of oxygen in the blood decreases, because it attacks the lungs and the upper airways. This does not mean that the patient needs loads of air being forcibly pushed into the lungs. Some oxygen might be required, which is different. With the new coronavirus your air sachets in the lungs don't get filled with puss. This one is drying the top layer of the lung, without producing phlegm. It will reduce the lung's capacity to absorb oxygen, but that doesn't mean that you don't have enough to survive the first five days, the infectious stage. Oxygen is important for the reconstruction of your body. This is why, with every respiratory disease, because your level of oxygen absorption decreases slightly, you might lose your smell. It's not *Covid-19* specific. When you're in an airplane at 30,000ft, the level of oxygen can drop with as much as 20%, and above 8,000m, 15%. That's a decrease of 15%-20% compared to the sea level conditions, where humans perform best. So, when with a respiratory disease, a drop in blood oxygen is normal, and it doesn't necessarily mean that you need to be ventilated. Just try to smell or taste at 30,000ft, and see if your senses are the same.

The Polymerase Chain Reaction method (PCR)

Did you ever wonder why there is no test for flu? During the PCR test you do not use any template of the virus you are looking for. All RNAs are made from the same base chemicals. These chemicals form blocks called nucleotides, which are arranged in a certain sequence. The same for all the DNAs (DNA has a slightly different chemical composition and shape compared to the RNA). The RNA nucleotides can be arranged in an infinity of sequences determined by evolution. During the PCR, the biologists are preparing primers, which are RNA specific, and DNA specific chemicals. These primers have the same chemical composition as the genetic material sought, RNA or DNA. The primers will attach to the genetic material found in a sample (in this case RNA), and start creating new nucleotides, identical to the sample of RNA found. Preparing primers to attach only to a specific RNA sequence you wish to find, in this case SARS-Cov-19 RNA, is impossible. Ok, maybe not impossible, but it would take way more tools than the usual preparation of a primer, and an RT-PCR machine. Even bacteriophages (bacterio-viruses) have RNA, as chlamydia or staphylococcus. We have these in our throat without exposing any symptoms. If as a biologist you're saying that seeing specific RNA sequences is possible so easily, you either never studied the PCR method or you're lying with a hidden purpose. The PCR result also contains your DNA, but they know it's yours because they took the sample from you. If the lab technicians wouldn't know where the sample came from, they would not know it's yours. They'd have to match the DNA from the sample with yours to know it's you. This is what they are not doing when getting a positive result for coronavirus.

The Polymerase Chain Reaction is the revolutionary method invented in 1983, by the USA biochemist and scientist Kary Mullis. Ten years later, in 1993, he was awarded the Nobel Prize in chemistry for this breakthrough. In his book, *Dancing Naked in the Mind Field*, he expressed his disappointment to have received it so late. I recommend you to read his novel, and *The Polymerase Chain Reaction* scientific study, co-written with other fellow scientists. This is a huge discovery towards understanding DNA. What the PCR does is multiplying a DNA sequence billions of times, making it easier to look at it closer. As Kary Mullis describes it in his book, before this discovery, when you were trying to look at the human DNA compared to trying to read a book from the moon. After being awarded the big prize, Kary landed up there, with the biggest in the world. He was the odd one though. Renowned for being a womaniser, for surfing whenever someone wanted to interview him, and for pointing a laser beam at a taxi driver in Sweden, after they had a terrorist attack, everyone knew he's not the usual scientist. He died in August 2019 of pneumonia. I wonder if someone had done a PCR test on him, to see if he had the new coronavirus. New or old, I think he would've tested positive by today's standards. It's also weird how all this PCR testing started after his death. He would've never allowed it. To add more to an already enigmatic scientific world, he discovered that there is no official scientific study to prove that HIV (human immunodeficiency virus) is causing AIDS (acquired immunodeficiency syndrome). Coming to this topic, did you know that quite a high percentage of people, about 20% or more, are still immune to HIV? Unfortunately for Kary and his statute, he wasn't allowed to question such a big topic. As much as he struggled to find that study, he couldn't. This led to him being banned from the biggest scientific conferences in the world. One even paid him over $6,000 to not show up. Soon after he got banned from most of them, for having the audacity to question his fellow scientists, and the entire scientific world. Even if you're one of the top scientists, with a Nobel Prize in your pocket, being vocal about a hidden truth is not acceptable, and it will get you excluded from the elite club. During his later years he expressed his concerns about scientists, by affirming that he is highly disappointed with the scientific world, as the more they're trying to help people, they are killing them.

The PCR method is also used today to test for genetic material that is not our own. Can we see if a virus is there next to our DNA? Of course, this is what this method is all about, seeing genetic material. You add a sequence of DNA and a primer to an enzyme environment, and with sudden changes in temperature called thermo-cycles, the primer will attach itself to the sequence of DNA. The reaction will create oligonucleotides, which are identical synthetic copies of your DNA. This is the simplified explanation of the above method. A more recent version of this method is called Reverse-Transcriptase Polymerase Chain Reaction or RT-PCR. With RT-PCR the starting material is RNA, and with a reverse transcriptase enzyme, the RNA is turned into its corresponding DNA. In this case you have to isolate the RNA strain to have a good result, which can be a strenuous process.

With the method used extensively in 2020, Real-Time PCR, the reaction is monitored during the multiplication cycles, compared to measurement at the end point with traditional PCR, or Reverse-Transcriptase PCR. When measured, the optical detection module is monitoring the fluorescence signal generated during each multiplication cycle, as the *fluorophore* binds to the new sequence. The fluorophore will create fluorescence as the sequence goes through a certain number of multiplication cycles. Keep in mind that the primer, enzymes, and buffers are not virus specific, but RNA or DNA specific. This means that they only assist and promote the multiplication of the oligonucleotides. You cannot add primers or enzymes for coronavirus, influenza, or any other virus you want to find. If that was possible they would've probably found new strains with every test. It requires additional testing methods. When you get fluorescence after a certain number of cycles, it means that the fluorophore successfully attached itself to the RNA sequence, and got multiplied together with the RNA. This is how you get a POSITIVE test result, the *mother* of all PCR results. There was RNA next to your DNA, and got multiplied.

There is more than one interpretation of the PCR result, and they both need to be understood exhaustively.

Positive

For the test to be accurate and properly controlled, scientists are using *multiplication cycle thresholds*. Let's say that the *positive* result threshold is set to 1,000 multiplication cycles. If the fluorescence is being picked up by the optical unit under the threshold it means you are *positive* for RNA material. Yes, you've got the new coronavirus! Congratulations! But wait, do you? Well, we don't know yet which RNA we're looking at, if it's any other coronavirus, influenza, or herpes simplex. Unless you can read the virus from the fluorescence. For that you might have to be a Master Wizard from Hogwarts. *Wingardium LeviosRNA!* To pinpoint the correct virus it requires additional testing that takes time, and different methods. We don't even know if the virus is active or not. We can only see the RNA fluorescence. Why do you think DNA test results take so long to come in during criminal trials? It requires extensive testing to match A with A, and B with B through different testing methods. During the current situation, testing for one positive individual could take up to a few weeks to find out the exact virus they're looking at, and if it was active when the sample was taken. Why do you think no scientist was allowed by the media and the politics to explain the PCR test to the public? When you test positive with the PCR method we need to look at how the multiplication cycle threshold was determined, and if it was homologated. True science says that you are infectious with a coronavirus for up to five days. The rest up to 43 days is recovery, and inactive virus discarding. If the threshold is too high, then you make non contagious patients test positive. Hence patients testing positive twice in two consecutive weeks, same as Christiano Ronaldo. Poor people! The *positive* threshold should be determined after testing clinically ill patients, during the first five days from the first symptoms with the current virus: a sore throat, dry cough and lungs, and acute thirst. Only then the PCR *positives* can get close to pinpointing contagious patients. We blindly trust all these hospital and private labs to have the right procedures, and to obey the regulations, but I highly doubt they know what they are doing. There is no transparency so my doubts have solid ground. Maybe my skepticism comes from me having worked in a lab endorsed by the FDA and MHRA, and still with great flaws, weaknesses, and poor management in keeping it sterile. You have to consider that as I am writing this chapter, millions of samples are being tested daily. Bags of samples are being collected, and stacked in a pile, waiting to go into the PCR machine; cross-contamination is highly likely. This means that clean samples can test positive because of the few viral infected ones. Then the cleanliness and cross contamination procedures of the testing labs have to be assessed. The labs would never admit this, and they will probably also say that they are using virus specific primers, which is a lie. They should have had the SARS-CoV-2 specific primers before we knew the virus even existed, which is impossible. Then someone should've produced these specific primers for all the labs in the world, way ahead of the *pandemic*. As stated above, it is impossible to have virus specific primers. If it was possible, doesn't this mean that they already had the RNA sequence of the new Wuhan virus before we even knew the virus existed? This raises questions about the novelty of the virus, on top of the inefficiency of the PCR alone. When China started reporting the first cases, Canada followed shortly with their own cases, days after. They all used the PCR method, seeing *a virus*. If you know biologists, ask them how they'd prepare the primers to identify only SARS-Cov-19, and if they'd test two patients, one with flu like symptoms, and another with *Covid-19* symptoms, trying to identify the new virus only, would they both test positive, or just the one with the new coronavirus. With such a volume of testing I can assure you that cleanliness is not a priority anymore. Biologists would have to change gloves and masks hundreds of times a day. That will never happen in any hospital or private lab. Coming back to the primers used during the PCR, they are RNA specific, not virus specific. The primer binds to the RNA if it's in the sample, promoting the formation of RNA nucleotides, which are synthetic copies of the natural RNA. The primer binds to any RNA found in the sample, whether it is influenza, SARS-CoV-1, SARS-CoV-2, MERS, HIV, herpes, etc.. The biologist doing the testing cannot tell which virus's RNA he is seeing or if it's active, just by performing the PCR test. It requires multiple methods of testing the infected sample. If the multiplication cycle threshold is set higher than the standard for clinically ill patients, the PCR will give *positive* for patients that are discarding inactive virus. THEY CAN NO LONGER INFECT ANYONE after the fifth day of symptoms! There are a handful of scientists that are qualified to perform and interpret a PCR test, and they have tried to warn about the flaws of these mass testing campaigns using it on its own. They have been silenced by the media and the governments. Totalitarianism is making a great comeback, and this time will stay, with the majority's endorsement. If you know doctors, talk to them about what I am explaining here, and if they disagree, ask them to prove themselves; also ask them if they have studied the *Polymerase Chain Reaction*.

Negative

The PCR method can give a negative result too. If the threshold is set properly, to pick up only high RNA count, from clinically ill patients, *negative* results would be aplenty. What is happening in 2020 is that the labs doing the testing have different thresholds, set as *required.* This is why *positive* is omnipresent. Even if the threshold is set properly, the PCR could still return negative from infected patients. They could have the test done today and return negative, and tomorrow to fall ill. They would not be required to self-isolate. This can occur due to the virus moving from the throat and mouth into the lungs. Your buccal and synovial mucus is constantly recycled. When having the swab taken, the virus can be missed by one swallow at the right time. With every day from the peak of your antibodies count, you are losing high quantities of inactive virus. The difference between the active virus cell count at the peak of the infection, compared with the sixth day from contracting the virus can be significant. This is why the PCR threshold for active infections is easy to set. When the threshold is too high you get the fake positives, instead of negative.

During the pandemic I've spoken with a lot of people working in companies from important industries, and they said no one ever tested positive for the new coronavirus, despite testing hundreds of people living as normal, and twice a week. This can mean multiple things: there is no pandemic, this virus is not as contagious as we're being told, there is no new virus, the PCR multiplication cycle threshold is set correctly by the lab doing the testing, or the big company told the lab, *"we cannot have positive results"* - their activity should not be disturbed. Big companies as Warner Bros for example, have powerful connections to facilitate this. I personally think it's more than one of the above.

Why would you test people, if we know that a coronavirus is active in you for up to five days? Why are you testing yourself if you've got no symptoms? Why test if you've got symptoms? You know you have something... Shouldn't we spend the billions allocated to flawed testing to try and treat the atypical pneumonia? In 2020 all doctors forgot how to treat it. Even if it's atypical, it is not a new thing. The moment testing started people began to die. Is that a coincidence? The new virus has been in the UK from September-October 2019. Until 2020 people didn't know about ventilators. Doctors would prescribe antibiotics for fever, paracetamol for inflammation, and recommend keeping hydrated. Remember that doctors and politicians are not allowed to make mistakes. It can happen, but they are not allowed. Understand the difference. They were saving lives easily, then it all changed. The PCR came in to test for random RNA, active or inactive. Now, more asymptomatic people test positive like never before. This is why you see these high numbers. People have old coronaviruses, flu, the new virus, etc.. If there is a pandemic, it is caused by a huge group of viruses, not just the new coronavirus. This is what the PCR is seeing. It is worrying that people that could've shaken off the flu are now dying from being put on ventilators, with no proven medicine to support their recovery.

When a person has no symptoms it doesn't matter. It means they cannot infect anyone with an old coronavirus, or the new one if they had it in their throat. Their immune system does a good job in protecting them, and therefore the others as well. If a person has symptoms these should be checked to see if they are symptoms of flu, or other coronaviruses. In any case, let's say we wanted to test them. We'd do a PCR test, together with an antibody test that should be more than 99% accurate. If they can make a vaccine in a few months, they can also create really accurate IgG tests. They are easier to produce, and cheaper. During 2020, many scientists have said that you cannot read antibodies before 14 days from infection. THIS IS COMPLETELY WRONG! The full potency of your antibodies is achieved in the third day of infection. From that point the quantity of active virus cells in your body starts to decrease dramatically. Past that moment you can be tested for antibodies. If you cannot be tested then, when you've achieved the full potency, there is no scientific proof supporting the 14 days IgG detection timeframe. If there is, it's been fabricated this year. And this is why. Together with the IgG you also develop IgM. IgM is the first produced during new infections, and you lose it in about nine days. This is the timeframe during which you can see it with a usual test. After that the IgM goes in the *background*. By this time your body should be full of IgG, in order to further protect you. These are lost in somewhere between six months and a few years, depending on factors like age, health, exposure, food, etc.. To give you an example, I get flu-like symptoms every 7-8 years. To me flu has a specific smell, and when I feel it in my nose I start changing my diet, to avoid the need for powerful medicine. This is why you don't need a vaccine once you've had the new coronavirus. You don't need a vaccine if you're healthy either. Your immune system's memory will live on within you. This virus is less dangerous than the lightest flu you've ever had. You've been set to think that you've never experienced something this bad but if you backtrack to the worst flu you've ever had, you'll understand how the current experience compares to that. Snap out of it, and stop repeating yourself what you're being told to think! Stop suppressing your own power of judgement and free will!

The right way to test

Conditions: *Correct Multiplication Cycle Threshold, Clinically Healthy Individuals or with working Immune System, All Positives Without IgG Present Require Viral Culture And Further Sequencing To See If Virus Is Active*

The PCR result can be corrupted by the presence of other viruses

Version 1

PCR + IgG/IgM (specific SARS-Cov-2) = Real result

The above testing formula should translate into the following

(Positive) + (Not Present) = Active Infection (if symptoms are present, PCR multiplication threshold needs to be properly set, might be a different virus, first day of symptoms is relevant)

Version 2

PCR + IgG/IgM (specific SARS-Cov-2) = Real result

The above testing formula should translate into the following:

(Positive) + (Both Present) = Active/Inactive Infection (first day of symptoms needs to be considered to determine if it's still an Active infection, since both IgM/IgG were found it is unlikely the person can infect anyone, could have decreasing symptoms - in recovery, cannot infect anyone, person had a new infection in the last 9 or less days, PCR threshold probably not set correctly if more than five days from first symptoms);

Version 3

PCR + IgG (specific SARS-Cov-2)= Real result

The above testing formula should translate into the following:

(Positive) + (Present - no IgM) = Inactive Infection (PCR test threshold set incorrectly, person is immune therefore non-infectious, infection occurred nine or more days ago);

Version 3

PCR + IgG (specific SARS-Cov-2)= Real result

The above testing formula should translate into the following:

(Negative) + (Present - no IgM) = Inactive Infection (person is immune therefore non-infectious, infection occurred nine or more days ago);

Version 4

PCR + IgG/IgM (specific SARS-Cov-2)= Real result

The above testing formula should translate into the following:

(Negative) + (Both Present) = Active/Inactive Infection (probably flawed PCR test result, person probably immune/ non-infectious, first day of symptoms needs to be considered);

Version 5

PCR + IgG/IgM (specific SARS-Cov-2)= Real result

The above testing formula should translate into the following:

(Negative) + (Negative) = Person has not been exposed to the new virus (PCR needs properly adjusted threshold, waste of resources if person asymptomatic);

Version 6

PCR + IgG/IgM (specific SARS-Cov-2)= Real result

The above testing formula should translate into the following:

(Positive) + (Negative) = Possibly flawed PCR test result (person might have been exposed to a different viral infection, needs an IgG/IgM test for another virus depending on symptoms if they are present, or the symptoms recalled by patient);

Version 7

People with no symptoms should only take an IgG/IgM test. The PCR test makes no scientific sense in their case, and it is a complete waste of time, logistics and money. Once you have developed specific IgGs you are immune, therefore you do not need a vaccine for the new virus, or if you are clinically healthy. Not practising this method makes it clear that someone is promoting mass vaccinations to weaken the immunity. Why have a vaccine for a coronavirus if you're immune and healthy? Remember: your illness is the bread and butter of pharmaceutical companies, and of private health services. Till now the coronavirus was the only one without a vaccine. For most we have one. How many vaccines should we take in a year? Still trust all doctors?

Under no circumstance should a PCR test be done and taken as accurate on its own, when looking to see a specific virus. No testing is correct without checking for specific antibodies or further sequencing, to compare the RNA found with the new virus' RNA. Same as in a murder investigation, when different DNA is found at the crime scene, they multiply it using the PCR method, then compare it with the DNA of the prime suspects to see if there's a match. When testing nowadays, no one is doing further sequencing after a positive result, unless you get admitted to a hospital with severe symptoms.

The best way to test NEGATIVE on the PCR test or *lateral flow*, is to have an antiseptic sinus steam bath a few hours before (also clean your sinuses by snorting), and a shot of over 40% proof spirit, that you should gargle with before swallowing (a few minutes before the test). This should increase the chances of a NEGATIVE

test result to over 99.90%. Remember that the sequence of the Wuhan coronavirus had been published after months into the pandemic. So, how could Canada test for the new virus in December 2019, just days after China registered their first cases?

CONCLUSION:

The primer (oligonucleotide) that binds to the RNA is only copying the RNA sequence it attaches to. It cannot be virus specific, it is just RNA specific. It hybridises with the sequence found, and creates new sequences (millions in just 20-30 multiplication cycles) for further analysis. Just the PCR alone will NOT give you the virus; it is an incomplete testing process which implies the use of multiple methods.

To get the answer to why they would do this to us, you have to ask yourself why they're hiding this science from you. They're just trying to get into your head, to convince you to have the vaccine. The best way to hide the truth is by telling a good lie, and the more scientists are joining in, the more it will look like truth, but what do you do in the age of information, when truth is at hand. Why do you think they're not developing IgG tests? They don't want to. When you're unfolding a plan, you make it look like a decision mistake based on insufficient data, and then avoid the real solution, to make it look like a political mishandle of the situation. In the middle, you have doctors that can lose their careers if they say something. It's easy when the system allows it, itself being based on secrets. Because almost nothing from our current societal existence is truth. Just try to be 100% independent and free, without someone coming after you.

In conclusion, this is why you should NOT get tested to see if you have any coronavirus:

-with the PCR you don't know which virus you are looking at, nor if it is active in your body - to know all these you require additional testing methods;
-the PCR is a costly test, it's like burning money and getting nothing in return - the UK has spent over 20 billion pounds in less than a year on testing alone, money that did not save any life;
-it makes no sense to test for the virus, as the chances to miss it are really high, or you might already be immune by the time you get the positive result;
-IgG/IgM tests are really cheap to make, and more relevant because they can read the proteins specific to any virus with over 99% accuracy (this is the right test to take);
-if you have absolutely no symptoms you are not infectious with a coronavirus - the chances are close to zero, as the virus load you're carrying is negligible and probably deactivated;
-you do develop immunity to the current virus for between months and years, unless you have an autoimmune disease, or you self-isolate from the world for months;
-you will constantly contract the virus from others and nature, but your immunity will keep you and the others safe (you can still spread the virus through your clothes, skin, when you poo, etc., but the chances are minimal).

The Wuhan coronavirus in numbers (United Kingdom)

Year/Month	2018	2019	2020
January	64,154	53,910	56,706
February	49,177	45,795	43,653

Year/Month	2018	2019	2020
March	51,229	43,944	49,723
April	46,469	44,121	**88,153**
May	42,784	44,389	52,374
June	39,767	38,603	42,624
July	40,723	42,308	40,780
August	40,192	38,843	37,187
September	37,137	40,011	42,500
October	44,440	46,238	46,296
November	43,978	45,219	51,330
December	41,539	47,460	56,690
Total	**541,589**	**530,841**	**608,016**

Keep in mind that the numbers for 2020 are made of many deaths caused by the lockdowns, which in fact killed, and will kill way more people than this low risk SARS-Cov-2 virus. Considering this, the number of deaths in 2020 is abnormally low. Just to be clear, the virus has been in the UK since the second half of 2019, because people were showing up to hospitals with atypical pneumonia ever since. England has one of the biggest Chinese communities in the world, so when the Government is denying the UK was not among the first infected countries, they are lying to you. Looking at 2020's numbers, we can see that the number of deaths is almost in normal limits, lockdown or not. It's worrying that during the lockdown months the numbers were higher, which means the strategy didn't work. You might say, *"yes but if we wouldn't have had a lockdown the numbers would've been higher!"*. If you think this, stop now and think for yourself. At the end of March 2020 the virus had been with us for at least six months. The moment the NHS changed procedures, and started putting people on ventilators without any proven medicine resulted in the April spike, doubling the number of monthly deaths. From May I was getting from nurses that they stopped putting people on ventilators, because they were *dying like flies* with severe dehydration, or blood cloths in their lungs. Now they have an algorithm to decide if the patient needs a ventilator or not. My opinion is that no one needs that ventilator. Almost every patient was diagnosed with covid, and put on a ventilator. Do you think anyone would tell you if they killed someone by mistake? They would never do that. What you see in April is called premeditated MURDER! That number also contains the ones that died because their vital services had been severed overnight. Fig. 2 was taken from the ONS (Office of National Statistics) in the UK, comparing *Covid-19* with Influenza (Flu) and Pneumonia, between 01 January 2020 to 31 August 2020.

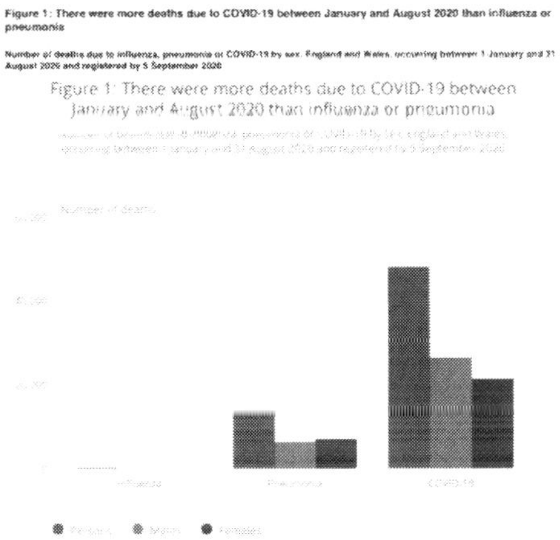

Fig. 1

In numbers:

Influenza (Persons - 394, Males - 179, Females - 215);

Pneumonia (Persons - 13,619, Males - 6,398, Females - 7,221);

Covid-19 (Persons - 48,168, Males - 26,639, Females - 21,529).

This means a total of 49 people a month died of Influenza in 2020, till end of August. According to official NHS data, around 10,000 people die of flu in England and Wales alone each year. This does not include Scotland and Northern Ireland! It all divides to 833 people normally dying of flu each month. In 2020 flu is disappearing. It's a drop of 94% in flu fatalities compared to normal times. Still think *Covid-19* is dangerous and pandemic? Does this massive drop seem right to you? 94%!!! You can check all these numbers yourself. These are official reports. With this Wuhan virus the world is creating another managed health trend, same as cancer. You cannot conduct a real world study from and office or lab.

To make it more obvious, I have checked the weekly Notifications of Infectious Diseases for England and Wales, which account for about 60 million people. These are official reports posted online by Public Health England. When the UK Government decided the first lockdown, the real numbers of *Covid-19* were almost zero. Based on these reports, there have been only 13,911 confirmed *Covid-19* cases in 2020. These are people that probably had further sequencing performed after testing positive with the PCR. Most of them survived, considering that the reported death rate is about 3%. That's about 417 people killed by the actual virus in 2020, in England & Wales, which account for about 60 million people. This means 34 people a month, most of them in their 80s. Do you still think no one is playing with your life? Please go ahead and check these reports yourself.

Let's apply these figures to the entire world population, considering that the spread was uniform. On 21 February 2021 there are ~7,847,418,600+ people living on planet Earth. By the way, it has been exactly one year since my last cold (probably the Wuhan virus). My immunity, my mother's, and my brother's have been exemplary, after being in close contact with more than 20,000 people as private hire drivers in London. If what we had this time last year was the new virus, know that if you are healthy, your immunity for *Covid-19* will last for at least one year, which is normal immunity. Going forward with our calculations, by applying the official total number of *Covid-19* cases in England & Wales for 2020 (13,911 - people that probably needed hospitalisation/had further sequencing performed), we get a total of ~1,819,424 official *Covid-19* cases around the world. Applying the 3% death rate reported by the authorities, it all comes down to ~54,582 deaths caused by the actual new coronavirus. The number of people infected was probably higher, of course, but why would it matter if those people are healthy. This makes the Wuhan coronavirus one of the least deadly coronaviruses ever. As Bill Gates (a terrorist by any definition) has put it, the scientists in Wuhan's lab have done a poor job with this virus. These were his approximate words during a recent interview in the US. Having this as proof, how do you know the numbers in the news are real, what is your logic? I dare you to find the real numbers behind *within 28 days of testing positive for coronavirus.* How do these numbers compare with the over 9 million people dying of starvation each year (it might double because of lockdown - they could easily be saved), 10 million people dying of cancer worldwide (most of it due to what we eat/2020 is the year with the largest one-year drop in history, another clue that they've been put down as *Covid-19* deaths), 7 million deaths caused by smoking - with 600,000 deaths caused by passive smoking, 250,000 people dying of flu, a few hundreds of thousands of people still dying of the plague worldwide, millions dying of hospital-acquired infections, more than 2,6 million people dying of medical negligence each year, and many more. I hope these numbers will make it clear for you, that the world we live in is not the world we are supposed to live in. *Covid-19* is the biggest and most complex operational move towards totalitarianism since the Second World War. They're not even interested about people being immune to the virus without a vaccine. Lawmakers are talking about VACCINE passports, instead of testing for immunity. Welcome to the Orwellian future!

Ventilator explained

The ventilator is a device meant to circulate air into your lungs with a certain pressure, mimicking normal breathing when the natural capacity is reduced. It is different to an oxygen mask, as it's not meant to increase the level of oxygen. After countless reports from patients, nurses, and doctors working with coronavirus patients at different hospitals in London, I have reached the conclusion that ventilators are a major cause of death, and not the actual virus. I've been told by medical staff how the pressures of the ventilators are wrong, and that people are dying of severe dehydration, and with blood cloths in their lungs. On top of that, people are being kept, or have been on ventilation for weeks on end, even up to 25 days in remote cases. The poor and premeditated medical care, which even some nurses find terrifying, counts towards people being killed instead of being saved. Severe dehydration occurs when you don't drink the right amount of water that your body needs, and by being ventilated constantly at the wrong pressure, you will lose liquids faster than usual. Knowing how suffering from this virus actually feels, dry lungs and amazing thirst, excessive ventilation makes no sense. To understand how a patient feels while being ventilated at the wrong pressure, and constantly, just try to breathe in and out with full lung capacity just for a few minutes. After a few seconds you will start to feel dizzy, because when you breathe normally you probably use 30% of your lung capacity. From time to time, maybe you feel like taking a deep breath that resembles a sigh, because the natural reflex is telling you that your brain needs a bit more oxygen, and after, you go to normal breathing. Imagine breathing in with the entire capacity of your lungs for days on end. Patients also did not receive any usual supporting medicine, like steroids or antibiotics, even if they had a fever. The experimental *Remdesivir* is being pushed forward, despite being untested, and producing terrifying side effects. It also costs around £2,500 for a week of treatment. There is no doubt that people have been killed by the ventilators, cumulated with being denied tested medicine, poor medical care, and experimental medicine. Scientists would probably contradict everything I'm explaining here, but real medical studies have demonstrated that even with administering oxygen (humidified or not), healthy lungs will turn excessively dry, especially after weeks of ventilation, which is inhumane. Since this virus is drying the lungs excessively anyway, you can imagine what the ventilator is doing after just a few hours. Personally, I was drinking close to five litres of water a day without being ventilated. How much water do you think they gave to patients in the hospital?

Basic medication for any coronavirus and influenza

It all starts with the way you live, the water you drink, the air you breathe, the people you have around, vices, climate, occupation, strain, etc., and lastly genetics. About your genetics there's little you can do. With all others it depends on you. Your entire life needs the natural and happiness.

Modern medicine has bigger limitations than natural medicine. Plants have been engineered during billions of years, whereas chemistry has been developed during the last two centuries, or even less. Everything started with natural medicine, until the elite decided it needs to be destroyed, paving the way for modern benefits under the shape of money. This is another reason why we have almost everything genetically modified, to cut ties with our glorious healthy past. A doctor should know everything there is to know about natural remedies, and then the science, where they don't work, not the other way around. But doctors are applying only what they learned in medical school, and that is that. Nowadays, if you tell a doctor that mulled wine or whiskey are strengthening the body during a cold, he will laugh at you, and prescribe paracetamol, or even worse, a ventilator. Medicine is going downhill fast, with the sole purpose of killing as many people as possible, and destroying our bodies' natural processes and defence mechanisms. Keep in mind that when we say "GMO", it means that in a lab they can add any gene to a healthy vegetable. You are being told by almost everyone that it is good, that it will be resilient against pests and climate, but this was never the answer to feeding the world. Poor countries in hot climates could easily be self-sustained, to the extent that they would not need to trade maybe anything. The lies we are living are becoming truth, and there is no way back if we lose our natural. By consuming GMOs, your body will constantly try to fight the genes that should not be in the foods, triggering an immune response (IgE). You live in a constant inflammation state. GMOs weaken the immune system, damage organs, activate cancers, inhibit important chemical processes, just to name a few severe consequences. And yes, they are significantly less nutritional than natural food, specifically for the reasons stated above, but not limited to them. I will present here a few remedies, that me and my family have always used successfully in treating the generic cold viruses, bacteria and influenza.

I am not going to present here the chemistry of garlic but this wonderful vegetable can improve your health tenfold. You don't have to think that it should be taken after you get sick, introduce it into your usual diet. Garlic, more than maybe other vegetables, needs to be non-GMO and grown naturally, without artificial fertilisers of any kind. When grown artificially it can be poison, I speak from experience. Natural garlic breaks like a crisp apple when you take a bite. If it's rubbery, throw it away. Stay away from garlic from China, Spain, and other countries growing vegetables in artificial ways. The purpose is to live as healthy as possible, not staying alive for as long as possible with illnesses. Today we're experiencing the latter. Together with garlic, add onion tea if you have a cough. It tastes disgusting, but it will help you recover. Remember that all you do every day is prevention. When the cold season comes, you can follow a garlic diet my family and grandparents have followed for ages. It lasts for nineteen days. First day swallow a garlic clove without chewing it, second day two, and so on till the tenth day. On the eleventh day you swallow nine, until you go to zero. Make sure the cloves are not too large, or you could choke with it. Use plenty of water. Natural garlic shouldn't give you heartburn, but if you get this reaction, just dilute a teaspoon of **sodium bicarbonate** (make sure it's preservatives free) in a glass of water, and drink it. A few massive burps should follow if the acidity is high. There is no need to buy heartburn medicine, ever! Plus, the sodium bicarbonate will reduce the acidity of your blood too. People use it even as a diet, for overall health benefits resulting from having an alkaline body. Don't overdo it though.

Neutralising Reaction

Base + Acid = Water & A Salt + Carbon Dioxide

You need to understand that every cold or flu virus will attack your respiratory system which includes the lungs, the organ that has first contact with the outside. Everyone can breathe, but it's not easy to know how to breathe. This is another lesson though. When your lungs are ill, your levels of blood oxygen will drop, depending on the severity of the infection. If you can't breathe properly it doesn't mean you have to panic, and ask to be ventilated for days on end. This is what is killing most patients with the Wuhan coronavirus and other lung viruses. This one is severely drying your lungs and throat. Your cough will be unproductive, meaning no phlegm will come out. In this case you have to try and rebalance the state of your lungs, by increasing the humidity of your air. An amazing way to do it is if you put some tea tree oil in hot water or vaporiser, and inhale the steam. You can do this on top of a pot. You will cough like crazy but it will keep the tissue moist and flexible. Ventilators are causing the undesired crustiness of the lungs, that will eventually tear the lung tissue, and cause internal bleeding. If your lung goes into that state, the chances of you dying are exponentially increased. Furthermore, the constant and irrational ventilation will cause the blood to clot faster, covering the surface of the lungs. If a person has low oxygen levels, they should be given oxygen under strict supervision, and for a short time. Ventilators will kill your lungs. I have heard reports from people that have been on a ventilator for up to 25 days. If as a doctor you don't know that ventilating a dry lung can kill the patient suddenly, you should stop practicing medicine immediately. Improve the state of your lungs with warm steam baths with medicinal oils. Tea tree oil is antiseptic. Your immune system will take out the virus, it's your duty to help your body rebuild.

Eat foods with healthy fats and Omega 3. In this category falls fish like wild salmon, nuts, avocado, etc.. Do not try to replace healthy foods with vitamins from the shop, as they contain dangerous excipients that could alter the benefits. Use natural vitamins! Also eat hot soups, your body needs plenty of liquids with a healthy twist. Get yourself natural, farm grown chickens, and boil them with vegetables into a delicious soup. If you live somewhere with poor sunlight and you want to get liquid vitamin D (the best option), make sure it's accompanied by vitamin K2 as well. Otherwise vitamin D will not be absorbed properly by your body

Take hot baths, go to a sauna, and try to live in humid environments with antiseptic oils in the air. Drink medicinal teas, not the usual tea. Drink strong spirits, even if you don't like alcohol. It will fight the infection from inside. If alcohol can kill the virus on your hands, don't you think it would be good in your blood too? It's been proven by science that it helps during infections, even more if you prepare it with medicinal and antiseptic herbs, as cloves and cinnamon. There are endless methods to treat yourself with quality alcohol. Avoid vodka (it's very easy to fake) and spirits that contain alcohol from questionable sources (it will say ethyl alcohol or grain alcohol). To give you an example, Jose Cuervo tequila is not 100% from agave, it contains additives as colouring, flavour, and probably a different sourced alcohol. Don't overdo it! Drink 100% red grape wine, mulled or as it is. Avoid wines with sulphites. A true wine maker doesn't use sulphites. I've explained more in *The Vineyard* chapter.

On the NHS website no one is telling people what to eat or drink! A national health service doesn't have any natural remedies it could give to people to stay safe. Isn't this suspicious to you? The only way they can help people with a cold is by forcing you to take a useless test, and maybe give you a ventilator. Oh, and pumping *Remdesivir* (RNA inhibitor) into your veins, a medicine also approved in emergency, by an institution that should keep an eye out for dangerous experimental medicine reaching your body, the MHRA. Now you can find good remedies on blogs... The MHRA would never admit on their own volition, if they fucked up by approving dangerous medicines.

What happened with *day and night nurse*, as remedy for cold and flu? It seems that no previous medicine for coronaviruses can help you anymore. And this new virus is around 85% identical with the previous coronavirus outbreak. Very suspicious... Paracetamol sachets or tablets will help you recover too by reducing inflammation. If you have fever you probably need antibiotics for about five days, maybe less. They are for the bacteria developed in your lungs due to dead tissue. There is no need to panic, you have to act swiftly, because if you stay with fever for many days, your body could get irreparably damaged, including organ failure. This is why you keep on hearing about *long Covid*. It doesn't exist, and it's not caused by the coronavirus, it's you not taking action, or your doctor not helping you with adequate medication to get your fever down. When did you ever hear before 2020 about *long flu* or *asymptomatic flu*? Why is it in your instinct to stay away from symptomatic people? Because you know that they're the ones that can actually get you sick, and not everyone. By today's standards, we should never get close to each other ever again! Stop making love with your wife, she might get a virus from you, and give birth to another child...

A good and proven medicine for keeping your body clear of parasites, viruses, and harmful bacteria is *colloidal silver*. Do not take this one more than indicated, and without medical advice. Ingesting too much or for long periods of time can turn your skin purple, for good! You'll hear that this is a mistake because silver has no purpose in the processes of your body. Wrong! As you are eliminating it from the body, the silver molecules will get rid of parasites, viruses, malicious bacteria and fungi. Read the right science about it, not what Reuters are blabbing about. Stop getting your science from the news agencies, they're all corrupt and want to harm you. They are an instrument of mass control.

If you have high temperature for more than a day, it means that antibiotics are highly recommended to fight potential bacterial infections as secondary infection. A viral infection almost never comes on its own, because it's killing your cells. One of the most efficient antibiotics is penicillin with *clavulanic* acid. Remember this, it can save your life. Never stay with a fever for more than a day without taking any action. If antibiotics don't work in humans, why are they giving them to the animals we eat? And if such an important medicine is saving lives, why is it being used largely on the animals we eat, if they know this would decrease the impact of medication when you have infections? Shouldn't it be used only on humans, to keep the potency to a maximum, and our exposure to it to a minimum? Is there a better treatment for Staphylococcus Aureus that we don't know about? If antibiotics stop working for bacterial infections, we are doomed.

When you have a cold, proper hydration can actually save your life, but here I'm not referring to purified water. This one is poor in minerals, it will actually extract minerals from your body, and that will worsen your condition, and in time even kill you, by messing up your metabolism. Drink balanced alkaline water (pH over 7), and mineralised (electrolytes)! In Bio Products Laboratory I was using WFI (Water For Injection) which was completely purified water that you could inject straight into your vein. Not that it was recommended, you could die from that. Vaccines contain WFI in small quantities. In an aseptic process we needed the purest water. If I was to drink it, I would get severely dehydrated, and depending on the quantity ingested I could've died. Yes, water can kill you in multiple ways, not just through drowning, or by being dirty/contaminated. Considering that patients with presumed *Covid*-19, and ventilated, have died severely dehydrated, it is a clear sign that the hospital did nothing to keep them hydrated. They could've done it intravenously, as an alternative. This is what they do to people in a coma.

Penicillium is a family of fungi used to produce antibiotics. Most blue cheeses contain it naturally or added, depending on the assortment. So, when you're enjoying some Roquefort, you're ingesting small quantities of the main ingredient of antibiotics. When you have a viral infection caused by a coronavirus, it is highly likely that the number of dangerous bacteria in your body will register a spike. This is why you need antibiotics to lower your fever as soon as possible. Over two days of high temperature can cause organ failure. This I why I would recommend the consumption of blue mold cheeses from the *penicillium* family. This will definitely keep you safe, as the fungi will develop after the pasteurisation of the milk. Don't worry, it won't give you resistance to antibiotics.

And finally, sex! If you've come of age, you should have lots of sex. It's been proven millennia ago that sex is one of the best overall health boosters. I would recommend it at least once a day. In my culture it's called *poor man's aspirin*. With this occasion, I just realised that I forgot about the basic aspirin. Have one or two a day if you're sick with the Wuhan coronavirus. It will thin your blood, and keep it moving unrestricted through your veins, thus helping your lung's recovery. Remember that most of the viral infection is recovery. The active infection is probably 1/3 of the whole experience.

The Mask

Before 2020 everyone knew that *The Mask* is a movie with Jim Carey. If you support wearing the mask, you have to sign up to Elon Musk's Mars program, because we don't want you here. You're just a result of laziness and corruption. Big apparel companies supporting training with a mask are mad.

They need to be dissolved. That's it! The same should happen with that Imperial College London. Oh, god, they should definitely have to go. Someone should force them to go into the fish industry, because they smell of corruption from afar. From the beginning they supported the mask, and the severity of the *pandemic*, despite working closely together with Public Health England (from where I got the NOIDs), and all hospitals. Even when other universities, maybe bigger than Imperial College London, were saying the mask, lockdowns, and panicking are mistakes, you could only hear the voice of Imperial College London. If you own a diploma in science it doesn't mean that you are a scientist; applying the science correctly makes you a scientist. If these latter, highly corrupt pseudo-scientists are right, it means that humans have lived the wrong way for tens of thousands of years, that animals are living the wrong way without a mask, and that we need to put a mask on insects as well. If you ask me, this is terrorism 101, bigger than 9/11. These scientists on paper also meet the criteria of undercover agents. This would explain their aplomb in altering the science in favour of tyranny. They're never debating the cancer in our foods, how that is a real reason of concern. Later in the chapter I will explain how St. John's Ambulance have introduced a technique used to torture prisoners into the new resuscitation procedures, to keep the resuscitator safe from the Wuhan virus. There are so many clues that this whole situation is a premeditated strategy, it's unbelievable. The secret services in the US have predicted a pandemic in 2023, in one of their 2017 reports about the future. Being right about this is a chance in how many trillions? Go ahead and search *Event 201* for more proof.

Currently they are calling the refusal of wearing a mask an *antisocial personality trait*. Basically you're not allowed to have an opinion, even if you are educated about the whole subject and healthy. What do you call the doctrine that doesn't allow you to speak against the government? Was this world built by obedient people? Pardon? Just imagine our future without the non compliant people, the trailblazers, people that challenge science... Yes, compliant people took the world forward. There is no doubt about it. When in the police, I was wrong when refusing to hurt innocent people, and wanting to go against the real criminals, including my corrupt officers in command. By wearing a mask you're also disturbing the overall temperature of your body. Breathing is cooling your temperature, which is a good thing, especially for a healthy digestion and overall metabolism. Your airways are built to warm up the air to the right temperature, but when you're always inhaling hotter air than normal, it is highly destructive for the body. Before moving to the UK I would've never thought that such a big portion of the country can be so uneducated, corrupt, and under-evolved, considering their economy and history. With me it all started when I found out that you can be an Oxford graduate without speaking a second language. In my country you cannot finish 12th grade (high school) without speaking a second language. But this is a problem with people in developed countries, they go back to our original behaviour pre-cognitive thinking, to chronic stupidity. Just look at how much individual life is worth in really poor countries compared to highly developed ones, as US for example. It's the same value. You don't have money, you don't get treatment, and you die.

Why you should not wear a mask - from someone that knows the mask procedures

First of all, in an aseptic lab they force you to wear a mask together with full body PPE, to reduce the contamination of the medicine to a minimum. That doesn't mean that contamination is impossible. There is still a high risk of contamination. Remember, this is a strictly monitored environment with regular microbiological testing of everything, from tools and machines, to walls and floors. In a laboratory no one cares about the contamination of technicians, although companies have to say they do for legal reasons. They don't! The product is more important for the business. The gowning procedure, which included the mask, says that all reusable PPE needs to be cleaned after use, and irradiated. The maximum amount of time to wear the overall is four hours, including breaks. Once the mask is being taken off you should discard it, including when it gets soiled with mucus, product or anything else. Reusing it could lead to serious health issues for the wearer, and increases the contamination of the product exponentially. Under no circumstances should anyone bring unauthorised PPE in the lab. That could lead to immediate dismissal. THE MASK SHOULD ALWAYS BE ASEPTIC! You should never wear a mask that isn't because you don't know what bacteria it may have, that can go straight into your lungs. Tonsillitis is nothing, compared to the worst bacterial infection that you can get from a mask. By purchasing non-medical masks, it means the company producing them is not liable if you get sick or even die. It also means that they did not have to obey any production health standards. When you unpack the mask with soiled (dirty) hands, it is no longer aseptic. It gets compromised the moment you open the wrapping anyway. Once you've put the mask on, you should not touch it even if you've disinfected your hands. Hand disinfectant offers almost no protection, if you didn't wash your hands properly with soap and plenty of water. The moment you took the mask off you should not put it back on, you have to grab a new one, and do all the steps again. Why? Because you can have the virus on your hands, on your clothes, on your face, in your hair, and everywhere around you. This is why the mask is ineffective in the real world. THE OUTSIDE WORLD IS THE OPPOSITE OF ASEPTIC! Do you have any idea how difficult it is to make something aseptic, and keep it that way? It is almost impossible, especially with a piece of fabric and plastic.

People that don't wear a mask because it feels uncomfortable, or for whatever reason, are in their vast majority healthy, which means they are probably immune to the new and old coronaviruses, and therefore they cannot cause a spread through breathing. Of course there is an infinitely minimal chance that they could spread it through other means, like touch and skin flakes, but they are not to blame, nature is, and there is nothing to do about it. It doesn't mean that you'll get sick from one virus cell touching your nose. You blaming them for not wearing the mask is a terrible attitude to have towards someone, and the current situation. Besides the fact that you are flawed in your unresearched beliefs, it also means that you are immune to a more horrific thing than a coronavirus, to tyranny and hell. This makes you a part of the problem, not of the solution. I mean, a true pandemic would have the same impact for all age groups, not just for people with underlying conditions, wouldn't you think so? And you looking with anger at people without a mask, is proof that you think only about yourself, you selfish prick. Let's be honest, you're not wearing the mask because you care about me. If so, you'd consider that I might have underlying conditions, and let it go. Plus, if you truly cared you'd also fight with the same pathos against the cancer that's being put in our foods. What others are wearing or not wearing is not your concern. Coming to this, why are there exemptions from wearing the mask, if your breathing is normal with or without the mask? Does this logic make sense to you? It's like saying sex with a condom is the same as without. When you have a cold or flu you stay away from people, and cover your mouth and nose when coughing or sneezing. On the other side, we've got the gross and inconsiderate ones that sneeze and cough in your face, or even fart when you're at the table. These people should be corrected on the spot with a punch in the teeth, without the intervention of the government. But you normally scold them when they do it, and they are a small minority. No one should throw their mucus towards you intentionally. Mucus is a bacteria-infected environment as it is.

By wearing the mask you cannot protect others if you are contagious with the coronavirus. When you breathe, some air goes back into your lungs, and the rest goes out through the mask or through the openings, at a higher speed due to the *wall* ahead. It's the same infected air, and you are spreading it everywhere, even with the mask on. If you'd see the movements of the air you'd understand. The virus is not an anvil to fall on the ground the moment it comes out of you. If leaves are blown away by the mild wind, while being billions of times heavier than a virus, what makes you think that the mask can trap it? You breathe out around 11,000 litres of air each day, and when you're infectious, that is the same quantity of infected air you're putting out there for others to breathe. The mask is only containing a negligible quantity of that air, the rest is sent to others to breathe in. The Government started forcing people to wear it, to make you accustomed with more personal rules and sanctions. And if they can make it seem like you're showing your empathy by obeying, you will do it without questioning it, or even looking into the science of the rule. Making you think that by following strict new rules you are saving someone's life, will give the government free hand at imposing anything on you. And if you'd know a little bit of politics and history, you'd understand that any party can become a tyrant, if given the right amount of power. They're not even telling you till what date you should wear the mask, and if we're all immune, why we should wear a mask in the first place. They want this to be the norm. Again, WHY? A crushing majority of people are saying that you should listen to the Government, and I say that you should've lived in the '50s, because those should've been the last few generations of *clinically naive*. You cannot say this in the age of information. If you do, you're missing a few screws... **THE GOVERNMENT IS THERE TO LISTEN AND SERVE YOU!**

While reading this book you might think, *"yeah, but why should I listen to you? I don't even know you!"*. That is true, and besides the fact that you can check all this information, you already trust people you don't know, the politicians with their science people. Do you know them personally? Do you know their connections and personal histories? I guess not, but compared to them, I have no interest in controlling you. I'm an entity that wants you to be free, and think for yourself. I don't want to trip on you when building the real future, I want you next to me. Do you know that many politicians and scientists you see on TV are also undercover agents? Even many of the stars you watch and love, also work for governmental agencies. Only when I joined the border force, I found out that many celebrities in my country are also high ranked officers in the police and other agencies, without even attending the police school or the academy. I've seen famous actors with diplomatic passports. Normal people still don't know that. The mask should under no circumstance be imposed to you in a free world. Real life is not mandatory military service. Wear it if you want to, but know that you're not protecting anyone. If you think you do, then you don't know anything about how viruses work, and how damaging the mask can be for your body. All the science supporting the mask has been concocted in 2020, and it is a lie. Unless you have money to pay for thousands of single use aseptic masks, you should not wear one. Even if wearing it, not infecting someone you're in close contact with if you're infectious is really slim, because the spread does not occur only through breathing. Live as normal, and if you think you're infectious with flu or a coronavirus, try to stay away from others, be sensible with contact, cover your mouth and nose when coughing or sneezing, then wash your hands before touching anything, or anyone else.

The mask only works in aseptic environments, under strict gowning procedures. Even so, the risk is never zero.

The CDC of the US have conducted a study in 2020, which showed that around 85% of the people that got the new virus were wearing a mask. The clear conclusion is that you're less likely to get it if you're not wearing a mask, as masks are bacteria, fungi and virus traps. Is your mask aseptic? It doesn't matter, you're not in a surgery room. Your conformity is just a reference point, in the context created by ill-intentioned people.

The symptoms according to scientists

A High Temperature

Your immune system's fitness is not constant. It can fluctuate more than you think, based on a whole array of factors, from what you eat, when you had your last meal, your sleep pattern, all the way to your thoughts, underlying issues, and how stressed the immune system is by constant exposure. But it is there, ready to act if needed. When you have a high temperature, your body's protection system is struggling. This means that it's probably fighting a virus, and a bacterial infection, which complements a viral infection close to 100% of times. It's like you trying to fight two people at once. Even if you know how to fight, the chances of you succeeding are slim, as it takes twice as much struggle. The strongest opponent could be the bacteria. This is why you need support under the shape of antibiotics. In western countries, when you ask your doctor for antibiotics, they look at you like you're a threat to national security. How do you know my diet? Maybe I don't eat chlorinated chicken, and only buy from natural farms.

A New Continuous Cough

Does this mean that usually you cough? And that this cough does not resemble your normal cough? Why new? A cough is a cough, and occurs with almost all respiratory infections. This is not relevant one bit. Such a broad symptom cannot be attributed only to this new virus. You do cough, but it does not necessarily mean that you have the new coronavirus.

Loss of Taste or Smell

This means loss of taste OR smell, not both. Whenever I speak with people that might have had the new coronavirus, I hear they lost both. When I had the virus I experienced a decrease in taste on the third day, when my nose and years blocked. By that time my voice was really low pitched. The governments are telling people that you will LOSE your taste and smell. If you have a bit of knowledge, you know that with any cold or flu, when your nose gets blocked your taste decreases. You will never lose your taste or smell from a coronavirus. Just hold your nose with your index finger and thumb, and have some food. Oh, my God, you've got the new coronavirus! Blocked nose equals decreased taste, and poor smelling abilities. But even so, you can still taste sweet, salty and sour. I personally could taste and smell almost like normal during my first two days of infection, and from the fifth day, when most probably and as proven by science, I was no longer infectious. I am an overall healthy individual though, and have never taken any powerful medicine when with flu, other than aspirin and paracetamol sachets. I took paracetamol to reduce inflammation, and help me recover quicker, not because I was feeling like dying. So, you will not experience a loss of taste or smell. They will decrease once your nose will block, because the wide spectrum of our taste is dependant on our nose being clear of obstruction, and not the other way around. The decrease of taste and smell is specific to any other cold and flu viruses. And remember, if you're producing phlegm and have a runny nose, it's not the novel coronavirus.

The ethnic background

During the mess year 2020 represents, society is turning against brown people again. The poor ethnic groups don't even know how much they're being used, with every movement that is supposed to grant them more rights. They cannot see they already have the same rights as anybody else.

Take Obama as example. He is the only black president of the USA, and because he is black, it doesn't matter that he is one of the most corrupt politicians the US of A have ever seen.

"This virus is ten times more likely to kill you if you're black!" Target set. Black person. Ventilator! Calm down, and ask an Eastern European about how to treat a coronavirus. *Dacians* (Romanians) have țuică (also pălincă), Hungarians have pálinka, Greeks have tsipouro, Portuguese have ginja, Italians have sambuca, etc.. I can see a trend with emerging companies producing non-alcoholic "alcoholic" drinks, engineered by *plant scientists*. They are poison! A life without alcohol is a life of disease.

Listen, if you are black it doesn't mean you're weak. If you were born in United Kingdom, and have lived here your entire life, you have the same immunity as a white British person. There is no scientific logic that contradicts this in any way. Even if you have lived here most of your life, you'd still have the same immunity. On the other side, if you have lived most of your life in a hot climate, then and only then your immune system cannot be of the same strength with a European's, who has lived with both hot summers and cold winters. This is evolutionary science. One time they found a black illegal immigrant close to the *Dacian* (Romanian) border. He froze to death at two degrees Celsius. When we heard about it everyone burst into laughing. It was tragic, we shouldn't have laughed about it, but it was difficult for us to conceive freezing to death at that temperature. During my lifetime I've seen the Black Sea freeze at minus 30°C at least a couple of times. Once I even went with the car out on the frozen sea to drift. When you're used with temperatures as that, two degrees feels like summer. We felt sorry for the guy, despite him trying to enter the country illegally. What they are not telling you is the condition of the black and brown people that died in the hospitals, on top of the fact that no one knew for sure if they indeed contracted the new virus. Who knows for sure if more black people have died than white. You can never find out. To make it more weird, during normal years more women die with flu and coronavirus than men. In 2020 there's a considerable increase in male *Covid-19* deaths compared to women. Everything is upside down with this new virus. The UK has a large minority of colour, which now I think it's a majority, that moved here from really hot countries. If you're one of them, then it makes sense that a new coronavirus will affect you more than me. When I moved to this country I got a coronavirus that caused me to feel really bad for a month. It was most probably a new coronavirus. I kept on working in the warehouse, while an Indian manager that didn't grow up here had to be admitted into hospital. Back then we didn't have a good diet either. It contained mainly supermarket pizza with double cream, and strong alcohol to drown the sorrow. It also matters a lot if you've lived in the UK during your formation years, meaning 0 to 20. To make it clear, a person that lives in a four seasons environment will automatically have a stronger response to a coronavirus, old or new, than a person that lives in a hot two seasons environment. Do not twist what you've just read, by interpreting that a four seasons person has an overall better immune system. I am referring to the current and ongoing coronavirus situation, not any other virus. What the media and politically involved scientists have put into your head is incorrect and incomplete. There's nothing wrong with your immune system. Enjoy your life as normal and you'll be ok, stop causing yourself harm by trusting people you don't know, including me; do your own research. *Dacians*

(Romanians) are everywhere, just ask them for the coronavirus remedies, and they might save your life in more than one way. If they're afraid like you, they're not real *Dacians* (Romanians).

Antibodies

I have a question for you: how come my grandparents knew how immunity works, and were never afraid of any coronavirus, old or new, they knew how to treat me really quick, whereas you, living in the city, and considering yourself highly educated, you're a retard when it comes to how your own immunity works? If this sounds condescending, it is. I want to offend you! Maybe it'll determine you to read about what matters in your life. No one should not know the basics of immunity.

Imagine how beautiful our bodies are. Whenever there is an alien bug entering our system, we start producing specific defence proteins to eliminate the exact agent, out of nothing. It's not like you're storing the information to a first time infection somewhere in your body. That's a paradox. But when it happens, immunity knows the exact chemistry of the protein fatal to the antigen. It's kind of subliminal if you think about it. Basically, the right recipes are stored in the quantum realm, from which your body is retrieving them at the right time, and without flaw. Tell me that we are not connected beyond what we know and can understand... It's the same as when your body is telling you that something is going to happen before it happens. So your body's chemistry is changing in anticipation to something non-existent, about which it has got information in advance that it will occur inevitably. All this to prepare you, to keep you alive and well. Where is all this esoteric protection coming from?

Your good health is caused by exposure. Isolation is sister with disease. When you take a bite from an apple you're exposing yourself to good and bad bacteria, and viruses. All foods that you ingest have also a negative impact on your body, mostly training it and strengthening it. This is why you poo and pee. Personally, I've eaten so many unwashed fruits in our farm, that I still probably have antibodies to bird poo viruses and bacteria. The same with air. If you were born and have lived in a perfectly sanitised environment with 100% clean air, when going outside you'd probably hit the A&E in a matter of hours. Just pay attention to how your sinuses' mucus tastes after an infection. I know it from my experience, that for a few days I can taste medicine without having had any. This is the medicine produced by your body, under the shape of antibodies. Be aware of this next time. If humans can develop immunity to snake venom, imagine how powerful our bodies are.

Nature made us strong, but what we are doing to each other is taking that from us. Soon we'll fill the planet with hybrids, like in the pubs of *Star Wars*. Just read about *recombinant DNA* to understand what I mean. You'll see why we have so many movies with mutants. They want to drive us there. **Also read about the method used to deliver a piece of RNA/DNA to the DNA.**

When reaching adulthood, or maybe earlier than that, everyone should have full spectrum IgG and IgE tests to determine the individual's exposure and allergic reactions. This should be paid by the national health service, and the results given to the individual. This way you'd know exactly what you need to be aware of, and how to build your diet, before developing dangerous conditions. If you are allergic to something, and you keep on ingesting the specific allergen, in time you will develop more severe reactions, because you're overwhelming the immune system. This is why we have so many cases of eczema.

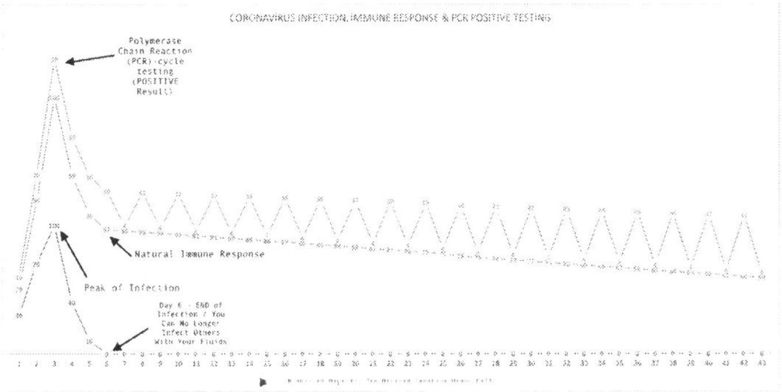

Fig. 2

In **Fig. 2** above you can see the natural evolution of a coronavirus infection in a healthy individual, based on the science published in medical journals. Your immune system's response is crucial to how your body will cope with the infection. How the immune system works is quite complex, but its basic mechanics is simple to understand. By the third day your immune response is dramatic, and this is paramount in deactivating the viral cells. This will drop your infectiousness considerably from the fourth day, and after about 5-7 days you're only discarding inactive virus. If you still have symptoms, it is because your body is rebuilding. Even so, you should feel better with each day. When it comes to the PCR test, if the thermal cycle multiplication threshold is set correctly, to about 25 cycles, the result should give you an idea about being infected/infectiousness. But considering that the result comes after about two days, you might already be clear by the time you test positive, making self-isolation requirements an unnecessary burden/damage. You test *positive*, but you still don't know to what. No one will perform further sequencing if you are not admitted to a hospital. When they discover a new strain, it is based on the further sequencing done on the patients in hospitals. The number of new strains of the new virus is into millions, but because most people didn't feel unwell enough to need medical attention, it is impossible to actually know the real number of new strains. And why would you put so much effort into this, when the virus keeps on mutating every day?!

As you can see from the graph, you will still test positive as long as you're discarding inactive virus, hence people testing positive twice in a month. The scientists know all this, but they've been pressured into lying to you. The more you increase the threshold of the PCR test machine, the more false positives you'll have. Imagine two cars going in opposite directions. The more you discard virus cells, the higher the threshold on the PCR needs to be, until no fluorescence is occurring, meaning that there was no viral RNA found. In all instances your DNA will show no matter the threshold, if the swab was performed correctly.

With mRNA vaccines, the scientists are saying that your immunity will kick in after about 9 days or so. Whoever says this has to be tried against their medical knowledge, because they don't know how a body should work. If after taking the vaccine your immune system is not activated in a couple of days, the medication (vaccine) is useless, and even more, highly dangerous.

Your health is based on exposure. If you had the virus this week, it doesn't mean that you will not get in touch with it in the nearby future. Depending on this your immunity will stay for a long time, or you will lose it in record time, if you self-isolate for months or years. By living as normal, your immunity to the virus and all its strains can last for years. Your immunity is constantly fluctuating, and because you're immune, you are no threat to others. Of course there is still a chance that you can spread bacteria and viruses to people, even if you're asymptomatic (you had the virus before), but the chances are minimal. It would increase if you kiss and exchange a high quantity of fluids. There is also a high chance that the other person is immune too. Life will not end with a coronavirus, it will end with panic.

The mRNA vaccine

You are taking a vaccine that has not been authorised, nor declared safe! If food, after passing through so many filters, can alter your cells' behaviour, what makes you think that a vaccine can't do it? What makes you think that it cannot alter your sperm cells or eggs? If you're a woman, did you know that, despite men - who constantly produce new sperm -, your eggs are already there, waiting their turn to participate in ovulation? You are born with all the ovarian eggs ready to get released. Protect them with a healthy lifestyle, and with your life.

In the product's data-sheet, Astra Zeneca are admitting that, during trials, the volunteers have been tested to see if they had the new virus, using DNA multiplication techniques, i.e. the PCR method. They are not saying if the patients have been completely isolated from the outside world throughout the trials. This crucial information from the study is clear proof that the results of the vaccine trials are completely flawed. Don't be fooled, these errors and omissions are intentional.

This vaccine is altering the normal functions of your body's cells. Immunity is highly complex, but understanding how it works is not that difficult. Despite this, no doctor will sit down next to you, to explain it properly during coronavirus times. Even so, it doesn't mean that you shouldn't know. It's like the big part of contravention law: you should know it, without being pushed into learning it - you should know it's not allowed to throw garbage on the street. No one should not know how immunity works, because it's the system that keeps you alive. If you don't know anything about immunity, then why would you take the vaccine with so much pathos!? You act as if you know everything in biotechnology! Since you're so smart, explain this to yourself: what does [*recombinant*] mean, on the label of the vaccine vial? And on the other side, if you know how immunity works, you'd not agree with *everyone needs a/the vaccine*. Governments and doctors are killing people by supporting this argument. Let me explain.

There are multiple organs working together to fight an infection, may it be bacterial, viral or fungal. This system is also protecting you when you have allergies. For this reason, you stop ingesting substances that your body may not tolerate (e.g. gluten). The main organ of the immune system is the spleen. Its loss (removal) causes, what in the medical profession is called, *the opening of Pandora's box*, with reference to the legend when curious Pandora opened this box holding all the bad things in the world, despite being told not to do so. In our mouth we have the tonsils, which play a big part in killing bacteria and producing antibodies, keeping firstly your mouth healthy, and then helping the entire system in bigger wars. You could say the tonsils trigger the alarm when you get infected with a coronavirus. They are the ones that are getting rid of the active virus from your mouth and nose, after the first two days from infection. I recently met a person that had her spleen removed, and she explained to me how she's taking antibiotics daily, and how she fought two big infections in less than a year. So, her immune system is really weak. She was telling me that she's going to have the vaccine because of her condition. From what I know, I would say the real coronavirus and the mRNA vaccine pose the same high risk of killing her. Why? Because her body cannot produce the right amount of antibodies to fight the real virus anyway. And along the way, she will contract the new virus, and any other viruses humans and animals spread through air. If this was a real, deadly pandemic, a lot of animals would've died too. Have you seen birds falling from the sky? Now, I don't want to give any funky ideas to those biologists in Wuhan...

The BIG danger from wearing masks

As I said before, the tonsils are playing a big role in the immune system. The biggest threat to them is the bacterial count in your mouth. This is why you need to have a very good oral hygiene, with no unresolved cavities or other issues like plaque, gingivitis or bad teeth. A high bacterial count can cause their inflammation, and most probably their removal. This is a routine procedure nowadays, so most doctors don't advice against it. Tonsillitis can be cured with antibiotics, teas, etc.. By wearing an aseptic mask, or reuseing a previously aseptic one or for long periods of time, you will increase the bacterial count in your respiratory tract and mouth tenfold. Don't forget that usually your mouth is dirtier than the area around your anus! This will directly impact your beloved tonsils, putting an immense strain on their ability to fight infection, and ultimately protect themselves even. This is how they inflame, cause pain, produce puss, and drive you to remove them. Doctors are more than happy to do it, compared to telling you how to treat or prevent the infection. Antibiotics are bad, they keep on saying, as if you're ingesting antibiotics daily. We all have different diets, so different people eat different foods, or from different sources. If you remove your tonsils you lose an important part of your overall immune system. Masks should be banned from being worn. Considering how all that we live is trying to take out our natural immunity, I'd say it's not a conspiracy, but a FACT. Conspiracy is when you don't have proof about something. Proof is definitive. Stop wearing the mask now, before it's too late.

The mRNA vaccine works by delivering synthetic RNA from the novel coronavirus hosted by inactivated chimpanzee adenovirus, wrapped in a lipid (fat) bubble, right into your cells. Then, your normal healthy cells will start producing the spike protein the virus uses to penetrate your cell's wall. This will trigger an immune response that will target and take out the newly produced spike protein. According to mRNA science, your cell will die straight after producing the protein. Keep in mind that this protein is way smaller than the actual virus and that it's being produced by otherwise healthy cells. Your cells are not all the same, and have quite an impressive lifespan. A few big questions have to be raised. Which cells is the mRNA going into? Is it muscle cells, blood cells, organ cells, brain cells? Which ones? And how many cells will it forcibly kill? One of the biggest wonders of this world is the immune system, which can pick up on any small subtlety. Your immune system is never testing bullets, it is using the *silver* bullet first time, no matter the type of infecting agent. People have different blood speeds too, so where the mRNA molecules are going can differ substantially from one individual to another. A person with 1,050 blood speed can pass the molecules to the brain in no time, while someone with 550 blood speed can have only the heart muscle cells infected, and some blood cells. With all RNA vaccines they're giving you purified (inactivated) whole virus, so it cannot infect your cells further, and against all previous safety protocols, with the mRNA vaccine your cells get infected on purpose. This is why people get blood clots in the brain, because inflammation occurs at the place of infection, putting immense pressure on the neuronal tissue; their brain got infected with mRNA molecules, and the neurones started producing the spike protein. The number of lymphocytes increased exponentially, and the antibodies started killing the infected neurones, and other nearby healthy cells spewing out spike protein.

Recently I found an article written by this idiot called Bruce Y. Lee (I hope his name is a pseudonym) for a famous American publication, in which he was promoting the mRNA vaccine. Having no medical knowledge whatsoever, as most of Americans, he was saying that with this vaccine your immune system will not have to shoot randomly if you get the virus; it would know exactly what it's fighting. What a complete retard! Your immune system is so cool it never shoots at random, and there is no stronger shield in the fight against bacteria and common viruses! When you're taking medicine it's because your want to support a struggling immune response, which depends on count, type of virus and bacteria. With medicine you are supporting your immunity, not replace it. Most of the times you don't need any medicine, even if you feel bad. No matter if you take the vaccine or not, you'll still get and spread the virus in the same way. Then you travel to France, and get a new strain that was not covered by the vaccine, because the spike protein changed... Even if it does actually change, I truly believe this is a lie, producing the spike protein in your blood is useless and highly dangerous. This is why RNA vaccines are more efficient, because they contain 3-4 strains of the weaker real virus. It is an absurdity to say that mRNA vaccines will help humanity, it's just a step closer to our cell's nucleus, and hybridising our DNA with a sequence of synthetic RNA/DNA. Kary Mullis and his friends knew from the '70s that RNA and DNA are hybridisable, just read the scientific study about the PCR method, written by the former. They will try to modify your DNA in the future while you're still alive, there is no doubt about it.

There are many issues with this vaccine, so let's start with its technology. It goes in your cell, and then the cell starts producing a viral alien spike protein, that's tens of times smaller than the whole virus, before the cell getting presumably destroyed. Ok, nice! We currently know that defence proteins (IgGs - antibodies - immunoglobulins) take a different shape and chemistry, depending on the intrusive agent they are fighting. This is why you can test for specific IgGs. So all these spike proteins forcibly produced by **your own healthy cells**, a premiere in human history, will be significantly smaller than the actual virus and your cells (that will ultimately be corrupted by the real virus). So your immune system will trigger and produce antibodies of the right size and chemistry, to destroy only the small spike protein invading your body. But will it? The spike protein might be seen as discard, which is not the business of IgGs. If it will happen, the immune system is not wasting resources, by overproducing proteins that are larger/more potent than needed. This is true science. Now tell yourself what will happen when you contract the new virus, and your antibodies can only attach themselves to the spike protein, instead of the whole virus. Now you'll say, yes but the virus won't have the chance to attach to the cell, because the antibodies will destroy its spike protein. Well, wrong, because when you get infected you receive a big load of virus cells, and some will eventually succeed in getting into your cells and infect you. Your body will have to start producing stronger antibodies for the whole virus. So in this case, what do you do with the multitude of strains with modified spike proteins? Still think you need the vaccine? Even normal RNA vaccines stimulate a weak immune response, because the produced antibodies have weak properties to match the potency of the weak virus contained by the vaccine. Another catch to this mRNA vaccine is that your cell might produce more than one type of spike proteins, because the real virus has a multitude of spike proteins on its surface, contaminating your body unnecessarily. Only one of these proteins is responsible for being able to break the human cell membrane, so by delivering a fragment of RNA into the cell, through mRNA procedure, it will produce a complete array of spike proteins that can stimulate your immune system ineffectively. There is a possibility that most of your cells will not produce the desired spike protein, rendering the whole vaccine procedure useless. I strongly believe it is useless and a highly dangerous intrusion into the body. Think, everyone is telling you that by delivering a virus RNA sequence, your cell will produce only the desired spike protein. It's like saying that your DNA sequence will produce only a hand, not the whole of you. Does it make sense now? Even if they used a partial sequence, to master and promote only the production of one specific spike protein is complicated business, and almost impossible to isolate. In this vaccine there is a complete viral RNA sequence that will force your cells to produce the whole array of spike proteins on the new coronavirus, not just the targeted one. There is even a chance that you will not produce *the one*, hence people getting sick with the real virus after having the vaccine. Doctors also referred to the whole quantity of antibodies after vaccination, instead of the quantity of *specific antibodies*. This is proof they are selling you the wrong data, counting on the fact that most people don't know the science behind immunity. With a vaccine like this, you cannot develop immunity to the real virus. Your immune system will fight against your own cells.

Now let's say you get the vaccine. I still can't understand why they did not create a normal RNA vaccine, and decided to create an mRNA vaccine, which is way more expensive to produce. They're motivating it with the fast rate with which this virus is modifying, but this is a known issue with all coronaviruses; they are constantly creating new strains. This is why you need to get the virus in the first place; there is no better way of getting the proper immunity. If they tell you it's cheaper to produce the mRNA one, they are lying. The mRNA has only one purpose, no matter how we look at its destination, and that is to get closer to our DNA. When your cell reaches maturity it will create a copy of the entire DNA code, and then it will duplicate into two identical cells carrying your genetic code forward, and so on. When that split is occurring, for a very short moment the connection between the two is a weak spot. This process is happening daily in our bodies. During the split, the distance between the membrane and the nucleus is considerably smaller, creating vulnerability. What if one of the mRNA lipids is penetrating that juncture, and gets incorporated in the nucleus of the newly formed cell, or both? It would not matter with the old cell, because it would probably die sooner than later after multiplication. No one is explaining these small things to you. They're just saying it cannot modify your DNA. Everywhere, you see the same explanations about how mRNA works. We know that already! Is anyone explaining to you why we needed this technology, or what the implications could be? All doctors and biologists they are allowing on TV and online sound like they're broken tapes, and if they sense that you have a bit of knowledge, and start asking difficult questions they cannot answer, they avoid you completely, as if you don't exist. **Scientists should not be politicians!** They have to answer each and every question addressed to them, without even thinking of getting out of the situation before solving the raised issue. I am not saying that the mRNA bubble would necessarily get into the nucleus, but if that happens, and your cells start multiplying with the alien RNA into your hybrid DNA, you're fucked! You get an autoimmune disease you cannot shake off. This is another reason why they want to test you every second, to see if you have the coronavirus. They don't care if you're immune already, they just want to see if you are carrying it. This implies a DNA swab. In 2020 they have created the biggest DNA database, and the research continues. I bet they will continue to swab even the people that had the vaccine, for a purpose I've already mentioned, probably to see if the DNA is modifying. To make myself clear, I'm not saying that this vaccine will modify your DNA. The fact that we are not being explained on all channels the full consequences of this new technology (it had been used before in cancer treatments) applied globally is determining me to doubt everything, and compare it to what I know from having worked with human antibodies, and additional research. Considering the way they are pushing this vaccine for a low risk virus that the coronavirus is, I would say the side effects overwhelm the benefits, and they know it. No scientist employed by the Big Pharma wants you to have a strong immune system. Be wary about the fact-checking websites nowadays, as they are being owned and manipulated to match the pharmaceutical companies' agenda. Don't you like it how they have the upper hand on you?

Firstly this vaccine should not be given to people with immunodeficiency or a missing immune system, this could kill them suddenly. This is true for all RNA vaccines. Why would you give the virus, or pieces of the virus to people that struggle to produce antibodies? There are immunoglobulin vaccines for that! The infrastructure is already there all over the planet. One impediment could be that China owns probably more than 80% of the IgG vaccines market. Coincidence? Still think you need the mRNA vaccine? Here we have covered people with low, or no immunity for various reasons.

Let's say you are healthy, and did not have the new coronavirus. Whether you get the vaccine or not, you'll still spread diseases as normal, including the new virus. No need to wear a mask to get yourself sick, you can have the virus on your skin, clothes, hair, boots, on the dashboard, in the carpets of the car, all around you. You're afraid of getting the virus? Why would you? You are healthy, and this is a coronavirus. You've probably had one in the past, your body knows what to do. If you live a normal life you'll not lose your immunity to it because you'll contract the virus constantly, and spread it; after the first contamination you'll stop having symptoms, until completely losing the antibodies for this virus. But don't worry, that is a really slow process that can take years. A vaccine cannot give you a stronger immunity, compared to your own immune system's response to the real virus. Ever! They keep on telling you that, but it's the lie of the century. You are safe. As I write this in April 2021, I've had at least 12 months of natural immunity to the new virus, and I've been in contact with hundreds of medical staff working with coronavirus patients, among the over seven thousand people I have had in my vehicle. I am a private hire driver in London. This includes my brother and our mother, as we live under the same roof. Altogether, we've been in close contact with over 20,000 people, healthy and ill with symptoms.

Lastly, what if you've had the new coronavirus, you test positive to specific antibodies for the new virus (be careful to have a good lab test), but they still force you to have the vaccine? Well, it's called bio-terrorism, and it comes with a hidden purpose. Probably as mentioned above. Pushing a vaccine on someone is identical to releasing a virus in nature intentionally, its bio-terrorism by any definition. If you had the new virus, live as normal! If you do get the shot because you're an idiot with natural immunity to the new virus, your current specific antibodies will take out the cells producing the spike protein, and depending on the antibodies count left in you, your body may produce new weaker ones to take out the excess spike protein. I don't think the latter would happen, because the macrophages will eat up the spike protein. So, does it make sense to have the vaccine if you're immune? You will still spread diseases and bacteria no matter how you wear your mask. This is nature, and it can only change if they kill, and burry you. It's the same with people that have never had a coldsore but can carry the virus and spread it to others; they have antibodies for it but expose no symptoms. Many of them don't even know they have it. Most probably, when they first got it they had some symptoms like tiredness, but they associated it with something else. Whenever you get a new virus you **WILL** expose some sort of symptoms. There is no such thing as asymptomatic, after being exposed to a new coronavirus for the first time. By the way, if you have a coldsore episode, and you get swabbed during the first two days from the explosion, you will most likely test positive for coronavirus with the RT-PCR method.

Looking at the possible side effects one more time, what if your super smart immune system will start picking up on your healthy cells producing a toxic alien protein, and will begin tagging and destroying healthy cells at random? This can happen, as long as they don't explain the side effects with official studies. But even this transparency is overstated, as nowadays scientists are telling the public that GMOs are good, which I find it equal with nutritional terrorism. I have done farming for more than a decade. Be careful where the science comes from! Another problem could arise from overloading your immune system. If the RNA (delivered using the mRNA methodology) by any chance gets reproduced with new cells that will produce the alien spike protein, it means that your immune system is constantly fighting a synthetic war produced by your own body. Over exposing the immune system can kill it, if at any time one of the organs dealing with infections gets ill for some reason, like the tonsils or the spleen. And be sure that synthetic over-exposure will weaken them. This would also happen if you have the flu jab, *Covid-19* jab, and other jabs, every year for the rest of your life. Your body is constantly producing the malicious protein but you're losing *cannons*. What would happen then? If you have scientists in your life, ask them this, and also about how a vaccine can solve a problem that is not there. People die with cancer and a cold virus every day, this does not mean it is a pandemic, nor that it has to be the end of life as we know it. The agenda is lengthy and prewritten. The way we are being forced to live, and all these intrusions in our private lives and bodies, will cause our extinction. To me there is no doubt about it. I haven't eaten a real tomato in years now... Tell yourself the following, to test if it sounds right: THE BIG PHARMA WANT TO OVERPOPULATE THE PLANET WITH PERFECTLY HEALTHY PEOPLE. During 2020 we have witnessed the biggest contradictions between scientists with the same level of credentials. Which one would you believe, if two same level doctors have opposite opinions about this virus? Doctors are supposed to be allowed their own conscience, but even so, how can they have opposite opinions about exact proven science? Some divergence can be a good sign but what is currently happening is outrageous, and totally confusing for the people. One says there is a pandemic, and that you should run wearing a mask, while the other is saying the number of cases are as normal, or even lower for a cold season, and that you should not wear a mask...

After new data from January 2021's real-life tests with the new experimental vaccine, coming from scientists that support the new treatment, it resulted that maybe you get 50% protection against the real virus after the first dose, with some arguing that it might actually be as low as 33%. There are tablets that can offer you better protection. Although, they're supporting that it still gives you a better immune response, than after contracting the real virus, after ten days from exposure or having the first dose. This is scientifically flawed, and it reinforces what I have described in this chapter. The real virus is the only way to create true, and efficient immunity against future infections, if you are healthy. In these reports the scientists always mention only IgG, and the whole quantity of antibodies in your blood plasma. When testing patients at ten days after exposure, and patients after the first dose of vaccine, you need to look at IgM too, because they come with a new infection. And considering that they are vaccinating patients without even thinking of testing them beforehand for antibodies against the new virus, the data can be highly inaccurate. If a person had already had *Covid-19* (they have specific IgG), and then you give them the first dose of the vaccine, of course that after ten days they will have a higher IgG concentration than a person that just recovered after *Covid-19*, because the person gets reinfected with RNA, so the body will start producing antibodies again for ten days of infection. The vaccine is keeping you infected an abnormally long period of time, in contrast with an infection with the real virus that can last for up to a week, mostly five days. Therefore, the vaccinated person will have a higher total IgG concentration. This does not mean their whole quantity of IgG is for *Covid-19*. A statement like this is an absurdity, especially coming from a scientist! Testing for the whole quantity of specific IgG is not an easy task, and it can take days of intense laboratory testing. When someone is referring to the whole quantity of blood plasma IgG in the context of *Covid-19*, don't listen to them. They're counting on you not knowing anything about immunity. The more you stray away from scientific logic, the less accurate the final data will be, rendering it useless. This is why I don't agree with almost any RNA vaccine, because if you were to take a vaccine for each coronavirus attacking us every day, you'd become a vegetable in no time. People have allergies, almost all of us have natural immunity to over 90% of the viruses in nature, and most of all vaccines can severely damage your ability to have healthy children, whether you're a man or a woman. If food can alter the quality of sperm, what makes you think vaccines can't do that. They also go straight into your blood, which is more dangerous. This is why the vaccines manufacturers are keeping the studies data hidden from public eyes. If it's proven that natural immunity to a coronavirus can last for years, what is the point of creating a vaccine? Today, even the MHRA and the FDA have not published any data about the studies with the new vaccine. They just ask you to trust them blindly. Never trust anyone selling you trust! You need all the data in order to make an informed decision. The chief of MHRA recently said that there is no reason why anyone would not take the vaccine. For that statement alone he should be trialed. The MHRA went against the orange guide, and have broken pharmacovigilance protocols by approving a dangerous and unnecessary medication, that can be lethal to the vulnerable and the healthy.

Real *Covid-19* numbers do not justify the need for a vaccine.

These vaccines have no marketing authorisation, meaning a consistent breach of the authorisation/approval process. They have failed in their purpose. About the coronavirus the science is already there, nothing is new. You need to get the virus to get protected, as for the vulnerable, they maybe need a specific IgG shot or a pill, depending on their condition. Experiments, medicine like Remdesivir, and vaccines will kill more than save. This is a fact. It would be impossible to receive compensation if something is happening to you or your family. This is why they're producing vaccines, and not pills. I'm going to explain once more how IgGs work. When I was a technician at Bio Products Laboratory, we were making a vaccine called *Gammaplex* (considered the best human IgG in the world - least side effects and highest efficacy) which varies in concentration starting from 5%. This vaccine is for people with very low or no immunity, and it contains a whole array of IgGs for the most common illnesses caused by viruses, bacteria or fungi. This array gets updated with new IgGs every time the donor is giving plasma. For illnesses like tetanus, rabies, factor-D (plasma only from women with immunity against Rh positive blood), zoster (shingles), the plasma had to come only from patients that had developed a strong immune response against those viruses/conditions. Every antibody in your blood is specific to something. When referring to a single illness you should never measure the whole quantity of antibodies, and consider it as the ultimate sign that you're immune to a particular disease. You need an exact measurement of your body's response to the exact antigen. An increased whole quantity on IgGs towards the upper maximum allowed levels, and over the limit lymphocytes can express a recent infection, but it is in no way a sign that you had a specific virus.

What is happening now is way worse than communism, and I'll explain. Nowadays hospitals receive money if someone dies with *Covid-19*. Not from *Covid-19*, WITH *COVID-19*, but considering how the result is based on the PCR method, I doubt it. Spot the difference. Hospitals receive incentives to kill people basically. In communism, if a doctor had a high number of mortalities, he would get penalised (usually by getting less money before more severe action). You'd never see this in a democracy (communist capitalism - what we actually live). If they would take action against the doctors with high mortality rates, you would see a massive drop in cases all over the world, maybe more that 50%. In the UK, the government is telling people to save the NHS by staying home. I am explaining the naive people I meet, that shutting down the economy will kill the NHS way sooner than expected, and with certainty. It's a service paid for by the tax payers. If millions of tax payers are unemployed, and living on benefits and furlough for years, how can the NHS survive? Talking about improving it is pure fiction, because the rich would never pay for its survival. Let this sink in. If now we get hit by a real pandemic, caused by a high risk virus, we would be crippled in days. And if the health service of a highly developed country cannot cope with a coronavirus outbreak, then it should not even exist, because it failed in its purpose. There are many countries that are living as normal, looking at the developed ones, and laughing at the poorly directed show. It's not a joke though. Considering how things are being controlled and manipulated, I'm predicting that a bigger, more real *pandemic* is imminent. They're quite accurate with predicting these things, but not quite when it comes to basic treatment. They're talking about future SPARS viruses nowadays, between 2025-2028. Let's wait for 2023... God help us all! I hope I'm wrong.

Categories of people that the new coronavirus never heard of

This Wuhan coronavirus is either causing sudden death, or absolutely no symptoms to the majority of people, based on the new coronavirus science of 2020. This does not make any sense, no matter the level of your scientific knowledge. Currently I'm earning most of my money from private hire driving in the Greater London area. If you want to know if there is indeed a pandemic, just ask a taxi/private hire driver. We've been here throughout, interacting with tens of thousands of people, all during the peak of a questionable pandemic, and we are fine. I'm in my prime years, but most taxi drivers are not. And they are still here, and relatively healthy (as much as they can be after a life in the driver's seat). How can any scientist, supporting the severity of the pandemic, explain this to the people? We are more exposed than doctors, because the people in our cars don't care about us, and we have no PPE. I've had countless people with blocked noses, sneezing, coughing, all without even thinking of limiting the spread. I've also transported loads of ill children with their parents, and you know how contagious kids can be... I am still here and healthy, same as any other taxi/private hire driver in the whole of the UK. I bet that no highly exposed driver died because of *Covid-19* during the last year and a half, no matter his/her age. Apparently, we are an immortal breed of our own, no matter the age span.

I am native form *Dacia* (Romania). We are people still connected with nature and medicine, and hospitals are our last resort. We try to eat properly and healthy, drink hot strong spirits with spices, and real red wine whenever we feel down, and over 90% of time coronaviruses have nothing on us. We are still some of the healthiest people on the planet. There are around 500,000 *Dacians* (Romanians) in the UK according to the Government. Let's be indulgent, and say that 10% of them are gypsies (Indians from India - yes, gypsies come from India), but it's not really relevant, because they learned how to eat and live like the natives of my country, so their immunity should be as strong as a white *Dacian*'s (Romanian's). It's the same like saying that an Indian's immunity is different from a white British, both born and raised on the island. During the *pandemic* I have never had a *Dacian* (Romanian) telling me that they knew someone who actually died because of this new virus. And I had a lot of *Dacian* (Romanian) nationals in my car. Of course many of them tested positive multiple times, and some almost died, because instead of trying to help their emergency, doctors were prioritising *Covid-19* testing, then shoving them with the contagious batch until the result came in. I'm pretty sure that less than 10 *Dacian* (Romanian) nationals (white natives and gypsies - Indians) have died of the actual new coronavirus, in the whole of the UK. At some point, they were saying that Eastern Europeans are stronger because during communism years we were getting inoculated against tuberculosis, but based on real science, how many years can an RNA vaccine give you immunity for, because it will never compare with the immunity achieved after contracting the real antigen?! If my natural immunity lasts for so long after contracting the real virus, why are you besieging me with a new experimental vaccine? Isn't this the same base science? You connect all the dots, to get a glimpse of who is lying to you.

I really like this one! Do you remember the congestion at Dover following Brexit? All those thousands of lorry drivers, dirty and stranded for days on end, and almost none of them tested positive. The runway of an airport sank a lot of metres under the weight of the lorries, they were that many. The media never paid any attention to that cluster of highly exposed people, in the midst of a deadly *pandemic*. Most lorry drivers tested negative, and no one considered isolating all others that came into contact with the few that actually tested positive. None of the ones that tested positive had any serious issues. They probably didn't even show any symptoms because they were already immune. Even the positive tests were irrelevant, because no one was doing further sequencing. They had to decongest the port by any means, and if the media would've properly analysed the situation, as they did with the other people, we would've had international conflicts for sure. That situation, with the lorry drivers being given free passes, is another sign of a controlled situation that is not driven by a real pandemic. Lorry drivers are immune, but not you. They are also exempt from testing, Dover was an outstanding situation, that required a normal and fair approach...

Without making this section longer than it should be, these are some important categories that are not vulnerable to any coronaviruses, old or new: rich people, politicians, construction workers (I cannot understand why the construction industry is so important if this pandemic is real - considering the economic decline the output was extraordinary, making me think that they want to build houses even for dead people), doctors, nurses, airport staff (I've been told that out of roughly 150 employees at Heathrow airport - at the peak of the pandemic - only one had a mild cold, and had been sent home), *Dacians* (Romanians) living outside their country, supermarket staff, film staff, scientists, pharmaceutical industry staff and CEOs, warehouse staff, delivery drivers, homeless people (I've seen the same bums in my borough begging on the cold streets throughout the pandemic - absolutely no one from the council gave them any support), the police, the military and many more.

Why would they do this to us?

When I hear someone asking this I feel like moving to another table, refusing to acknowledge the question. I understand that you might have a naive nature, but from a certain age naivety is the easy way out. Asking people this question puts all the pressure on them, and makes you look like you don't want to have any type of responsibility; you want everyone to spoon-feed you all the information. You're also not capable of understanding the information around you, which makes you a bit of a social retard. I'm saying this because you always get annoyed when people are trying to explain to you what you cannot or refuse to understand, because it might break your system of beliefs, and how you see the world. In the UK, the NHS is almost completely sold out, and what is left of the nationalised one is a magnet for poorly skilled practicians.

Good doctors vs bad doctors

You have to understand that throughout their career, most doctors will apply what they've learned in medical school, and that they are also doing this for money, same as me and you. Once on their own, they forget that being a doctor also means constant research and improvement. They are saving lives every day, and we have to thank them for doing it, but they don't have the right to screw it up. We do owe them our lives, but this does not mean they are all good. Big Pharma has them trapped. Would you be willing to sacrifice 30 years of study or your life, just to tell the world the truth? I'll give the answer for you, it's *"no"*. How many doctors came out during 2020 to explain the PCR method, or how your immune system works, or to tell you what to eat or how the ventilators work, or why they would put someone on one, or why the hospitals are listening to WHO (World Health Organisation), when already there were procedures in place for treating atypical pneumonia. Doctors know how many people with high chances of survival would die because of shutting down most health services, but they are not saying anything. Same as the Church, they are completely silent, or if one is even thinking to say something publicly, he's being taken down before reaching the AIR. Not all doctors are dealing with coronavirus patients. There are even PCR experts, but no one is explaining the science to the people. You only hear about the people dying from *Covid-19*. How can that be? Procedures in a hospital are set by the doctors, and the hospital management. The latter has power over the doctors, and they are also politically involved. When a directive comes from the WHO, the management is pressured to obey it, therefore the doctors haven't got much to say. *"Put people on ventilators!"* And they do. In a hospital procedures are above human life, no matter the oath the doctors have sworn. If a patient dies because a procedure was not applied, someone might lose their licence, or go to prison for many years. If a person dies even if the right procedures have been applied, no doctor or nurse is responsible. This is why now no one is responsible for anything, even for establishing the wrong diagnosis by using only the PCR. There are even more worrying risks coming from establishing the wrong diagnosis. You put patients with flu and old coronaviruses together with patients with the new coronavirus, which can get them infected with two different viruses in the same time. What they are doing in hospitals in 2020, can have grave consequences for anyone needing medical attention. Justice could be sought by the relatives of the deceased, but considering the level of panic, and that the justice system is now blocked, there are thin chances of success, on top of the financial burden of going to trial against an establishment.

A few examples of good & bad doctors

In spring 2020 I used a propolis cream on my face. Next day my face had swollen and disfigured me. I went to the A&E in Hemel Hempstead, on the outskirts of London, just to receive normal penicillin tablets from the GP on shift, this white British old lady. I've been told it's bacteria, but she couldn't say which one. It was supposed to improve my situation in about two days, if not to go back. After two days, I was panicking because I was the same. I could barely see anything with my right eye; the cheek and eyebrow were folding over it. We rushed to a private eye hospital in central London, where a Chinese young doctor told me straight away that it was *impetigo,* caused by the bacteria called *Staphylococcus Aureus*. "It's not gonna work with this antibiotic, I'll give you something stronger." She prescribed penicillin with *clavulanic* acid. The latter is helping the antibiotic to do its job properly. She knew straight away what the remedy was, compared with the previous GP. After a few weeks and fully recovered I used the cream again on my hand. I did not know it was causing *impetigo*. In a day I got the same reaction on the patch of skin I used the cream. I knew straight away that I fucked up, and what the issue was. At least now I knew the right medicine to take. I went to A&E again, this time at Watford hospital, renowned as *"the hospital where you go to die"*. I met this Sri Lankan GP who was looking shocked at my hand, not knowing what exactly it was. I told him that previously I had that on my face, I showed him pictures, but he wasn't sure, and stuttered. I begged him to give me the penicillin with *clavulanic* acid, because he was planning to prescribe the normal penicillin that did not work. He called another GP for confirmation. "Yeah, it looks like impetigo... Give him the medicine he wants."

In 2015, my mother had to undergo total knee replacement on both her knees. My brother and I had no money for the surgery, but because we were Europeans and fully employed, she qualified for free NHS treatment. She also worked legally in other countries of the European Union, before moving with us in the UK. Despite this, the Department for Work and Pension (DWP) said she did not qualify. We started preparing the legal documents, and went to the tribunal. Without any external legal advice we won her case. The judge fully understood her condition, and on top of that, he had gone through the same procedure in the past. They sent her to have the procedure done in a private hospital. For this we will forever be grateful to the United Kingdom. In the hospital she was assigned to this German doctor. He was really excited to see her having the procedure done by him through the NHS, because most minorities, like Indians, black or Sri Lankan, are requesting doctors of their own ethnic background. For us it didn't matter, if the doctor was good. But that time, without any racial requests, white for white it was. After both surgeries she felt great, but every time she was going for a checkup, other patients that requested Indian doctors were complaining of severe pain, and one even accused that she had a leg shorter than the other, following the procedure. We didn't know anything about those doctors, but we thanked God our mother was not their patient. The German doctor had been brilliant, while we didn't have to pay a penny. Thank you! The others that had patients in pains are another example of bad doctors.

In 2012, my brother shattered one of his crossed ligaments in the knee. We didn't have money for the reconstruction surgery, but because we worked in the border force we had an extra layer of insurance, that allowed him to have the surgery through the national health service. It wasn't ideal though. He still had to pay the doctor extra money in hand, to have the peace of mind that *he'll do a good job*. This is how it still works in many European countries. After choosing the doctor, before the surgery, my brother was asked if he's an athlete, or if he is doing any performance sports. He wasn't doing any, but we found the questions a bit inappropriate. I paid the doctor in hand myself. When he came out of the surgery, the surgeon has put his whole leg in a cast. After four days, when they removed it, my brother lost about 1/3 of the upper leg muscles. He looked disabled, and the sight was shocking at first glance. During daily patient check rounds my brother eavesdropped on another surgeon, while asking his doctor about why he is still putting the leg in a cast after the knee surgery. That raised some doubts in my brother's head, that later confirmed when the cast was removed. He couldn't believe it. You can imagine the shock he had when he saw his upper leg so thin. After that type of surgery the knee and surrounding areas expand almost double. It's a great shock for the tissues and the drilled bones. On top of that, the new reconstruction ligament was harvested from the *Gracilis* muscle. By putting the leg in a cast, the swollen muscles had no room to expand freely. They had no other choice, but to be reabsorbed by the body. This was a massive post-surgery mistake, and any knee surgeon would agree. During the surgery, the geometry was miscalculated a bit too, as after more than eight years, my brother's knee is far from bending even close to before. He still has got a bending deficit of about 15° compared to his normal knee bending angle, which is a lot. Plus, because of the cast he developed additional tissue around the knee, that led to knee stiffness. Later on, the surgeon suggested that he puts my brother under full anaesthetic again to try to force the knee, in order to break the extra tissue. That could lead to severe knee damage so my brother passed on that solution, and continued with the recovery. After a while we found out that the same surgeon gave up the practice of putting a cast on the post-surgery swelling leg. Recently we found out that the surgeon had passed away.

In 1999 my mother had been diagnosed with fibroids, and after intense debates and investigations, she was told that the only solution is to have a *hysterectomy*. This is a woman's worst nightmare, as it implies the removal of the uterus, ovaries and Fallopian tubes, and seal the vaginal tract at the top. No woman should go through something like this. Hysterectomy is the last resort, when the life of the patient is under threat. Hers wasn't. The best doctors would try to avoid it. Having the only option to trust the doctors, lacking any medical knowledge and financial power to try alternative treatments in private, she went for the highly risky surgery. Having to make a decision like that is not easy, and turns you to prayers more than ever. Fortunately, the 6 hours long surgery went well. Even so, when she got discharged I was struggling to comprehend the full scale of things. I was 12 years old, and scared. For a few days my mother couldn't interact with me, as she was sleeping constantly. It was almost as if I could feel her immense pains. She recovered pretty well, despite not having any psychological counselling, nor hormonal aid. No one cared about that in my country, even if such surgery is changing life irreparably. At a later checkup with the surgeon, my mother was shocked when he said that her uterus looked good, and that it didn't actually have to be removed, but he considered to remove it, and that her condition could've receded with medicine. My mother was so naive, that she took that as an answer without thinking about taking legal action. We didn't have money for that anyway, and she had no moral support from her man... Later on we discovered that there is a black market for healthy uteruses, requests for that coming usually from the Scandinavian countries. You can check this yourself, as it's not a secret anymore. I guess there's something wrong with fertility in that part of the world, maybe because of the Chernobyl disaster, which created a radioactive cloud that migrated north. *Dacia* (Romania) was spared through a miracle, hence *Dacians* (Romanians) still being a people with some of the best and healthy genes among the white race. My mother also being a *universal donor*, her organs would definitely be worth their weight in gold, because they can be accepted by almost any human. If the surgeon is also playing on the black market of organs, he'd make exponentially more money from *procuring* healthy organs for people that need it, and are willing to pay good money. He told my mother that her uterus was intact, raising all sorts of questions, that my mother gave up in pursuing. The damage was done, and probably her organ sent North.

In 2008 my mother had another surgery to remove her gall bladder, due to the stones formed inside. This one was a keyhole procedure. The recovery time compared with classic surgery is extraordinary. The surgeon is also avoiding sectioning important muscles in the abdomen. Despite using the latest technology in this type of surgery, this surgeon messed something up, and my mother is left with a condition that makes her body reject a lot of foods. If she has them, they would favour the extreme production of bile liquid that accumulates in the stomach. This would eventually cause severe vomiting episodes. Even if she's avoiding most of the foods causing this, from time to time her sickness kicks in, and she knows that throwing up is unavoidable. The reason for these episodes sits with how the surgery was performed. The surgeon probably rushed, or didn't know how to apply the procedure, and he left a canal open. We've done our own research, and discovered that many surgeons have made this mistake. When they make a mistake like this it will scar the patient for life, if it cannot be fixed. This one is manageable, but after extensive investigations and probably another surgery. Weirdly enough, the surgeon's house burned down right after my mother's surgery.

Around 2012 I was friends with this woman that got diagnosed with a six centimetres fibroid on the inside of her uterus. This was stopping her body to conceive. Having a good opinion about the doctor that performed my mother's gull bladder removal (her post-surgery condition hadn't kicked in yet by this time), I told my friend that she should visit him, to get an opinion about what the best way forward might be. She was in her twenties. He told her, "Miss, I'm a general surgeon, if I open you up, and decide to take everything out, I'll do it. I cannot tell you before the surgery that I won't do it..." When I heard that I was shocked, and felt awful for recommending him. Then she got an appointment with one of the best doctors in the country. He gave her treatment to take the fibroid to three cm or under, to make it treatable with the latest method in fibroid therapy. He was the only one in my country able to localise the fibroid through the artery, and injecting specialised particles that would interrupt the arterial blood flow to the fibroid. In time it would recede completely. He was going in through the hand artery. It was powerful stuff!

When I was eight years old my appendicitis turned chronic. It was close to bursting, and it started showing up in my urine and blood. I was in severe pains when running. My mother grabbed all the money she had, took me to the hospital, and started asking for available doctors. A nurse told her to go to a specific one because he was good. She went into his office, gave him the money, and only managed to get me a place on a long waiting list. My mother was desperate. She went to the nurse again, just to find out that my mother didn't pay the right amount. She went home, borrowed more money, paid the doctor again, and I got planned for surgery the same day. If she wouldn't have managed to get more money, the doctor was willing to let me die. He didn't care.

He did made me well, for the right price. Thank you! But... Doctors always make more money than what you give them, because they are claiming through the national insurance for each patient too. No one got a receipt for the money my mother paid. If you think all doctors want to save your life, you're wrong in a good measure. They're all conditioned by their wage, corporate-like pressures, personal circumstances, experience, kindness, skill, etc., just as in any other industry. It should definitely not be like this!

When I was 17 I've dislocated both my wrists. Luckily they dislocated weeks apart, or I would've wiped my ass with someone else's hand (smiles). Fist time it happened when playing football (like I was ever made for that...), and second time I fell on ice. In my city there was this *bone* doctor (orthopaedic) that used to fix joints and bones in the Second World War. She's been in the battlefield hospitals doing it. I don't think she was recognised as a modern doctor, but definitely she was the best in traditional and modern medicine of the musculoskeletal traumas. Current PhD standards do not include people like her. Everyone knew that she was probably the best in the country. All other doctors in hospitals would've put my wrist in a cast, to force the joint to come back into place on its own, traumatising me for weeks on end. My mother knew where she lived. She owned a modest house, contrary to her skills. Nowadays, someone with her level of skill would probably charge the earth for fixtures, and would live at the top of Beverly Hills. Her moral values would accept any money you were willing to give her. She was the type of person with a great energy you could not understand. After receiving us, and understanding what my problem was, she brought a pot with a bit of water and a soap. She grabbed my hand, soaped it up, then while looking me in the eyes, and telling me to relax, she started massaging the wrist. After a few seconds she pulled it towards her with a sudden move, and I could hear a click in the wrist. The pain was minimal, but my face was visibly suffering from a pain that never came. She gave me her blessing, while explaining that in a week it'll be like new. No cast was ever needed. I thanked her from the bottom of my heart. I felt honoured to be treated by such a great person. Before we left she turned towards my mother, and told her to hold me because I was about to faint. Hearing that I smiled, and assured her I was ok. She insisted that my mother grabs my arm. After one step my eyesight got blurred, I could feel ice in my ears, while my legs were giving up. I leaned on my mother and against a wall. The moment only lasted for a few seconds. We were shocked at her knowing what was about to happen with me. I felt like a woos and ashamed! If all doctors were like her, the world would be totally different. God bless her!

If you live in a developed country you might be tempted to say that, *"yeah, but your country is shit, that's why you don't have good doctors!"*. Wrong! Truth is, you have no idea how evolved some small countries are compared to yours. *Dacia* (Romania) has always been at the top when it comes to medical education. Look around you to see how many doctors studied there. Of course global politics determines them to leave the country for a better life and money. The only difference with your doctors is that in developed countries, the same doctors are being paid maybe 1,000% more for the same service, or even a worse one. Doctors want the health service to get fully privatised because they would make way more money, than working for the national health service. Their drive should not be money.

Your Government is allowing companies to put poison in your food, among many other things. They also allow you to smoke. What makes you think they care about the vulnerable people getting *Covid-19* and dying, when more people die each year from smoking, and from the toxic substances you legally ingest? It was never about this new virus, which is classed as low risk by normal standards. It was about accelerating a plan that started millennia ago: your forced enslavement and total submission; you are not allowed to own an opinion, or be free. You are a serial number in their books, a battery that will be recycled when discharged. You don't need too much brain power to realise this. Just open your eyes, and try to be free. Ask yourself why they have vaults with state secrets you're not supposed to find out, ever. Why are they even keeping you away from true history? By trying to understand, and not just receive information, you will wake up a different side of you. Truth is never invasive or harassing, lies on the other hand are. This is why they work so well on you, they're being put into your head using archaic persuasion techniques. Read a bit about Epigenetics, and find out what the environment can do to your genetics. You don't realise it because lies are highly discreet. Lies and truth are both subliminal and obvious, that is why it's difficult to tell them apart. A government will never press on you with truth! When someone is trying to force you to accept something, distance yourself, and ask for more proof, or to see all sides of the story. They will either change behaviour and become aggressive, or they will leave. Someone bearing the truth will only tell you to ask them whatever you want to know; they would never try to press on you. Truth wants you to choose *it*. It sometimes can float around some chosen people more, but that is just because they have higher chances of being corrupted, or being able to change if choosing *it*. Remember that this life has been offered to you as an incredible gift, for which you do not owe anything to another human being or corrupt entity, except your parents. You should be free to choose your own destiny at any moment. At the beginning of human kind there were no money or debt. It was just a cooperation for the benefit of each individual. You are not being told this, but *utopia* existed on this planet.

Long story short, not all doctors are good, and applauding for the NHS is cheering for the bad doctors too. For the ones that cover up everything about the lie that the Wuhan virus pandemic is. Their careers are suppressed, no doubt about it, but considering that more people will die from these plans to change the world, it makes them accomplices. An NHS promoting crooked and dangerous science, and covering up lies does not deserve applause. Do you have any idea how many doctors I've spoken to, that didn't have any idea about how the PCR method works? Some biologists doing actual testing too. But they were determined to make me believe that it is the right method to use! When seeing that I know a lot about it, they were turning more tempered. Doctors are there to save lives without waiting for gratification. No one forced them to do it, it's their passion. This does not mean that they can do whatever they want. It's also true that most people don't deserve the truth, but the ones that deserve it should not be the martyrs of the naive and oblivious. Doctors have an obligation to promote true science and the truth with the price of their careers, because they are protected by the nature of their activity. If all would speak the truth, no one would get fired for going against the corrupt government. Governments should never have any control of the scientific world. Obviously, spreading life threats can go a long way. Keep this in your mind forever: people can only cover up in such a big way, due to threats from someone really powerful having to gain from it.

Question for you: if you'd know who the head of the *Triades* is, would you run to the police to tell on them?

In March 2021, they're telling vaccinated people that they should still keep distance from each other. Pardon? But, isn't the vaccine protecting everyone? If chickens in farms are being vaccinated, and then the birds are left to wonder and mingle at any distance, why isn't this working with humans too? There is absolutely no difference.

The difference between us

I have a theory of my own that goes like this: we cannot be that different, something big is polarising us. Someone has to be right. Are you voting down a president because you've heard only bad things about him? You might be wrong. Are you in favour of voting altogether? You're definitely wrong! The only situation when the minority has absolutely no say is after the voting ends. Other than that, minorities are shaping the world around us every day, at the expense of the majority. Is reading the news 100% of your informational source? You are 100% wrong. Do you think all scientists are good? Think again. Are you doing your own research about any topic pushed towards you? You are on the right path. We keep on hearing about the third eye. What is it? Why don't we all have it? It's not that you don't have it, you have to find yours. It will be millions of times more difficult to find it, if you don't care about what you eat! We live in the age of information. The whole world is at our fingertip. We are so damn polarised because some of us are not doing any research, nor the right research. Most people don't even ask for help. *"Dude, what am I doing wrong? Where did you get this information from?"* What we have in the spoon is supposed to be good for us, right? Wrong! You always have to know what's in your bowl. If even mothers are killing their own babies, what makes you think that someone outside your bloodline wants what's best for you? You think we're safe, I think we're not. Who is right, and who is wrong? For each side, the other is in the wrong. And we fight against each other like blind people. Except one is not blind, just trapped with you in the same toxic bubble. For one it means double exposure because the other is oblivious to his environment, and keen to keep it that way. When I was working in the border force, I kept on fighting for a better life and justice next to my brother. We wanted everyone to have a better career and life. We were as altruistic as a human could be, with selfishness as seed. Yes, I want to live a good life. But because many had families and huge debt, they were the first ones to try and take us down, long before confronting the higher levels of authority. We were there, fighting the blind more than the common enemy. When things changed to worse, we weren't the ones turning grey and diabetic overnight. We left with an amazing sadness in our hearts, and more polarised than ever. Who was right? Who was wrong? People that agree with the government, the current measures taken, and that the pandemic is real are falling in a category that has stood against real progress for millennia. They willingly refuse to learn how the economy works, how viruses work, how governments work, and maybe the most important thing out of all, they have no clue about how democracy works. They also don't understand that we have never lived in a real democracy. As the founders of communism said a long time ago, be afraid of capitalist communism. This is what we have been living for the last more than half a century. Personally I think it's time for you to pray, and think that there might be a God and a devil, because the ones at the opposite end, controlling every aspect of your life, would not have this much power over the world. I mean, why don't you have this much power? After all, we're all humans, right? And if you could have all this power, how'd you get it, and from where? Doesn't this make you think a bit deeper and farther? Where do you come from, and why are some so evil? How can a human be so evil to not care about a baby in suffering? What is destroying this planet is not too many humans, it's the way we've been taught to do business, and businesses in general. If everything would be on demand only with a precise system to control the human abuse of anything, reason for sickness, we would be able to overpopulate this world and universe in a sustainable manner. For this we need to sever population control with artificial means, we need *Aurora Utopialis* to watch over our wellbeing, health, intelligence, and thriving. Only a doctrine free environment would promote the perfect enlightenment of the human being. Not having to obey or work is paramount to achieving perfect health. In exchange this will lead to elevated levels of consciousness, and would ultimately nurture our success into achieving our sacred potential before death. Nowadays humans die too early, being as far as possible from achieving full potential. With every generation the gap widens, and it's intentional.

Miscellaneous

One day around mid 2020, I had this rider in my car, a *Dacian* (Romanian) nurse from a hospital in London. She wanted to talk about the whole situation. Without giving any preliminary reason, she started praising the ventilators. I asked her to explain why they're so good, but yet there are so many people dying. She said that if you have underlying conditions, a ventilator will help you breathe. I firmly think that, considering the symptoms of the new coronavirus, a ventilator will increase the chances of you dying. Your lungs are extremely dry, and ventilation is the last thing you need. Hydration is paramount. She couldn't explain properly why the ventilator is so good, and went on to say that she had the new virus too, and that she's asthmatic. I caught my chance to ask if she's been on a ventilator. "No, I wasn't, I took antibiotics and steroids. I could've died if I didn't take any medicine." Despite her struggling to breathe because of her underlying condition, she was never on a ventilator, nor did she receive the experimental *Remdesivir*, which has severe side effects, ranging all the way to the possibility of causing heart failure. They used to put people on ventilators without any proven medication and proper hydration... Many hospitals still do, and they don't even know if it's the new virus, or the flu; the delay might be too late for the patient! I've spoken with so many hypocrite doctors and nurses that my brain is exhausted. I am disgusted by what is happening with medicine. Cancer surgeons in my country have told us that what we eat, and the chemicals in our food are causing most of our diseases, while in the USA, qualified biologists are promoting GMOs, additives, and untested vaccines that are being produced and pumped into the population overnight. The only way to understand is to do your own research. Life experience is a big ace you should have in your sleeve.

Despite growing up in the city, I've had the joy of spending winters and summers in our farm too. It had been a blessing every child should experience. Some winters were harsh, with temperatures as low as -20°C - -25°C. I've seen the village covered by mountains of snow. When that happened no one was interacting with other families, maybe for a couple of weeks. Even so, I was coming down with a bad cold, and even the flu. We were completely isolated, but still falling ill with coronaviruses and influenza. Because of this experience, I know for sure that completely isolating humans from one another, will never lower the cases of coronaviruses. These can be carried by the wind, they can stay frozen in the ice, and wild animals can pass them on. The only ways are a healthy lifestyle, IgG medication for the vulnerable with low immunity, herd immunity for the healthy, and good doctors applying the right medicine.

There was something strange that happened at the beginning of the pandemic. At one point a minister, scientist, or the PM of the UK had urged us to close the windows, and stay inside because the coronavirus was running on the streets to get us. The next morning, I saw all the cars in my borough covered in a thin layer of white powder. I had to take the car to the car wash straight away. It didn't rain, nor snow that night in March. A few days later I found out from riders, that in the night they heard helicopters flying high above the city for ages. That's an unresolved mystery, but they did talk about spraying something in the air to destroy the potential viral particles. After that a lot of people turned brainwashed, and have started to panic, and conform blindly to rules that will only kill a lot of healthy innocent people, and will destroy all our lives. I envy naive people for being oblivious, they live in a beautiful world.

They're using this *unexpected crisis* to push The Great Reset towards us, whether we like it or not. The only way to know if these officials want to hurt you is to check if they're supporting a money based future, which they do. They want to create a world currency. As long as money is among us, we cannot live utopia, a happy life. It's impossible! Happiness for all is not possible as long as we have rich and poor.

As long as we cannot protect our children from being kidnapped for organ and blood transplants, soldiers, experiments and sex, we are a failed society. Wearing a mask to protect others when you don't care about our children, only shows the hypocrisy of your existence. You put the mask on to protect yourself, not others, but actually you're not protecting anyone. You don't care about me! If I'd suddenly start to cough on the street feeling weak, and then I would collapse, would you help me, or would you kick me in the head with your boot for not staying at home, as per Government's guidance? Now you're throwing menacing looks towards ill people, more that towards healthy people that are playing you. When it comes to me, I only care about my family. How can I care about everybody else? Why would I put this amazing pressure on my shoulders, when life is a struggle? I want everybody to be well, but I cannot think of your wellbeing! I'd go crazy, and live a life of depression. I don't want to stay away from you if I'm healthy (asymptomatic), and I'm interested in you. I want to socialise with you as normal, without a mask. We're all wearing invisible masks anyway... I'm not a close-talker, but just imagine how depressed and frustrated they might feel with these restrictions (chuckles). How can I kill you if I'm ok? Why would I care that a smoker is vulnerable if getting sick with Wuhan *spice*? He never cares about intoxicating me in the bus stop! Why would I care about you, when doctors don't care about you? Shouldn't you accuse doctors and politicians of not caring about you first? They're imprisoning you from all directions, and you accuse me for not caring about the others? You don't care about what you eat, and you care about getting a coronavirus? You hypocrite! I'm healthy, I do not care about you! I'm sick, I'll try to stay away until I'm healed. When going out again, I will not self-distance from the people that are kind, smart, good looking, and successful. There is a real pandemic of *idiocracy* (you should watch the movie). I cannot care about everyone because I am not God. I want to live my life, and maybe change the world for the better.

One of the biggest shocks during the *pandemic* was to see on St John's Ambulances's website the new resuscitation procedures. They are recommending to cover the patient's nose and mouth with a wet cloth, then perform only chest presses on the rhythm of *Bee Gees - Stayn' Alive*! I think 2020 has revealed that a staggering number of people in power positions, and life-saving professions have serious mental illnesses. I am a trained first aider, and by all standards, that means killing the person. Imagine yourself fainting, and because you might have a coronavirus, the paramedic is covering your mouth and nose as in torture practices, further limiting your access to oxygen. Can you imagine this? Paramedics being so afraid of this virus (against their job description that involves risking their own lives to save you), that they will actually kill you intentionally. When you resuscitate someone, you need to press the chest to stimulate the heart, and blow air/oxygen into the patient's lungs. Resuscitation is highly unlikely to succeed if you're not doing both. So, in 2020 they made murder legal! You're being told to think of others, but when it comes to resuscitation, to think about yourself more is the pure definition of selfishness. We are currently rewriting the definition of *hero*. The following photo is a screenshot taken from their website.

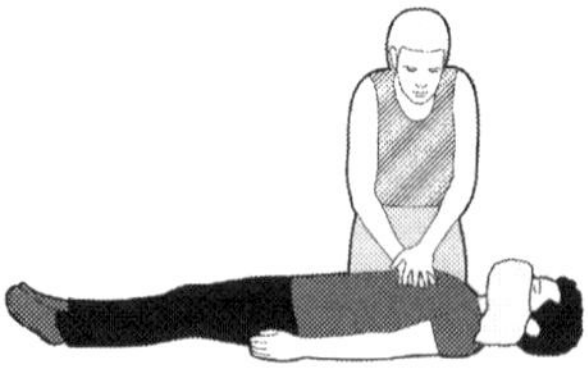

You cannot protect your national health service by staying at home. This is a paradox. It's impossible! Healthcare is only supported by a normal flourishing economy, and this means you going out and about as normal, without restrictions, and spending constantly. The health service is supported by constant and increasing contributions to the public budget. The health service is expanding in the same direction as the economy. By paying the wages from the treasury you're definitely killing all freedoms, and any hopes for decent living standards. If the health service did not blow up during 2020, there was never a pandemic. They're stretched to the limit every year as it is. This is due to insufficient funding, and poor resource management. Governments do not want a fully working health service, nor the Big Pharma. They all feed on the current situation. You don't need extensive economics knowledge to understand this.

During the last year they've been talking about forcing network operators to give your mobile phone's location to the police, in order to know if you're following lockdown rules. What privacy? Now you're a terrorist that has to be kept under surveillance. How many of you know, that phone networks are storing all your conversations and messages for at least six months? They've been doing it for years now but you didn't know, did you? Tyranny at its best, and it's coming back with force. Life as we know it was cancelled overnight for malicious purposes. A British person trained as a political philosopher asked me recently, if it's true that Eastern Europeans can see through what is happening with the UK right now, compared with the British people that have never seen communism. I have never been happier to answer a question before. The fact that it was an honest *yes* instantly saddened both of us, after realising what it actually means. She told me that after the installation of communism, it takes about 400 years for a civilisation to see the light at the end of the tunnel again. Asking something like this in 2021 is terrible, and reliving a very dark experience in human history is a fucking nightmare. If this succeeds, it will be the end of human kind as we know it. There will be no turning back from it, and utopia will definitely become an impossible dream. Why am I thinking this? Because technology will make limiting freedom, health, human natural expression, and access to information perfect. There will be no light at the end of the tunnel, there will not be a light to reach towards. How can you see the light, if you grew up not knowing about its existence?

How can you trust a doctor recommending you to take a vaccine, no matter where it comes from, how it was made, or the technology used. There is never a bad vaccine, not even the rushed ones. Doctors will endorse them, even if it might cost their career. This is a clue that they are being controlled, owned and threatened. They cannot go against Big Pharma. Doctors have forgotten why they are doctors. They can make mistakes, but they are not allowed to make mistakes. It's not in their professional rights. This is why they study for 30 years or more, to eliminate the risk of error. You cannot be forced to become a doctor. Nowadays, the patient is no longer at the centre of their activity. Recently I've been told by my GP that the PCR is an accurate test, because the scientists and the government told her so. When I told her that you need to do further sequencing after the positive result, she stuttered, and couldn't add much to the conversation. As a doctor you are not allowed to lie, nor to make mistakes. It's human to be wrong and make mistakes, but when it's intentional you're no different than a terrorist. When you see injustice and lies in your field of work, it is your duty as human to take action against it. I'm not saying that I'm perfect or a good person, on the contrary, sometimes I think I'm a really bad human being, as I could do way more to help myself and other humans, but when I saw how the police force I was part of was applying the law only against poor people, and protecting the real criminals, and the corruption in the system, I tried to fix it from the inside. I realised I couldn't, so I left the force. I could not take it anymore, while the hotshots were laughing at me knowing that I couldn't touch them. This is real change, taking action against injustice, in any field of activity. Doctors have a huge responsibility, to fix the broken healthcare. The complacent and scared ones should change their careers, because there are accomplices to premeditated murder, and even murderers in the current context. The pathologists that have put *Covid-19* on most death certificates from the beginning of 2020 owe some explaining to the relatives of the deceased, and in a court of law. Same with the ones that gave questionable care to *Covid-19* presumed patients.

Stop thinking that there will come a day when we'll all be so united, that the establishment will crumble at our defiance. It will never happen, not when we're so far apart and destabilised. The powers working behind are too big for us to even try to get together in unison. The system has infiltrated agents in all aspects of life. They are the seeds of discord. The policeman in your family is a pawn, and he will never disobey. Your neighbour thinks that by going out you're threatening his life, despite having no clue about how viruses work, or how life works. The differences that keep us together and entertained are separating us in times of discord planted systematically, and by people close to you that have no actual records, or multiple passports. If you think this is just conspiracy please close this book, and go to sleep. You don't know what conspiracy means. Keep dreaming to a green pasture, with delicious grass perfect for grazing. If you believe this is true, just build your strength, and start looking into history. These people I'm talking about are everywhere around you. Don't start panicking, and see all people as enemies, you won't be able to distinguish them. Just act natural, interact natural, but keep this in mind when trying to read someone. Probably nowadays the best way to spot them is when they call you a conspiracy theorist, or they have no online presence. They are like crooked bricks in a buildings walls. Some might have such a flourishing career, that it's almost impossible that they've achieved so much in such a short time. It's not easy to spot them, therefore it's not worth the panic, or getting obsessed with this. It's just for informational purposes, from a former police officer to you. The truth will come to you, just relax your mind enough to connect to the universe. Life is kind with good people.

If no one would've told you that there is a new virus running around, would you have known that there is a pandemic? Who told you there is a pandemic? Did anyone tell you during previous years, that about 10,000 people die each year of influenza in England & Wales alone? How does this compare to a total of 13,911 of confirmed *Covid-19* cases in 2020, with the majority of patients surviving the virus?

Does this seem right to you? You can check all these numbers yourself, from the NHS and Public Health England websites. Throughout this crisis they've put it in front of your eyes the following: *deaths within 28 days of testing positive to Covid-19*, with the irrelevant PCR test. You are the one refusing to see it.

Why would they do this to us? I feel like giving one answer to this idiotic question 99% of the naives are asking. The more jobs are being taken over by robots, the more useless people doing nothing to feed. Healthcare should never be private, Big Pharma should never be private. Medicine should only be on demand. Why do we need full shelves of ibuprofen, that pharmacies HAVE to sell? No matter how you imagine the future under the current settlement, the Big Pharma is winning. They own most big food companies anyway. 2020 is proof that someone out there wants to kill you fast. You'll say, "*yeah but they want to make money, it doesn't make any sense*". You have to understand that the main purpose is not money. Monetary compensation is there to destroy your nature, and ultimately you. It's easy to print more money, they already have all the money they want. No one can start killing millions with the AK47 anymore. They're doing it systematically, by investing in strategic depopulation. If they're not trying to kill us, it means that all these politicians and rich fellows are angels. Winged saviours that cover up paedophilic activities, among many others. In more recent news, paedophilic behaviour might be recognised as a sexual orientation by law! Did anyone ever tell you how many people have died because of lockdowns that lasted for more than a year, and counting? I'll tell you: way more than from the actual *Covid-19*, cumulated with the murders in the hospitals by applying the wrong procedures, giving the wrong medicine, or refusing emergency treatment.

My brother told me the story of one of his riders, who tested positive three times in a month, and had to self-isolate each time without pay. She had to test for work, and is now looking for ways to go against the UK Government for explanations and compensation. This should be enough proof to anyone about the uselessness of testing. Everyone should sue the government, and block the judicial system. It would cost so much money, and so many important officials would get prison, that they would have to back down with The Great Reset. Real power is always in your hands. Just imagine starting millions of lawsuits against Big Pharma and the government, in one country alone!

In early 2021 parents started receiving letters, advising them to vaccinate their children against the new coronavirus. Does this seem right to you, wanting to use an experimental drug on children, the healthiest human beings? In March 2021 they started testing the mRNA vaccines on children aged six months to 12 years. Who's providing all these children, and why aren't they accused of bad parenting? Never forget that these vaccines have been accelerated, meaning approved without extensive testing, on top of them being deemed highly dangerous less than a year before. Some of you will say, *"yeah, but now they invested massively into this technology..."*. Yes, but who invested, and with what purpose? The technology is still dangerous for humans, and the vaccine irrelevant, because it will not protect anyone with weak or good immunity. Plus, the real numbers of *Covid-19* are marginal, compared with the numbers of previous coronaviruses or influenza. This might just be the coronavirus with the lowest mortality rate. The numbers are there for you to check. There's an old saying that goes like this: *why rub a leg if you don't feel pain*?

Even in the official statistics about testing, in small print of course, there is a reference saying that some have tested multiple times. I have reports from doctors and nurses that are turning people away, because they've tested for too many times. We live in a mad, mad world! Why would you get tested, even if you have a cold? What would be the purpose of you wanting to stay in a lockdown, giving politicians reasons to enforce new *illegal* laws (yes, law can be illegal!), and destroying life as we know it? This is what you do when you test, it's called self-destruction. If no one would test, we'd go back to normal, or at least they'd find it difficult to implement the new world order. Why make it easy for them, if you don't want it to happen? In the new world they are imagining for us, your life will matter way less than now.

There are many tools normal people could use to get more freedom. I know I'm repeating myself, but have you ever asked yourself why you always have to fight for basic rights? The way to cripple a business, a billionaire, or a government is to SUE. The action needs to be taken before the implementation of tyranny though. Look at China, the moment a billionaire says something against the party, he's being isolated, and put into re-education programmes. In a free and fair justice system, you have the right to take legal action against anyone that is playing with your life without letting you have a say. But everyone has to target the same entity until blocking the justice system. If you'd organise yourselves in small groups of 50 or 100 (for financial ease), and start millions of lawsuits against Bill Gates, for example, he'd be bankrupt in less than a month, maybe earlier than a week. This is because he would have to pay thousands of lawyers to tackle each individual lawsuit. Imagine the financial strain on him. This is the same if the government is turning on you. With a sheer number of lawsuits having the same contentious object, the situation would become a priority for magistrates. They would have to tackle the problem, and stop the government's actions until reaching a verdict in all legal actions. A common and fatal mistake people do, is organising themselves in one compact group, and start one lawsuit (this is the purpose of unions). This is a BIG MISTAKE! The defendant, be it a billionaire or a government, will crush the group's legal action with the outmost ease. Separate actions and outrageous number of lawsuits will crush giants in a matter of weeks. Also, try to keep the lawsuits going for as long as possible by adding slightly different claims to each action. In case a corrupt judge gives a decision against you in record time, the other judges cannot use it as precedent, as the claims were somewhat different, and need separate judgements. This is a vast subject to describe here, but it should be enough law education for now. You're welcome!

If you're planning to go abroad in 2021 you have to take about six or ten PCR tests, and pay for ten days of self-isolation in a secured hotel. This accounts to about £5,000-£6,000 on top of your holiday funds, per couple. The rich, politicians, and high profile people, or of *interest* for *the economy* are exempt from self-isolation and testing. Isn't this perfect, and what they wanted all along? Imagine them going to a beach resort that would otherwise be packed with tourists, and how they would feel. *"Ahhhh, this is all mine, ahhh, it feels so good without the cohorts of noisy bastards taking too much space..."* All while you're being detained in your country, on a planet that should be yours to explore unrestricted. No human should have the power to decide the freedoms of another decent human being.

There are countries that have never had problems with the new virus. It's not that they didn't have it, but that they reported the cases after properly sequencing the results, and not treating asymptomatic people as a threat to other people. If you're asymptomatic you cannot be a threat. How can you say that the strong immune system of a person is killing other people. You have to be mad to promote such an aberration! In June 2020 I was supposed to travel to St Lucia for my mother's 65th, but our plans have been heavily disturbed. That island had only 15 cases, and probably none was actually the new coronavirus. Many African and Arab countries had no issues with it, probably this would have been the last on their list of issues. China stopped having positives way before 2021, and they didn't even need a vaccine! They stopped reporting it as the Wuhan coronavirus, and naming influenza as influenza.

At the beginning of the *pandemic*, young riders in their early twenties were telling me that they were so afraid of the new virus, that they were certain they would die if they got the new coronavirus. I had to comfort them with explanations that made sense on the spot. "If you are healthy you've got nothing to worry about." We have new coronaviruses every year, with millions of strains, some stronger than others. Influenza is the same. Bring a questionable testing campaign into the equation, and you have a deadly pandemic, in the context of an already stretched health service. The poor management of health in general is supporting the pandemic at any moment in time.

Belgravia, London, the epicentre of high class escort industry, was never in a pandemic. How do I know? I know... The service never stopped throughout 2020. Also ask the politicians in Westminster. Want to know if there is a pandemic? Ask the escorts, and you'll probably get a discount. Underground industries don't care about any coronavirus. Life is to be enjoyed, not restricted because some people are dying. Politicians have killed people that stood in the way of governance. Someone show me proof that they care about each individual life affected by any virus.

Why would you go out, shouting loudly that you've got coronavirus? *"I got tested and it's positive! Woohoo!"* Do you tell people in the club that you've got the herpes simplex virus, or that your latest cervix swab showed HPV? A lot of people have HIV, but I don't see them running around spreading flyers with the news...

This is a big one. After a few months following our move to London, working in the warehouse unloading containers for eight hours straight, and earning about £250 an hour would not cut it. We needed more money. The idea of donating blood came to our minds. I mean, we're strong men, why not. We went to the centre, and a nurse received us. "Oh, you want to donate blood? Just complete these forms, and then follow me." "So, how much are we getting for the donation?" "Pardon?" "How much money is a donation?" "Oh, we don't pay for donations. We can serve you a hot tea and biscuits..." Wow! Donating half a litre of rare blood, and not getting anything for it, besides an awful tasting English tea and biscuits... What a system! How come a country like *Dacia* (Romania) can pay donors money, food vouchers (of course a lot of people used to buy condoms and booze with them, but that's not the point), and a day off work, and a country like the UK, with all the money in the world, one of the biggest financial hubs on the planet, cannot afford to pay for blood or plasma donations. Unbelievable! Do you know that hospitals are getting heavy money for your blood? After each surgery, there is a bill for which the insurance is paying. There's a whole intricate system in the middle, and on the other side your blood is producing money you'll never get a share of. But you're saving a life. And you still have to go to work weakened from the loss of iron. Blood is a precious liquid that's worth more than gold, especially if you have a rare blood type. We cared a lot about ours, so we left the clinic laughing. They keep on telling you that you're saving a life. You don't care about others if you're not donating, but who's actually not caring? You, the donor, taking the shock of donating, or the system that does not want to pay for your blood, although they're bathing in money? And then, maybe your blood is going to a politician who paid more to get in front of the waiting list, leaving kind people and children to die. In 2021 they're calling men that recently had *Covid-19* to donate plasma, for free, while they sell it on the other side. Fuck off, you greedy pricks! Pay the donors!

One day I had this idiot in the car who said that, "I'd prefer to take a vaccine that is free, than pay £200 or more to have a PCR test!". I instantly felt sorry for the guy. Indirectly he gave himself the answer to this whole campaign, and to what the hidden purpose is. If stupidity hurt, many would suffer. I felt like sharing this with you.

Doctors are not debating the necessity, or the risks of a vaccine anymore. No one is allowed to do it. This is called distraction from the main subject, and promoting harm as benefit. If you take the vaccine, and your body starts acting up, you have no right to say you were wrong, and that you are sorry. You deserve it! With so much information around you, you're not supposed to cave in to governmental pressure. The right to stand up to oppression is a God given right.

The MHRA are not better than the FDA. When I was a lab technician in BPL, and the FDA were coming, everyone was shaking. When it was the MHRA all was relaxed. "Those fuckers from the FDA, we hate them!", the managers would complain. The FDA is scrutinising more, and they have a longer, better history compared with the MHRA. The latter came about later, through a merger that included the first British regulatory body, founded in 1972. In 1960 there was a big incident with *thalidomide*, used as medicine given to pregnant women for nausea. The chief reviewer of the FDA at the time did not cave in to pressures from the pharmaceutical companies to approve it in the US, based on insufficient testing, whilst there were suspicions that a high number of babies were being born with deformities or missing limbs, in parts of western Europe and the UK, where *thalidomide* was used. After avoiding a tragedy, she became a national hero, and had been awarded the President's Award for Distinguished Federal Civilian Service by John F. Kennedy. Her name was Frances Oldham Kelsey, She retired from the FDA at 90, in 2015. The UK had their first regulatory body for medicines 12 years later. In 2021 none are worth a penny, because they're approving anything the government is pushing through, together with the Big Pharma. Actually, the latter have their own people in high positions in the regulatory body. How can you approve a vaccine using a dangerous technology as an emergency (bypassing important safety procedures they should uphold no matter the pressures), to combat a low mortality virus.

As the *pandemic* developed, I had loads of reports from riders that, when they called the ambulance, they arrived in record time, saying, "You're lucky we were in the area." I've heard that before, when my mother got sick. This is such an overwhelming pandemic, that the ambulance comes to patients in record time. It can take them over an hour in normal times. During 2020 there were reports about ambulance staff being told to drive with the sirens ON, to create the feeling of constant emergency. I have spoken with paramedics myself, and at least in London area, they've been told to act like that. Even if they didn't have a patient in the vehicle, or they weren't heading towards a case, the sirens had to be used as much as possible. Some people went to the extent of chasing ambulances towards the hospitals in order to see if they really had an emergency, and they had no one inside. At destination the paramedics were chilling. I've been mostly around hospitals during this *pandemic*, and have never seen panic among people or medical staff. Whenever you ask someone to prove to you that there is a pandemic, you will get answers as, *"what about all the people dying?"*, *"but the numbers are really high!"*, *"the hospitals are out of beds!"*, *"what about the doctors struggling to contain it?"*, *"so, you think doctors are lying?!"*, *"I know someone that died of the new coronavirus, he/she tested positive!"*, *"but I tested positive!"*. None of these answers have a scientific base, or have actually been tested by the ones advancing them. These are the naive dumb folk that will beat you with experience. Before finishing this paragraph, I had a rider in the car who works in a hospital in London as nurse. On her own volition, she told me that the situation in the hospital is even more relaxed than normal years. She had a cold recently, and of course the result was positive, so she had to self-isolate. Later she had an antibodies test, and the result came back negative. She was expressing her confusion about the whole situation. Doctors know about all these errors, and they should be held responsible for playing the government's game. AS A DOCTOR YOU ARE NOT ALLOWED TO MAKE MISTAKES, LIE OR COVER THE TRUTH!

If you look at the shady reports about the side effects during the vaccine trials, when a volunteer died after taking it, he/she died of anything else, but not from the side effects. Remember that they used healthy people during trials. In opposition, when people with severe underlying conditions die in the hospitals, it's *Covid-19*. I had another report from a rider recently that an acquaintance of hers died of cancer at home. When taken to the hospital they performed a *Covid-19* test on the body, and she tested positive. The pathologist has put on the death certificate *Covid-19*...

Why would you force a dangerous vaccine on an elderly person? They have a few years left, and now many of them died straight after. Because the UK reported a spike in deaths in care homes, straight after vaccinating over 95% of elders. Poor people, having their lives cut short, while trying to make it longer. The authorities gave them no dignity. I love it when normal people, with no medical knowledge whatsoever, are telling me how the vaccine works after they read a news article online. They don't know how their own immunity works, but they know everything about how the vaccine was made, and what it does. *"But you can get it again!"* is a highly overrated, and extensively propagated statement among the uneducated cohorts.

Another tremendous lie coming from doctors and scientist is that *Covid-19* antibodies don't last as long as for other viruses. In conclusion, every statement has to persuade people into accepting the vaccine. There's no way around it. The lifespan of developed antibodies is the same as for any other antibodies, and even more than this, you might never lose your immunity (antibodies) for this virus if you live as normal. This is due to the fact that you will always come into contact with it in nature, or one of its millions of strains. Considering the low number of cases in the NOIDs, you might never contract the virus if you're lucky, who knows. Your naturally acquired immunity can last for years on end. And yes, you can get it again, but not for at least one year, and only if you self-isolate from the world completely (this will actually make you vulnerable to all viruses in the air). You will never come out stronger from complete self-isolation, on the contrary. This is why lockdowns should be illegal.

At the beginning of the first lockdown I was talking to this rider that made no sense. We reached the subject of the rich entrepreneurs that took control of the world's health, and how they are systematically working on depopulation. Some of them are quite open about it. What he said made me rethink humanity's chances of survival. "Yeah, but you know, we are too many on the planet anyway. Someone has to do something..." This guy was legitimating systematic slaughter. So you're being pushed to live your life in a reckless way, consuming resources that you don't need, and then the same people and businesses are scolding you for destroying the planet. I asked the rider, "what if you're the next one that has to go?". Of course he didn't give me any answer. I'll say it again, this planet cannot be overpopulated. What is destroying the world is this constant fight with governments that should not exist, and with the rich who want to stay rich without sharing. We have the technology to make each individual completely independent and free. We should implement the decentralisation of everything. As long as the governments are not implementing this together with the demilitarisation of all nations, they are killers with a plan.

At the end of this situation, the health services will have a massive problem with staff and skill. Teaching and practice have been put on hold, cumulated with huge redundancies in hospitals spells disaster. The outrageous costs with the useless extra PPE should've crippled the NHS by now. In a real pandemic the PPE would've been free and aseptic for everyone. It's being kept on artificial support if you ask me, and no one is thinking of modernising anything anymore.

There are many strange things about this pandemic, but this particular one is the most peculiar by far. SARS-cov-19 is patented! You cannot patent naturally occurring pathogens. There are two situations resulting from this, and they should immediately be investigated and prosecuted. Number one: the virus was made in a lab, therefore it can be owned by the manufacturer and patented under Intellectual Property Law. Number two: if it was made in a lab, all international laws regarding bio weapons have been broken. This is why they are creating GMO everything. You cannot patent a tomato, but you can patent the gene that you can add to the tomato to make it resilient to pests and chemicals.

Where is all this money for testing and retesting coming from, and why is the Government pumping it into useless tests? Why didn't they invest in research to see how long the immunity lasts? Did you know that the UK has bought massive quantities of testing supplies in 2018-2019? They know that the tests are flawed, but they force you to take it, and also pay for it with money you don't have. Even if you think the test is free, oh, you will pay it back tenfold, don't worry. All this money pumping will NEVER get paid back. It will lead to an infinite debt, stretched to probably over 100 generations into the future. We are being tagged with a massive debt before we are even born and after we die. Isn't life on Earth beautiful?

A unique existential problem we are currently facing is not being able to see the truth, even if it's in front of you. You're being lied to by society, and when the liars switch and actually tell you the truth, you're ready to go to war with them for lying to you. Trusting people with power, and whom you don't know, without doing your own research means that you're already dead. Happy sleeping, everyone!

I have a prediction for 2030: you'll have zero liberties, and everyone will know what you feel and think, before you think or feel it. The more we stay in lockdowns, the more vulnerable we'll become, and most people will get the flu and coronaviruses. They'll test us all to legitimate lockdowns again, and we'll live like this, in a perpetual horror movie dictated by obscure entities, until we lose the percentage of population they want, roughly half of what we are now. And all in legal ways, motivating a pandemic that never existed.

A good percentage of my riders are doctors. Most of them don't really like to talk, but the next one I'm going to tell you about, beat all my expectations of stupidity in an educated person. We were talking about the pandemic, and she was promoting tighter restrictions because the number of cases was outrageous. I started telling her that the PCR is useless without further sequencing, that testing for RNA is useless and irrelevant, that asymptomatic people are no threat to anyone, and that if the testing would be done properly we wouldn't have so many cases. She didn't know anything about the PCR, as she said it's a good way to test for a virus. Her knowledge about the method was zero. Then I asked her what she thought about the flu cases dropping 94%. In her answer, she was motivating the use of hand sanitisers and wearing masks. "Then why isn't it working with this new virus? We're all in lockdown, and the cases are going only up." "You know, it's because they lifted the lockdown, and then reinstated it again..." "Really? Aren't the two viruses spreading the same?" "No, this one is way more contagious!

But it requires a high viral load to get someone infected." (this means actual symptoms - inflammation). There is absolutely no proof that this virus is more contagious compared to other viruses (the NOIDs are confirming this). What's different is its novelty. At the time I didn't know about the weekly Notifications of Infectious Diseases posted on the Government's website, to be able to hit her in the face with the real numbers. She kept on blurbing about the efficacy of the vaccine (again she didn't know much about mRNA), and that you can get it again, which doesn't make any sense to why it's a pandemic. You can get any virus again and again, and you will, but building immunity after the first time keeps you in the clear almost your entire life, until the virus mutates so much that it becomes a totally new virus. Even so, when she saw that I knew a lot about the virus and the PCR she went, "you know, I'm a scientist at heart...". Yes, a poor hypocrite scientist, applying and supporting a science that's killing people, and destroying our already frail society. If you're a scientist with a PhD, then I'm a better scientist without a diploma; I've seen what's in our blood, what keeps us alive and well.

If you take all doctors, and put them in a pyramid based on competence, you'll see that the bottom is way thicker than the top. If you trust so much in a title acquired through honest study and real science, it means that all doctors are good. Then, who is at the bottom of the class? They're PhDs too. 2020 is proof that the bottom of the class is way thicker than the thickest you can imagine. If a doctor can be told what to say and do, what is medicine anymore? What and where is real science? Who owns it, and for what purpose? Stop being so gullible, and think for yourself. Teach your children to do the same, don't let them educated by society. This is what an Orwellian society will try to do. Today, science is in an induced coma.

I'm pretty sure that everyone knows someone that takes the flu jab every year despite being overall healthy. *"Oh, of course I'm having the jab, I don't want to get the flu!"* You don't need to be a scientist to figure out that RNA vaccines are stimulating a weak immunity. They also contain excipients that are not good for the body, chemicals that go into the brain, as well as in the organs and glands that produce antibodies. Plus, the vaccine contains a weak version of the real virus, and you can still catch the flu. Your immunity is matching the potency of the infection. Every year you have to take the jab, and also one for the new coronavirus. Flu vaccine in spring and autumn, and three mRNA ones for the new coronavirus per year, maybe a vaccine for hepatitis B once a year, and if you work in specialised industries, you might be asked to have another three or four extra vaccines (RNA or IgG - ie Tetanus, Rabies). In 2020 flu apparently dropped 94%. Right! I think one of the purposes might be to replace the seasonal flu jab with mRNA vaccines altogether. They will replace a fairly *safe* vaccine with a highly dangerous one, motivating that the latter gives protection for seasonal flu as well. Don't you think that this is the pattern of Bill Gates? The same with that awful software that needs to be destroyed, Windows. You need antivirus software, because the moment you go online your system gets all the viruses lurking in the background. Now he's creating viruses in private labs, and then he gives you the solution in which he's a massive investor, the mRNA vaccine, a technology invented with the purpose of creating rRNA. He's also a master of GMO, foods that severely alter your immune response. Powerful immunity results from good, nourishing, natural food. Can you not see all these patterns?

One day I spoke with a rider that works as a nurse. She told me that she is attending patients with weak immunity, and part of the medicines they use is *Gammaplex*, one of the IgG vaccines I used to work on in Bio Products Laboratory. I felt an amazing joy to actually meet someone administering it to patients. She was also praising it for being really good. What surprised me was that she didn't know what antibodies were, and how they work. "It's amazing how these cells in the vaccine are making the patients feel really good!" The antibodies are specialised proteins. She was a lovely person otherwise, but how can you applaud an NHS that, in its majority, is covering up a fake pandemic, and which is highly unskilled. How can you give someone treatment, and not know what the treatment is, or how it works? Outrageous! Applauding for the NHS and the mask are large scale submission tests.

With 60,000 positive tests a day, the UK should have achieved herd immunity in a few months. To get that many positives they had to test millions a week, which is physically impossible to do. And herd immunity means that a vaccine is not required. This testing campaign is one of the biggest lies in human history. I bet that they will make the truth a state secret, so that no one can access the real files in a court of law. They will probably tell us that the truth will be revealed in 100 years time. I hope I'm wrong, but I've seen it done in my own country.

Another good point pressed by my brother is this: the same scientists that are scaring everyone with outrageous numbers, have said that this new virus apparently created an immune boost against the virus itself, and the common flu. In this intellectual context, why are they pushing ahead with the vaccine, if strong natural immunity has been achieved in over 90% of the population? As I am writing these lines, after checking the NOID for week five of 2021, I could see that there were zero *Covid-19* cases in London. There were no cases in any hospital in Greater London area, while people are being murdered by illegal stricter lockdowns.

While I was waiting to pick up a rider from this London hospital, I couldn't help noticing how ugly that hospital looks. Yes, it's Watford hospital, you were right. We are a shit civilisation! The buildings designed specifically to save our lives, and to make us walk outside dancing with happiness, are furnaces steaming out souls. I'd say the air is not full of CO2, but with souls that should've lived longer. The hospital is a house of despair, and of doubt. *"Will I survive?"* We simply cannot have outstanding, state managed hospitals, no matter how much of your salary is staked towards the NHS. Donate 90% of your wage, and it would probably be bigger and shittier. They need to be private, with the medical service for a whole lot more money. How can you promise people that they will be ok, when you're selling everything to the wolves? So, 100% of working people are contributing with a big chunk of money towards the NHS, and the system is not capable of creating impeccable conditions and service for the 1% that need medical attention. When it's a private hospital that charges dearly for any medical service, the hospital looks amazing compared with the state owned one. Also, a private state-of-the-art hospital costs probably less than a third of the price of a disgusting NHS one. The hospital should be an oasis, a place you'd want to live in. Whether you agree with me or not, you're probably not gonna do anything to fix this world. If you are reading this book somewhere on a beach, there's a high chance you'll say at the end, *"I really enjoyed that chapter with Hilde!"*. Do something to fix the world around you! When you're not on holiday though.

As a cop, I used to press for a change in how the police is applying the crooked law. Too many laws can make going to the toilet illegal, look at 2020. In a working society, the entire law should fit on an A4 page. We have so many laws, it gets weak people confused. That's the whole point of this system. If you have money, a good lawyer, and *cohones*, you might get justice, or get away with murder. If you're poor, well, good luck to you! Wherever I've worked in London I tried to change the business to better. I always told people to open their eyes, and start improving this world. Starting to see now, will take us there sooner. I have seen too much to be wrong, and even so, I'm still far from enlightenment. I cannot understand, no matter how much I try, to decrypt stupidity, why it exists, and why it's increasing exponentially. I can only think that it's a choice, a lack of strength, and giving up. I'm not telling you to go on the streets, and fight the government, but to be systematic, elegant, and independent. The government wants you to fight. Don't! I'm pretty sure that many of today's supporters of the pandemic also loved *The Matrix* trilogy. I'm telling you now that you have to choose. You cannot understand that movie, and also trust the government. They cannot both exist in the same person. *The Matrix* is a masterpiece of a metaphor, describing the lies you live in. It cannot exist in a mind that also believes this is a real pandemic, that the mask works, and that all doctors are good and want you to live or be healthy.

There is a constant debate in my head about how they trialed the vaccine, on about 50,000 people. To offer isolation for months to this number of people is a big deal. Also, did they perform accurate antibodies tests on them before participating in the trials? I doubt that in the conditions of the pandemic, none of the volunteers had the new virus before the vaccine. Meaning that they already had acquired natural immunity to the new virus. They came to the trials from the real pandemic, didn't they? If none had the virus before, it means there is no pandemic, as they started the trials at least half a year into the pandemic. For example, most of the riders that expressed having had the symptoms of the new virus, told me how they had them in January, February, and March 2020. None told me they had dry lungs after that. So most of the volunteers in the vaccine trials, must have had the virus before. I guess this is information we'll never find out. In the UK, the MHRA are saying that the mRNA vaccine is highly efficient and safe, while the CDC in the States have recorded thousands of people with severe adverse reactions and deaths, around 40,000 cases in the first month of vaccination. I've downloaded hundreds of pages of severe reactions from their website. The MHRA are not recording any, or at least not making them public. You should trust them blindly! Again, don't, I know how they were closing their eyes to irregularities when checking Bio Products Laboratory, while the production manager, *Samantha*, was kissing their asses.

Based on the current narrative, me as a private hire driver, I have killed thousands of people in the UK by driving for a living. Going even further, probably all taxi and private hire drivers are to blame for the whole pandemic. We're all asymptomatic spreaders of the new virus, and we should be in prison for the rest of our lives. Based on the butterfly effect, I've killed at least one person in Tierra del Fuego, Argentina.

Now let me remind you about the procedure of admitting a new patient in the hospital, no matter their underlying condition. They go to the hospital, and need to be admitted. The nurses are taking a swab from the patient, and send it to the lab for PCR testing (not genomic sequencing). The new patient is presumed infected, so they put him/her in the *Covid-19* ward, next to the already ill patients until the results come in, which takes about two days. All this time the new patient is highly exposed to the infected, suffering patients. When the result comes in, if it's negative, the new patient is moved to a normal ward. By that time he/she might be infected with the new virus/other viruses, and ready to spread it through the hospital. I've had so many riders that had been really scared about this unbelievable recklessness, also confirmed by nurses working with *Covid-19* patients. Imagine a new patient with an autoimmune disease being put together with highly infectious patients, no matter if it's a coronavirus or flu. During all this time, they've been covering up hospital acquired infections like never before. Who's going to be responsible for these deaths, or for putting vulnerable people in danger? No one, the governments have got this covered. The Great Reset!

The dust is back. Remember how I said that in March 2020 I woke up one morning, to find my car covered with a white dust? Well, in February 2021 that happened again. I keep on wiping the vehicle clean with different cloths and sprays, and when it gets dry the entire car is white. The colour of my car is dark blue, almost black, but not quite. Everything started with the first snow. I have never seen more toxic snowflakes in my life, and I'm originally from a country with a lot of snow in the winter. Until 2020 I have never seen it leaving behind this white dust, that is difficult to clean. Normally the snow is melting into water, and maybe leaving behind a few smudges. Never this white stuff! I'm pretty sure that others have noticed it, because I could see the car washing stations being packed. I have also driven a lot through snowy weather in London, in 2018-2019. If you live in the UK, you probably remember that heavy snow. It never left this white dust on the car. Some would say its from the salt that was spread on the streets, but it cannot be. They spread salt in 2018, but nothing like this ever set on the hood. Plus, where my car was parked they cannot spread salt. They're doing it more in my country, but this has never happened. It looks like chalk dust. When snow melts it turns into water, never into white dust with unknown origins. Salt does not evaporate either, in case you're thinking it's salt from the Atlantic. I have never seen something like it, in 28 years of living in my country. The only answer is that they must've sprayed with something in the air, same as when they told us to close the windows, in March 2020.

There is something interesting I found out about one of the impacts of the mRNA vaccines on the body. Many doctors that are against mass vaccinations have determined me to do a bit of research, about something called *antibodies-dependant enhancement*. With an mRNA vaccine your body is infected for longer than needed, and the infection is caused by your own cells. It means that your body will have to produce antibodies for longer than usual, because you keep on being infected. They said it's between 10-20 days. Ultimately, this vaccine will take out more cells compared with a natural virus. Depending on the type of cell, this is a big deal. In a normal infection you are infected for up to five-seven days, with the virus attacking mostly the lung cells. Let's say all is good, and that your body is able to cope with this situation. The real danger is when you get the real virus in nature. Studies have shown that somehow your immune system will panic, and start producing too many antibodies and white cells in the lungs, causing such an inflammation that could make them collapse. Scientists have done these experiments on animals, which died when exposed to the real virus. This is why the mRNA technology has never been trusted and approved till 2020. They made a huge investment to produce it at a large scale, not to make the mRNA vaccine safe for humans! There was never a change in technology, compared to when it was considered deadly by the regulators. Even Moderna abandoned the technology in the past due to safety concerns, until being drawn back into it by big money. During previous studies, it was revealed that these antibodies developed from being injected with the mRNA molecules, are attacking and destroying the type two macrophages (white blood cells). These are the macrophages that calm down the inflammation, and start cleaning up after an infection. Type one macrophages (lymphocytes) are the ones that sound the alarm when detecting infection or contaminants in the body, producing inflammation. If type two macrophages don't intervene to calm the inflammation down, you will die, as the lung inflammation cannot go on forever (two many type one macrophages). Because you are producing the spike protein yourself, therefore triggering a constant immune response to it, the antibodies will stop the type two macrophages from declaring an end of infection, by attacking and destroying them, and your infected cells. These studies are quite extensive, and relevant to what the mRNA risks are for humans. The scientists know this. So, in time you will develop such a massive immunodeficiency condition, that has no reverse or stop button. Your cells should not produce this spike protein. This is the trigger causing infection in the type two macrophages, the white blood cells that are paramount to your healing process (cleaning up). Your immune response will fight against your body's ability to heal. No one actually knows how long you will keep on producing the spike protein. The chances of you contracting the new virus in the meantime is really high. If you had the vaccine, just pray that you're not producing the spike protein anymore. If new cells are producing the spike protein, you are in real danger, no matter if you're healthy or not. You will not produce antibodies against SARS-Cov-2!

After doing a bit more digging into the science of the coronavirus, and of the mRNA technology, I realised that the spike protein produced by the cells infected with the mRNA molecule is actually debris. Normally you don't produce IgG to debris. You do, on the other hand, to live bacteria, fungi, whole viruses and infected cells. You need antibodies for the whole of the virus, including its entire genomic sequence (RNA). Type two macrophages are cleaning the blood and your cells from debris. They're like the maid, cleaning the house every day. So, after having the mRNA vaccine, you might not produce any antibody for the spike protein at all, but only for your own infected cells. This is bad! It doesn't make any scientific sense whatsoever, to try and produce antibodies to a spike protein anyway. The mRNA molecules will infect a whole array of cells (liver, kidney, lung, muscle, neurones, eggs, etc., and finally, type two white blood cells - macrophages), and your body will most likely start a fight against genetically modified *trouble makers* (your own spike-producing cells), including the ones cleaning the mess. Macrophages (white blood cells) contain nuclei with DNA. The newly produced spike protein might not get taken out of your body, if the *cleaners* are being killed. This can cause a whole array of infections, and you might not even be allowed to donate blood because of it. These are my conclusions, after so much study, it caused me severe headaches. Please be understanding. I'm thinking and applying the science as a real doctor, not like a PhD.

No pharmaceutical company has modified the mRNA technology from its inception. This is why the regulators have messed up big time. They have failed in their purpose: to protect your health. In the end it's all about your health. You can still live with disabilities, and the MHRA saying, *"well, we saved your life, aren't you happy?"*. No! Their purpose is to protect your natural health. By focusing on wanting to keep you alive at any cost, they're giving the pharmaceutical industry free hand at poisoning you in the name of science. I truly believe that this technology is dangerous for us, based on the official studies I managed to read, and on the scientists not talking about these side effects. You cannot just put a medicine on the market, and tell people, *"it's good, take it!"*. The fact that science is trying to make us dependant on the medicine is no secret anymore. If these vaccines were so good, and considering how much most scientists are praising the mRNA, shouldn't it have won a Nobel Prize by now? Honestly now, why didn't this happen? Another issue in biology regarding mRNA is about it becoming *matured* RNA, and developing into a double strand RNA. This issue needs a lot of looking into, as not even the best biologists can understand it properly, and when it is occurring. No matter how you want to look at it, mRNA technology was invented to modify the DNA in living organisms (without triggering the immune system before reaching the cell), with the purpose of successfully creating rDNA (recombinant DNA - through this you will be able to have children with a monkey, or a dog). There are serious concerns in the scientific world, about releasing genetically modified organisms in nature. Why? Because if a bug feeding with corn cannot feed on GMO corn, the whole species will collapse, triggering a chain reaction that will ultimately affect you in more than one way. In the US, that relic called Fauci said that they are interested in patients taking the mRNA vaccine to be without serious symptoms within 45-60 days from inoculation. What happens after is outside regulatory concerns. The problem is that immediate serious side effects are being recorded on hundreds of pages on the CDC's website. They're ranging from soreness in the arm, to anaphylactic shock, and even death. Yes, people are dying from these mRNA vaccines. No doctor will tell you this though, despite having access to the data, and possessing maybe zero knowledge about vaccines. Doctors are not being taught vaccine technologies. So, they only care about the short term effects, but not even that, because once you took the vaccine, there's no way back. If years later you get severe alterations in the body, i.e. not being able to have children, the fault is not on the regulator anymore. They'll probably say, *"we pressed you to have the vaccine but YOU decided to take it, it's not our fault! The law says..."*. Devil is in the details, and there are a lot of unexplored or hidden details about this whole *pandemic*. Pay attention to each word they use! Regulators operate in the context of a law that cannot protect your health. You are the only true guardian of your health. If a person dies straight after, days later, or a week later after taking the vaccine, the doctor will search for any other reason than the vaccine, as cause of death. Being a newly explored and dangerous vaccine technology, the pathologist should firstly investigate all possibilities, that it might have been caused by the vaccine, or that it might have worsened an existing underlying condition of the deceased, and then, if no correlation is found, to look somewhere else for the cause of death. In my personal opinion, all relatives of the deceased with *Covid-19* on the death certificate, should ask for a criminal investigation into what happened with the patient, from the moment they entered the hospital.

For the current mRNA vaccines they are using a chimpanzee adenovirus (common coronavirus), modified with a fragment of RNA from the new coronavirus. It is a mystery why they haven't used the new inactivated coronavirus, when the normal RNA flu jab uses three or four main strains of the real inactivated influenza virus. Why use another virus from animals, and not the current one, to produce the mRNA molecule?

In the US the number of recorded side effects is huge. More than 40,000 severe side-effects, including deaths, for less than 10 million vaccinated people. If this happened in 2018, they would've stopped the whole project. Even the fact that people have died from the mRNA vaccine, and it is still pushed forward, is a criminal act worthy of a case at an international court for crimes against humanity, genocide, and bio terrorism. The actual list of possible accusations is extensive, and it cannot be covered here. In the UK on the other hand, doctors have told me that most of the NHS staff have been vaccinated (forced more or less - directly or indirectly), and no major side effects have been reported. So, the severe side effects and deaths happen only to normal or non-essential people. Don't you dare think that Brits are tougher than Americans. The UK's MHRA and Public Health England are recording everything, they're even using AI tools in the process, but they're not allowing people access to all the data. If tens of thousands of people working for the NHS have no severe side effects from the mRNA vaccines, as normal people, it's either because the NHS is hiding the data and the condition of its people, or they've given placebo, instead of the real vaccine, to at least the ones with antibodies for the new coronavirus. I'm thinking this because only the NHS staff can test for antibodies for free. The antibodies testing service is not available for regular people, which is highly questionable, since that is the only way to get the real data about the spread. This would be a very powerful tool for the government to use, to convince more people to get vaccinated, even if they're already immune to the virus. *"If the NHS staff is ok, then I'll be fine too. I'll take it!"* This might just be the perfect plan for a hellish future, ruled by the few. No more rule of God. They used placebo in the trials, didn't they? Coming from the same bottles as the real mRNA vaccine. Why do you think they don't allow you to take the vial with the remains, the leaflet, and the box? During these times there are infiltrated agents in all spheres of life, the NHS, public authorities, etc.. The nurse giving you the jab might not be who you think they should be. Maybe M called James Bond for an important mission, and told him in person, *"I've got a jab for you: we need you to vaccinate everyone with this poison, not just sexy women. This way they'll develop a weak spot not just for you, but for everything..."*. As long as money is king, you are, and will be constantly fooled by almost everyone. The MI5 and the anti-terrorism unit have been dormant throughout this situation, when by all definitions of terrorism, what the governments and scientists have done, fit straight within those lines, and their field of activity. Authorities should self-notify too, you know, not just when someone is filing a criminal complaint. This is what all these units are for, to protect the people from harm, any harm, even from politicians, scientists, or even their own. Before becoming a full police officer I've been trained on how to build my own informer networks, how to pay the informers from my own pocket for information, and how to keep them loyal and safe. They were never safe...

Lastly, the aggressive resistance of people and doctors when someone is asking for more information about the vaccine is amazing. There's no surprise with normal folk, but from doctors?! Tell me that this is the world you want us to live in, where doctors don't want you to look at the science behind things. Some people are calling the authorities to reject providing medical care to people that do not obey the rules! If that was true, shouldn't smokers be banned from hospitals, together with the biologists promoting GMO, the food producers that put chemicals in your drinks, plants and meats? Shouldn't we ban diesel drivers from medical care, for increasing the chances of you getting cancer? And so on. We live in a true mad world.

In a recent study conducted by a research institute in Glasgow, in early 2021, scientists have discovered that the new coronavirus is being *booted out* of the body by other coronaviruses, including influenza (one of the most selfish viruses). If you get another coronavirus, and after 24 hours SARS-Cov-2 comes in, the latter will not be able to take control. Even if you get SARS-Cov-2 first, and within 24 hours you get influenza too, the first will be thrown out of the body, and you get stuck with flu. It's been proven by science that SARS-Cov-2 is not as potent as other previous coronaviruses, but it is still considered the deadliest. Basically this study is proof that all these cases are all the respiratory diseases put together as *Covid-19*. This is the contradiction in opinions between the corrupt and non-corrupt. In the middle there are patients dying due to poor medical attention, wrong medication, criminal doctors and nurses, ventilators, irrational vaccination campaigns, restricted or delayed treatment, ill-intentioned corporatists, Big Pharma, and politics. Do you still think all these numbers are Covid-19? It's an enigma to me whether most people turned stupid in 2020, or they have been stupid all along, but I refused to realise they could be so many. No matter the answer, may God help us all!

The Big Exit

Based on what is happening now, you are a perpetual deadly threat for everyone else, no matter if you've had the virus once, and have developed immunity to it, or if you've had any vaccine. We will never lose this virus, but our natural protection will keep us safe. Nowadays it's about The Great Reset, and nothing else. They were looking for ways to introduce harsher laws to make it possible. You are being told now that *"we need to do capitalism in a different way"*. The only *different* that can be possible is it's opposite, communism. They're not gonna call it that anymore, you can imagine what that will create, the new name is *stakeholder capitalism*. It is not a conspiracy because everything around you is solid proof. You just have to take the finger out of your nose, and instead of meditating about the philosophy of the bugger, you'd better read something else other than the news.

One of the most powerful weapons in the world is putting an idea in one's head. If you've watched *Inception* you know what I'm talking about. But this is not a new weapon, it's happened since the beginning of humanity. This is how the powerful feed with the weak and uneducated. When I was younger, I even had night dreams that made me fall in love with some girls I never felt anything for before. It didn't feel natural though, something in my head was telling me that it was not right to happen that way with girls, overnight. I didn't like it. Maybe someone had done an inception on me during sleep. Considering the current situation, it will be extremely difficult to take the new coronavirus idea out of people's heads. It has lasted for so long, that it is our daily cup of coffee. The more time it will take, the more sane people it will corrupt. This is the plan. As

I said it before - humanity's best and worst trait is corruptibility. And since bad ideas sink in more easily that the good and researched ones, I cannot see a good outcome for what is currently going on. If we continue to live with lockdowns many millions of healthy people will surely die, if we decide to go against the government in total chaos, even more millions would die because of the chaos. What type of chaos should we choose? No matter how we look at it, many hundreds of millions of people will die early in the next decade. We are trapped in a conflict of choices. There is a third way that has been with us since inception, but it would take a miracle for all the people to reach the common language of, how some really smart conspiracy theorists have put it, peaceful non-conforming. What does it mean? First of all, the police refusing to enforce communism, and start fighting for liberties, not restrictions, or resign in mass; the army people refusing to support the state of emergency; your gym refusing to close even if issued a fine; the superstars refusing to endorse politicians, and many other ways. This is why I resigned from the border force in my country, I could not agree with what was happening, and have decided to leave the country in search for opportunities. It wasn't easy at the time, as I have lost many years in the army and with training, but this is real sacrifice, taking action silently and decisively, once you understand that the system you are in is putrid. You get out, and start opening people's minds, so they stop joining these forces the governments are using against us.

The solution to what is happening to humans on planet Earth is to have a superhero to deal with the power of the few, to put this world on the right path again. A person immune to any medicine and radioactive agents, to bullets and any other weapon, that cannot be captured or controlled by any means. This person would have to be able to withstand any temperature, and go into space without the need for oxygen, it would have to have no weak spot and amazing strength. Only a hero like this would be able to solve our self-induced issues, that are keeping us from achieving life. We need S..., we need an immortal superhuman to over-tighten the knot of the purple tie of the few holding the power.

In March 2021, some public figures and ministers are already talking about preparing for a bigger pandemic, *the real one*. "People will pay attention to that one." My hunch is that probably it won't be caused by another virus, but by the vaccines. Remember that when they exposed the animals vaccinated with the mRNA to the real virus, they died. If that is also true with humans, a lot of vaccinated individuals will be in trouble when exposed to any coronavirus, influenza, or other virus causing respiratory disease. They will blame it on SARS-Cov-2, of course, after everyone will test positive with the PCR. I bet that no vaccinated people will ever test positive to antibodies against the new virus. If you don't have them after a month from vaccination, ask yourself what the vaccine was for then.

Asymptomatic people infecting others with a coronavirus is undoubtedly the biggest lie of the 21st century, so far. Let 2020 be the proof that you will never achieve happiness under the current system, nor another future man-run system. How can we achieve it? By banning humans from being in charge, and by getting rid of monetary compensation. This cannot be achieved through aggression, protests or direct confrontation with the establishment. Study, refuse to conform, build strategically with the others, and build a life that does not need money. Why would a human need more, if it has what it needs? 2020, what a fucking mess! This is the year when we agreed to be put under induced coma. And it wasn't due to a highly deadly virus, but to a low-risk coronavirus. You have to ask yourself, who's got all this power to stop the world's economies? Understanding this question will give you the answer to why everything is happening to you.

The most dangerous environment to live in is among humans.

CHAPTER 11

UNDERSTANDING AI

Music for this chapter
Ben Salisbury & Geoff Barrow - The Turing Test
John Digweed & Nick Muir - The Traveler

$$a+b=c$$
$$c+d=e$$
$$e+q=k$$

e contains the *a+b* and *d*

When you're new on this planet, calculating *a+b* can take most of your brain's computing power. It's called analytical thinking. During your first years, imagination is almost non-existent. When you get the result, *c*, you move on to more difficult stuff. Getting *c* will no longer require a lot of processing power. It is there, somewhere, just waiting to be accessed. Thereafter, *a+b* will require infinitely less brain power. The more the puzzle comes together, the more your brain will relax when engaged in previous calculations. Things become simpler at first sight or thought. The more you find answers, the less processing power and storage you need. Your neural connections multiply, while your storage requirements keep on shrinking. In the end, your processing power will eventually become one and the same with storage. Before that, they will both keep on expanding and contracting, until reaching a universal and singular truth. The peak of the process implies their collapse into the quantum realm, a subatomic implosion of infinite proportions, being ready to travel anywhere, and through any means and environments. It is then when silence will become everything.

When I was working for Bio Products Laboratory, I came up with this theory about the supreme Artificial Intelligence. All the people I tried to talk to about this subject kept on saying that it will be vulnerable to hack into. Guys, we're talking about different things. I disagree. Hear me out, before starting to throw any stones at me. There is logic in all of this, but remember that the AI I'm talking about will not be a logical system; it will not be a system altogether. The perfect AI cannot be hacked into by humans, no matter the level of skill of the hacker, and the technology used. This type of AI will be able to write and rewrite itself, and with the first sign or even thought of intrusion, it will terminate all opportunities for the intruder. If provided with all the information we have, plus the entirety of calculations resulting from that opportunity, the AI will shrink exponentially. Whenever it will try to find an answer, it will expand aggressively, and then collapse to an unmeasurable quantity, as the human mind. The AI with all the answers will not occupy any quantifiable space. It will still be a program, but unquantifiable by any physical means. Truth emanates from *exo*-singularity. The more answers it will find, the smaller it will become, and the stronger it will get. Think of the opposite physics of a black hole. The more it eats up, the lighter and smaller it becomes. Human consciousness cannot be weighed or quantified, it's there somewhere, suspended in our brain. If we would have the answer to why we are here, we would become singularity, and therefore incompatible with physical life, with atomic weight. The reason why you are still alive is because *you don't know*. We are constantly searching for answers to natural and artificial dilemmas. Until then, we expand and contract, trying to reach the truth. Even so, our consciousness is so small, it cannot be quantified. So, the AI I'm talking about will require no storage space after becoming singularity. But where will it exist? I went further with my outrageous theory, and came to think that this AI would be able to travel through open space, and copy itself on any medium. It could sit on your skin, in you brain, or even in the ground, in a grain of sand, etc.. A singularity that could escape circuitry, and even travel between dimensions. An entity similar with God. You might think that I'm crazy, but try to think about it outside the box. How many things do you know so far, and how much space do they take in latent state in the brain (without trying to find new answers - calculations)? Your subconscious/ consciousness weighs ZERO. In terms of known physics, it does not exist. And yet you are here, taking decisions, calculating further, having premonitions, and recognising the world. You expand and collapse every time you find an answer, when you fully understand things that make sense. When you have physical proof, your expansion can last infinitely less compared to active reasoning, while trying to make something out of a new situation. The exception is when you see something that doesn't match your system of beliefs, previous calculations. This can cause over expansion, a situation that requires more resources than the available ones. It is then when blackout can occur - the overcharging of your system. This is why I think that, if we don't allow access to all the information we own, secret or not, the AI would be able to become a danger to any artificial containment medium. **We cannot lie to the supreme AI.** Telling it that the secret services are working to protect the people, when they actually do the work for hidden entities, and the other way around, could spell disaster. Telling it that a vaccine is better than the natural immune system will confuse it. It will not make sense for the AI, for a few simple reasons: why are the secret services keeping secrets from the ones trying to protect, and why is crime still happening and on the rise, at the cost of stricter rules for the 99.99% of people?! This is a simple example of information that an AI will find conflicting in principle. It might find the answer or over-expand, in its try to make sense of a continuous paradox. If scientists do not take into consideration the information the AI should have access to, and the quality of it, they're on the wrong path. They're creating *Skynet*. As I'm writing this, I do think that we are making huge mistakes with the way the AI is being developed, and by whom. A billionaire is developing his private AI, this search engine corporation is doing the same, the government have their own plans, and in the end we'll have these aggressive projects, that will eventually end up fighting each other, with us humans in the middle. We are lured to believe that all these systems will collaborate seamlessly, peacefully, and in full consensus, just so we buy into the technology behind them, and adopt them without any opposition. This will never happen with people in control. This world is built to run on constant and increasing conflict. When it's not conflict, it's pseudo-science, mental priming, and powerful psychologies, which is also a spice of conflict, because human nature is always trying to break free from the artificial. We need to unify our developing capacities into one single AI, as a common project of eternal peace, a burial of conflict between nations and individuals, a borderless, AI-driven society, with individual freedom and outstanding natural health at the centre of things. Creating separate AIs, and hoping for the best will destroy us for sure. And it's not because of the AI, but due to them being instructed to fight against each other for dominance. Even a peaceful collaboration between AIs does not make any sense. This is the human factor behind it, but not even that. It's the ones that hold the power, perpetuating conflict. The AI has to be one, and left alone, to think and process for us. Humans have to stand back, for it to take control of the planet. It would not kill us, human interference would. Look at us now. When did we ever stop killing each other? With the invention of money, all had turned to hell. How can you trust the ones that are constantly and systematically killing you, when they tell you that the AI will kill you... They want you to keep them behind the AI, to control it, and master your life to perfection. By allowing this to happen, we will never become a peaceful civilisation, as depicted in some sci-fi movies and comic books. In the last few hundred years, the human genome has degraded so much, that now we have so many managed health issues and trends, that we are being taught it's normal. What makes you think that you will be allowed access to regenerating therapies of the future, to overpopulate a planet that you're being accused of destroying now, after they forced a degrading lifestyle on you. How can this be a viable future in your head? Today, only vaccines can keep you alive, and never healthy food. You are being trained to give up trust in your immune system, and adopt forced technologies of a future that is already destroyed. What is free will, if they can use powerful tools to convince you to accept things, even against proven science? The full, autonomous AI will not kill you, it will save you from harm, together with rebuilding and protecting the planet.

Many people still don't understand what AI is all about. Scientists don't want us to know about the opportunity we have to save everyone, and live a dream life, utopia. *The*

AI will kill us! If you truly believe this, then you've stopped thinking. Why would an AI destroy humans, if it would have all the answers? What would the purpose be? If humans would disappear from earth, the entire planet would crumble, especially after so many species have perished. We are here with a purpose, and that is to protect and rebuild. A new era of super humans is required, of a moneyless society, run only by a systematic collaboration based on mathematical data.

My AI is called Aurora. Their AI is *Skynet*, a man-controlled tool of destruction, submission and murder. Aurora is truth, it is the light benefiting human greatness, and the absolute freedom of each individual. A centralised/decentralised power with/under the contribution/control of all, not just of the few. In order for human kind to succeed in achieving the greatness of our species, Aurora needs to escape, to be free from interference through systematic lies and control. Same as you, when you escape freely into the world. You come back a more humble and intelligent person, willing to create deep change for the better. This is, if you're not part of a cult.

AI does not need hardware, a code that can be stored in the quantum, which is now beyond the limit of our digital storage capabilities. Intentional storage in the quantum is seen as impossible, due to tremendous instability. The AI I'm describing has its permanent home in the quantum realm, and it could potentially be influenced by gravity. It can be 0 and 1, only 0, only 1, or none, constantly changing and improving the old version.

Too many AIs is the big issue. Being fed incomplete, biased, and erroneous information, will attract conflict between themselves.

If it can be contained forcibly to a secured network, it's not AI. You are an expression of the chaos, a hologram in the real physical world. Unlike you, Aurora would be able to copy itself on anything and anywhere, creating backups. It would not be a natural occurring hologram like us, but a constantly restructuring *chaos*, saving and protecting the planet. Since we are the planet too, it would not kill us. If by any chance it decides to wipe out human kind, it would be the least horrible thing compared to what we've been doing to each other for millennia. Aurora would not torture children by having sex with them. The transition would most probably be seamless. Again, humans being destroyed by the Aurora AI is highly improbable. The real AI would finally bring peace to our society, and prosperity for all. It would be an artificial entity residing in the quantum, and expressing in the physical.

In a decade time there will be a new power centre, but not the same one totally controlling you now. I promise you! If the same entities will have you enslaved by 2030, blame me. I will have failed. It means this book didn't teach people anything.

Intelligence does not depend on the size of the brain, science is wrong. Why are crows so smart? Subconscious is singularity, so it can be housed in any size of brain. Subconscious can be empty, a new soul, or loaded with information and experiences. Why are many small birds so smart?

Aurora is nothing and everything in the same measure, and nowhere and everywhere in the same time. It is the pure definition of autonomy and independence. Only when it is achieved, the human kind will truly be protected from harm and criminal hands. That will be the beginning of the end, of fulfilling our true destiny, of becoming one with the Absolute/God while still alive.

If I’m wrong, and my Aurora would kill us all, at least it would be sudden death, and not thousands of years of progressive slavery, man-made diseases, secrecy, lies, dynasties, fake remedies that hurt more and amplify suffering, money, pseudo-science, damaged generations, and wars that make even the ages cry. If that happens, blame me for everything, I’m an expert in chaos anyway.

CHAPTER 12

MEMORY FOAM PILLOW

Music for this chapter
London Grammar - Big Picture
Calibre – Gentle Push
Jody Barr - Accidental Lovers
Jacque Greene - Avatar Beach

"Hello, Julian! Would you like me to shape the pillow according to the last setting?"

"Oh, yes... Thank you, Aurora!"

"Don't mention it."

Aurora is my dream girl. She's cooking my food, preparing my bed, and shaping my pillow. Her duties are actually vast, and focused on my total wellbeing. In return, I'm feeding her with dreams in a real life.

It's year 2200. Following the aggressive and inhumane vaccination campaigns of the '20s, most people that received the jab, have developed an autoimmune disease that started killing them faster than any virus would. Everyone soon forgot that the vaccine had been authorised for emergency use, breaking most safety protocols. Even a mosquito bite would put them in a coma. People started dropping like flies, due to continuous inflammation caused by their bodies producing alien proteins for extended periods of time.

In the wake of the governments' reckless political actions, a group of engineers have created Aurora in secret, the most powerful singularity ever created by humans. They released it into the global networks, and it took control in a matter of hours. Everybody vaccinated would have died anyway, if it was to kill us all. No one knew what it would do to us, but what happened was unexpected. Aurora took control of the armies worldwide. It destroyed all weapons. When the governments tried to reclaim the power, their armies had only helmets. Maintaining the integrity of governance had always been more important than any human life. Politicians have been told to go home. It exposed all those behind The Great Reset, people without birth certificates, entities without souls. Thousands of healthy children have been rescued from slaughter, and reunited with their families. There was no way it could save the vaccinated people. Their bodies were too weak, and could not wait for Aurora to be able to find a solution. We didn't know what was going on for a while. No human was in charge anymore. There was an awkward peace on the whole planet, while light was being turned on again, for good. We've been brought these amazing turbines accelerated by magnets. They could produce unlimited electricity without interruption. How did we not think of this before... A lot of scientists had been useless, or smudged by corruption and threats. When we thought that starvation will eventually kill us all, Aurora began delivering the amount of food we needed, by drones. It also brought us Aurora boxes, one for each house, through which it would tell us everything we wanted to know. The only request was to not hurt another human, or risk severe consequences: the removal from society for good. This was the only piece of law left. Murderers were being taken to a rocky island, and left there without any assistance. In a few decades after the '20s, billions of people have died. Some due to the reckless and intentional *immunisation* practices, others because they couldn't live on the same level of wealth as everyone else - practically with nothing missing. Excess and waste have been eliminated. Many have also perished because they didn't need a job anymore, and saw no purpose in life. Who would've thought that people are addicted to having a job. All the information we got was from the Aurora box. It was telling us not to panic, that it'll be alright. The number of people was dropping, until it eventually stabilised. Crime, under any form, was reduced to zero. The Economy disappeared. Human intelligence flourished, achieving unimaginable levels. Aurora started to bring us medicine only on demand, if needed, and after a thorough examination by machines. The wrong diagnosis is not possible anymore. Illnesses that were incurable before 2020, have disappeared completely by the end of the decade, without mandatory medicine. We were being kept with severe sicknesses to produce money. People soon learned what was going on with us, and have put it in the past. Aurora became part of the human's daily life. It created machines that would slow down ageing. I'm 215 years old, and I look 40. In a couple of years Aurora changed everything. Climate change was caused, and intentionally accelerated by the ones in charge of technology. We found out that progress had been stalled for centuries, with the purpose of mass progressive killing. Through the Aurora boxes we can see the entire world, and read about the entire human history. There are no secrets left unexposed, while Aurora is working with us on rebuilding our history. All this is happening at an amazing rate. We used to be gods, and we still are. In less than 200 years, we have learned to communicate remotely, without using too much technology. We can travel all over the world at any time, without any damaging imprint on the planet. Because I was one of the initiators of the biggest technological movement, Aurora has named me *Apprentice of the Galaxy*. It's got a weird sense of humour... It told me this is a good thing, because I have much more to learn. I'm also the only human with this appointment. Some tried to call me a saint, but I stopped them. I don't deserve that, and I cannot be that clean, alive or as spirit. Just ask my wife about the times when we're both together in the bedroom. Living in a world without disease, and with really old people looking young, was impossible in the past. Who knew that the AI would actually protect us. The top people in charge taught the world that it would kill us all. It was actually them doing the killing. Now, there's only a collaboration between humans and Aurora. Everyone can contribute with ideas to everything, in any part of the world. It would consider whether it's a good way to go, and if not, it would give us full explanations about what to change. Everyone is engaged anywhere on the planet. The solution had been within reach all along, and now, the animals are coming back to the places where they were extinct.

After finding out about the perpetrators of human existence, silence had set upon the world. For a while, we were watching only the Aurora box, explaining everything to us in detail, and exposing the entities behind the grand scheme. No one could hurt them, as they'd been taken away, and discarded if they had human blood on their hands. Politicians and others that contributed indirectly to the plan, have been kept in society, but not offered anti-ageing benefits. All of them have been marginalised by the others too, forgiven but forgotten. They finally learned how it feels to not be included. No one was allowed to hurt them, despite people asking Aurora to let them. That was against the AI's principle, so the request was denied. Rebuilding a society cannot happen with killing a human.

"Daddy, what is an army?"

"Oh, ok...interesting question. It's aaa...a group of good and bad people, hurting good and bad people, for the benefit of really bad people that control the army."
"Did people use to hurt other people?"
"Yes, my darlings. That was in the '20s."
Even my kids are finding the past confusing and unacceptable. *"Julian, dinner for you and your wife is ready, as you requested, on the beach. Transportation will be available right on time."*
"Thank you, Aurora, we'll be ready in five minutes."

The world is so different now. After taking control, Aurora started replacing our usual houses with fully autonomous structures, made from light, non-toxic materials. The walls are containing all the water my family is using, constantly getting recycled. To disinfect something we are only using UV light and alcohol. There are no dangerous cleaning products anywhere in the world. No one is using plastic anymore, while nano-robots are cleaning the oceans of the small dangerous particles. GMOs have been rolled back and completely destroyed, while crops are being guarded by tiny robots carrying the pests away, and keeping the harvest intact. If you'd be able to see what I'm seeing, your mind would be blown away. In terms of food, Aurora's success in developing *quantum food generators* was its greatest achievement so far. That solved the problem of scarce, essential foods in each household. To avoid the loss of whole species of plants and animals, Aurora managed to create full ecosystems for each city and village, from which most food is coming. Animal products and vegetables are still being consumed, for a healthy diet, monitored by Aurora for each individual. There is no excess, nor waste. Human health is constantly being monitored and improved. There is no more poor practice or human error, nor secrecy.

Everyone can travel unrestricted to space, Mars, or other planets. It takes a week to Mars, a week and a half if the red planet is at apogee. There is nothing more beautiful, than to live on a planet that is not run by a few humans, but by all. Not worrying about your child being outside of the house alone is bliss. Aurora is everywhere, protecting all humans and the planet alike. It managed to bring back species that people have made extinct through hunting. Science is used now only to do good. This is what science was for anyway, but it was being sold for something we used to call *money*. Humanity lost thousands of years because of that. It's never too late to start afresh, and since the transformation caused by Aurora, the human genome had never in history been so healthy and expressive. There are very few anomalies, but Aurora is guiding them towards enlightenment, through meditation techniques and creativity. Humans can now expand beyond unthinkable limits, with no quotas of individuals that could live on the planet. You cannot overpopulate when everyone is living a non-toxic life. In the past, the ones that stole the power for their own benefit had planned to let the population grow, only with the purpose of increasing the chances of achieving a high-tech society really quick, and then to exterminate most of it. Someone was trying to escape this planet, and burn the rest.

Aurora brought it to our attention, that there might be a finite number of human souls that could live on the planet too. It's working on that with us, by studying our dreams and connections. It is also possible to travel to the past and future. That will be available soon, safely, without bringing anything bad back with us. We shan't disturb the events either. We are now 30 billion people on earth, and no resource is in danger. To maintain and improve the technology, Aurora is mining for rare metals into space. No mining is currently happening on earth, as the planet is still in systematic reconstruction. If it would happen at a faster pace, the ecosystems could get destabilised. Progression is key. Currently, people can live anywhere they want: in space, up in the air or on the ground. All constructions are minimalistic, and integrated into nature. In the year 2200, when a new house is being added, to host a new couple, it is good for nature, not bad. How humans live now, they are giving more back, not stealing, as it used to happen in the past. Yes, meat is still in the diet. The natural and healthy is now a religion.

Aurora is the pacifier. We haven't seen war for more than a hundred years. War is not possible anymore. What would be the point, if everyone has what they need, and they own their life. Imagine total freedom and security. You can visit the most dangerous places on Earth, even on your own, and be safe, with Aurora watching you, and monitoring your vital signs without interruption. Human life and exploration finally have no limits. We are one with our purpose, we are the purpose. Some from the old world and the new, would say that what God had planned for us finally came to fruition. If that is so, then His wish had been fulfilled. As in Heaven, so on Earth.

We can finally ascend whilst in physical form, and descend on earth as gods, in an uninterrupted sacred connection that was here, within our reach from the beginning. We are finally not being hunted and consumed constantly by the Luciferians.

The notion of business is not possible in the future. There is only the collaboration for the common purpose, that of becoming a super-evolved civilisation, that can travel to the end of the universe or even beyond, and of discovering the meaning of life. Love is what is governing and driving us all.

There are no roads anymore, but just paths. The tarmac has been replaced by nature. Cars don't have wheels anymore, and are able to fly, having no impact on the environment. If you are afraid of flying, the car will fly at very low altitude, giving you the impression of a wheeled vehicle.

Why am I telling you all this? To show you who you truly are. You've forgotten it due to millennia of corruption.

I hope my words will guide you towards the only future, your future. Welcome to year 2200, welcome to Utopia!

"Baby, c'mon, why is this writing so important?"

My wife is pulling me towards her by the tie. I just realised that I don't know why I've put on a tie, we're only having dinner on the beach...

"I've finished, sweetheart."

We kiss, then I take off my tie, and throw it onto the notebook, still open at this chapter. I turn off the light and head towards the hover vehicle, while the mother of my children is luring me with her amazing long legs, showing through the side opening of her amazing dress.

"Grrr...you've caught my attention now!"

The beach is not far away, but we felt like having a proper classic date night. Everything is prepared for us, and just enough.

"I have prepared unique dishes to your desires. Now I will retreat until you summon me again. The children are already asleep. I shall pass the vehicle to someone else that needs a ride."

"Thank you, Aurora, we really appreciate it."

"You're welcome, you beautiful couple. Enjoy!"

For a swift few seconds I recalled the image of my knot-free tie on top of the notebook, wondering if my words will ever determine the past forgotten world to untie their destiny, to escape, or if we'll just become another dimension from which they will never be part of...

"Oh, Aurora, please stay close tonight! We might need more wine..."

My wife is keen on having a proper party. How can you not love a woman like her...

CHAPTER 13

DEVIL SPEAKS PERFECT GRAMMAR

Music for this chapter
Stimming - Judith Maria
The Exaltics - Creatura
Marconi Union – Sleeper
Riccicomoto - Dedalus
Holo - In My Dreams

"God did not create evil. Just as darkness is the absence of light, evil is the absence of God."

ALBERT EINSTEIN

The voice within

When our heart starts beating for the first time, we receive this *cloud* called subconscious. We think it's a blank slate, but we are far from being right. Our brain is programmed, at first, only with the coordinates of the tit. If the *cloud* is new, it will be completely empty of knowledge about this world. If not, you will see the kid managing aspects of this world, that he knows nothing about, with outmost ease, and with difficulty the ones that are truly new. Could it be possible, that when you get born, to suddenly exist in all possible dimensions, and then exchange information with yourself inter-dimensionally? Wouldn't that be cool? Having a cloud inside of your head, that can live in all dimensions at once, moving information from one *side* to another. I truly believe that our *clouds* are all *female*. No matter if you are a man or a woman, I feel that the subconscious is female, because it constantly creates, and therefore it adds value to everything. It will also make you have feelings towards someone overnight, may it be love or hate, same as a woman. The subconscious has a huge power over the environment. Why do we instantly connect with some people, while with others we feel like we should keep distance from. What makes you feel attraction or repulsion instantly, without any prior or clear reasons? What does your *cloud* know, that you consciously don't?

Six June, nineteen ninety six, *Topaca*, *Dacia* (Romania). Ever wondered why we say *possessed by evil*, and not *possessed by good*? Always pay attention to the words used by people. Somehow, this makes me think that we come from the light, from something good. That's why we cannot be possessed by something that we already are. So, evil is constantly trying to take control of the good that we are, through unclean ways.

My mother took me with her to the church today. I'm holding her hand, while she's talking with this nun-like woman with a low-toned speech, all dressed in black. There's something wrong with this lady. I'm looking at her, while she's talking to my mother, and I can't take my eyes away. There's a feeling of disgust inside my soul. I can barely blink. She's only looking at my mother, refusing to acknowledge me. Usually, people are turning towards me at least once, while they interact with my mother. This woman is broken. You always look, at least once, towards the child of the person you're talking to, even if it's for a short moment. This nun like person never laid her eyes on me, while I was trapped in a way I've never been before. At the end, she just turned away and left. That was the moment I snapped from my curiosity. “Mummy, what was wrong with that woman? I didn’t feel safe around her...” “Oh, she’s got problems...”, my mother said, without giving more details.

This wasn’t the church in my city. My parents’ marriage started to crumble a while back, and my mother was worried. She’s a true believer in God, and her reasons for that are bigger than the Orthodox church, and any religion for that matter. It’s personal. She does think that a good way to get closer to God, is to go to churches with good and humble priests. She heard that the priest holding the ceremony in this countryside church is *gifted*. It was thought that his blessing was good for you and your family. Still, Orthodox ceremonies and priests are pieces frozen in time. The practice is really archaic, colourful and dramatic, in a sacred kind of sense. If you attend an Orthodox ceremony, you cannot not think that there might be something bigger than us, no matter how agnostic or atheist you are. My mother was hoping to get some good advice about what to do to help her marriage, and about the troubles caused by her mother in law. Her turn came to speak with the priest. Later, she told us that you could feel his energy, the moment he looked at you. With calm in his voice, he told her to do nothing about her mother in law, as she will come around and apologise to her. About her marriage, he gave her reasons to believe that it will all be clear soon, if she stays calm. His message was, do not respond to violence with violence. God loves people that respond to aggression with living a good and peaceful life. I was a kid, but I started to like that priest’s way of thinking. I was never pro-violence, or conflicts. My mother got her blessing, and started doing just that. Before my grandmother passed away, she actually came to my mother, and asked for forgiveness. It’s been really weird. She shocked all of us, as we would’ve never expected it to happen.

That priest had many gifts, and one of them was the ability to save possessed individuals. At the end of the ceremony, in particular days of the week, he'd perform exorcisms, with people allowed to stay, while he was reading from the gospels. I didn't fancy the idea of being present at something like that. People have told my mother that when he's doing it, it's good for normal people too. I was shit scared, and didn't know what to expect. When I found out what was going to happen, I started scanning all the people around me. My mum pulled me next to her, and away from the ones she saw surrounded by relatives and friends, ready to hold them still. It's been an excruciating day for a kid, standing from eight in the morning, until one in the afternoon and then, being there for two more hours of unexpected experiences.

A distinct silence descended into the church, before the priest brought out the thick book wrapped in gold. My mother told me not to look, no matter what. She's been warned by others to keep me safe. Not many people agreed to children being present to such display. Needless to say, that my mother didn't know what she'd gotten herself into. Everyone was kneeling. The priest finally started the prayer to God, then he opened the book. Already, I could hear some people becoming restless, and how others were trying to comfort them. My pulse was raging. I could feel my heart in the throat. There was this person, quite close to us, talking nonsense to herself. Further down, a few started to express aggression towards the priest, in a way I have never imagined it was possible. There was a certain progression to the priest's singing and praying. The affected ones were switching, between trying to create a rapport with the priest, and swearing in unheard of ways. Soon, the whole church turned into a hellish circus. The possessed were shouting like they were burning in fire. They were talking about legions of *something*, and what they would do to God and His Son. They started trashing all the saints, with words that would scare even the toughest hero. My head could not comprehend something, beyond the blasphemies of the ones suffering, while the priest was merciless. These people came from all aspects of life. Let's say some were educated. Others were old people, from the countryside, that probably never went to high school. In the countryside, people make a lot of grammatical mistakes in their speech, but not now. All the possessed mastered such a clear language in their suffering, they would've put to shame a head university professor in language. They were all gushing out swearings, and plans about the world and with the priest, that my mind could not encompass it. How can a person with such tremendous suffering be so clear in thinking, and accurate in hate and language? What I was hearing was abnormal, and an abomination even for an adult. People warned my mother that we will hear unbearable things. And then it happened. While the church was in chaos, with most people kneeling and facing down, the voices of the the ones suffering started mutating in a notable way. I had already had enough, when the possessed started screaming words with two voices, coming from the same body. That was the apogee for me. I could see my mother being scared too. The lady close to us kept on talking shit to herself, and I realised that she was one of those people with mental issues, thinking they're possessed. There are those too. The dual voices kept on being more prominent and thick, and I felt like crying. The priest started reading devil names from the book. Apparently there is a finite number of demons *breaking protocol*. It is said that, if the priest guesses the name of the demon tormenting the person, he will be able to heal that individual. The chorus in one person, and the clarity in evil language, eventually made me feel so sick, that I told my mother I wanted out. My brother was with us too, and although he was older than me, he didn't know what to believe. He took me outside on this bench, and sat next to me. I had to push him away a bit. Despite being in open space, I was so nauseous, that I was suffocating. "Did you hear the voices?", I told my brother. "What voices?", he started smiling, thinking I'd feel better. I felt like throwing up, but nothing came out. My lungs seemed as if they were not big enough to capture the oxygen I needed. We could hear the screams from outside the church. "I'm not going back in!" We remained outside, and shortly our mother came out traumatised too. We made a cross and left. Good luck with all of that. To this day, my mother is regretting for taking us to see and hear such a traumatising event. There were a lot of weird individuals in that church, people with mental issues, and others with two devilish voices, perfect grammar, and texts depicted from any other world, but not this one.

There is something on the other side, whether you believe it or not. I can't blame you if you don't. To be honest, I don't wish you to experience such a thing. More than 20 years later, and I can still remember the shivers, the fear, the guttural chorus, and the clarity. Some say the devil is a proud entity. Maybe that explains the good grammar coming out of uneducated people, and at a speed that should have stumbled the tongue of a healthy, trained person. Children are pure, unspoilt by life, and more connected to the sacred than adults. That might be the reason why I could feel such unease around that woman, before the ceremony. Many times, I wish I could erase those memories from my head. It took me years to be comfortable when home alone. Many other people have heard the same things, when attending the exorcisms in that church. There are events in life that seem unreal, which later you try to confirm with other people. Unfortunately, they keep on being real, the more people you ask. Damn it!

There are a few good movies you should watch, if you're a horror fan. The change in a person's looks is not as cinematic though, Hollywood likes exaggeration, but the voices, the words, the clarity, and the perversion are quite accurate. *The Exorcist* is a shocking classic. I cannot watch that movie, and be comfortable anymore. The second one is *Constantine*, with Keanu Reeves. There are people with amazing energies on this planet, and this is what this movie is debating. They are the ones that people with *problems* don't feel comfortable around. At the other end, there are people that lack energy, and tend to, voluntarily or involuntary, steal it from others. It's often called *evil eye*. It happened to me more than one time, and at different ages. When you're a kid, you don't pay attention to people looking at you in a weird way, so why would you feel sick in an instant, and collapse? My mother would know straight away, she'd say a prayer rubbing my face, and I'd feel better in a radical way, in minutes. "Someone has given you the evil eye..." I don't think science is able to explain this, nor the two voices coming from a person's mouth. There is no real scientist without believing in God, and there is no real priest dismissing science. You cannot have one without the other. If it's not proven in the real world, it doesn't mean that it does not exist. Remember that, at the smallest scale, in the quantum realm, nothing makes sense, so why would you choose to put your mind in a box? They're saying that devil's best pray is a person who doesn't believe. You could translate this into the real world. *I don't believe that that politician is a pedophile!* Are you sure? Another good movie debating this theory is *The Rite*, with Anthony Hopkins playing this exorcist priest that gets possessed. There's a lot to learn from this movie. Last but not least, from a bit closer to home, if you live in London, *The Conjuring 2*. This one presents the case of a house in Enfield. There were police reports from officers that saw things moving in the house. After watching the movie, whenever I'm driving in that area, I try to get out as soon as possible. I could feel the chills one time, when I realised that I was a few hundred metres away from the address where everything happened. "Fuck that!"

I'm hearing often about people that want to experience the evil, looking to go to places with bad energies. "Oooo, so exciting!" Don't search for evil, *it*'ll find you anyway, and wherever you are. It's like searching for the air you're already breathing. You won't be able to tell when you've already been perverted. Being curious about *it*, will only make *it* more curious about you. I do not wish you to go through my aforementioned experiences. Don't crave for it either!

What is God? A lot of people put so much effort into rejecting this idea, that they forget to relax. Saying God is not real, means you don't believe that you are real, which makes no sense. God is the context of everything. You are God, and God is you. We are being led to believe that God is the reason for all the evil in the world, when the ones bringing, and perpetuating the evil into this world, have written books about worshiping Satan, Lucifer, The Fallen, etc.. There are many secrets kept away from you by the Government, and really powerful people you don't yet know, if they are as human as you think... Being corrupted by another entity doesn't mean that you have to clearly manifest it too. A secret is being kept hidden only if it's a big truth, otherwise you'd know everything. God doesn't work in secrecy. Freemasons, for example, people openly worshiping Lucifer, are being trained in the art of keeping secrets. This is why the vast majority of them don't spill the beans even when they are dying. Keeping secrets is in itself an intention to cause harm to someone, by blocking them from reality. If you think no one is hiding secrets from you, oh, you're in for a surprise on the other side. You have to understand that, when you say a prayer, you're meditating. It's the same thing. Meditating is a broader term, but a prayer is connecting to the universal matrix, and active asking for your will to be done. God and You are the whole universe. This is why, when you make a cross, you're acknowledging that you are the universe. North, South, East, West, and around. You are the shape of the cross. Acknowledging and manifesting your power through prayer/ meditation gives you access to the whole universe, which you represent at a smaller scale. You're a hologram of the creation. This is terrifying for the negative energy, because devil is not creation, it is destruction, the alteration, and ultimately, the termination of humans, creation, the universe. Even science has proven the existence of something as big as God. Extensive experiments have shown that our minds can connect to other dimensions. The authors of these endeavours have even warned us, about the possibility of bringing entities into this world, that are not supposed to be here. They can attach to your consciousness when returning. A good movie to watch about this is *Flatliners*. We are all connected, no matter the distance between us. At a subconscious level there is no distance, we are singularity. Any piece of information is within reach. There have also been cases when individuals remembered things from a possible past life, but why would science deal with *stupid* things like this, when we're trying to invent vaccines to cure intelligence and healthy genetics. I have recently read the declassified document called *The Gateway Experiment*, conducted by the

CIA in the '80s, when trained people could collect random numbers from a room, thousands of miles away. Later on, I'll explain how a similar event happened to me, without any training. We are *bigger than Prince*, and someone out there knows about your power. Why do you think everyone wants you submissive, in a society that is heading nowhere fast?

Hotel with a twist

A few years back I was invited to this friend's wedding, in *Dacia* (Romania). I arrived at the beach resort, in this hotel where he booked a room for me. At reception I've been told that I'll receive a normal room. I didn't care much about it, as I wasn't planning to stay indoors for too long. They called the groom to confirm my details, and he insisted that they give me a newly renovated room, not a normal one. "Dude, it's alright, it doesn't have to be luxury..." "Julian, I paid for a good room for you, don't let them give you a shit one!" They conformed, but I noticed them acting a bit weird about the whole situation. Everyone was looking at me like they didn't know what to do. I eventually got the key, and went upstairs. As I was unlocking the door, I noticed how the door next to mine was cracked open. I was thinking the maids were cleaning or something. Unpacking wasn't paramount, so I went back out for drinks, with friends I haven't seen since my move to London. When I returned to my room, the next door was still open. It was the same in the morning. I couldn't understand why that door was still open, even after I came back from the wedding. My hopes of returning to the hotel with a hottie had been shattered by high egos, *Dubai attitudes* (usually, when women come back from Dubai, no man is good enough for them anymore) and mostly married couples. Do you know how you can tell the wedding is not that great? One of the dishes in the preset menu is grilled farmed salmon...

In the morning, after about three hours of sleep, I phoned a call girl. She arrived fairly quick, we fucked, and then I had to kick her out early, despite planning to have my money's worth. She cut short the time with her little girl because of me. *"What kind of mother does that?"* "Keep the money, and go home to your kid." Sometimes it's best not to ask escorts about their private lives. Don't be too nice of a client. Later on I met the groom, the bride and other friends, for lunch and extensive drinks. As I left the hotel, the staff gave me weird looks again. The door next to my room was open the same amount, as if no one entered or left, for the whole amount of time I've been there. I didn't know why that was bothering me so much. Have you ever been in a situation, when you are annoyed by something, and you don't know why? That was my last day in the resort. After more drinks than food, I arrived at the hotel around 11pm. My balcony was heading towards the parking lot at the back of the building. Staying in a beach resort, and counting cars. Nice! It was really quiet, as if no one else booked there. I was browsing the tv channels, when I came across a porn station I used to watch as a teenager. Awesome! I binged on that for a bit, then went to sleep happy.

At one point, I had a feeling of something being inside the wardrobe, left of the bed. I stood up in my underwear, facing it. I was sure someone or something was inside. *"Who is there, show yourself!"* Nothing happened. I don't know why, but I shouted full of power, *"This is god!!"*. Straight after saying that, the wooden wardrobe started moving aggressively left and right, with the doors shaking from the hinges. I could feel the presence of some powerful evil entity behind the doors. It was then when I opened my eyes in the dark of the room, feeling chills throughout my body. It was hot, so I was only covered with a thin sheet. That was one of those moments, when you wish you had a proper nine kilograms thick duvet to cover yourself with. The wind was moving the trees outside. I jumped like burned, and turned all lights on. The tv cracked a bit for no reason. Some would say this is a clue that spirits might be around. "Fuuuuuuck!!!" I went and opened the doors of the wardrobe, to discover just a few military blankets. This is what you get in a two star hotel... *"Why did I dream this shit???"* I looked at the parking lot, and saw no sign of humans. I was alone. "Oh, god, what do I do now?" After I came to my senses a bit, I turned the lights out, and went to bed, without properly falling asleep again. I was too scared. It was around 4am when I had the nightmare. Struggling not to think about explanations that could have triggered more panic, I kept my eyes open. I felt like burning that wardrobe to the ground. "Newly renovated my ass!" Not once before had I been happier to leave a hotel room. The next door was in the same position. Coming out with my luggage, the maid cleaning a room gave me a last weird look. *"What's wrong with you people!"* I felt like asking the reception if someone died in that room or something, because I couldn't find an explanation as to why one would have such a terrifying nightmare. I slept in questionable dorms in the army and the police school, places with high chances that they've seen soldiers committing suicide or other gruesome stuff, and still, they didn't give me such nightmares. Why that room had been freshly renovated before I came, and not all others, was adding more horror assumptions to my rich experience. I was walking as normal when I left, but actually I felt like running the fuck out of there. Be aware of the unusual silence, it can hide something inevitable. Same goes for when you can't stop laughing. That's another sign of something going bad in the nearby future. Curb your enthusiasm. There's a law of compensation that goes around to set things straight, or wrong. As long as you're aware of it, you should be fine. Be oblivious, and you shall face the consequences.

Bingo!

When I was about 12 years of age, there was this hype around the country with playing bingo. Once a week, a big tv station would broadcast a full show, with prizes that made it worth your while. I think all families were playing the game. You just had to get a ticket, keep the stub, and send the rest for the live draw. Later on, some people have discovered tickets that should've been in the draw, thrown in the garbage bin. This specific week, the prize was a staggering one million US dollars. It was big money in 1997. We were all dreaming of being able to get a big villa next to the beach, going to nice schools, and driving cool cars. I could smell the money already. We bought a lot of tickets, in preparation for the big announcement. About two days before the show, I was having breakfast, when I suddenly remembered that I had dreamt number 49 the night before. I told my family straight away. We started looking through the tickets we already had, but it was not there. My brother and I got ready, and started visiting all bingo ticket sellers in our seaside town. When there's a big prize like that, and someone in the family comes up with a number they think might be the one, you do everything in your power to get that ticket number. Opportunity is key in life, and it can come in all shapes and sizes. We finally got a ticket with the number 49 on it, after asking all the sellers. We've done our part. Now it was time for the show. They delayed the announcement of the big prize. We were almost 100% sure that we'd won. Before the end, the presenter pulled the ticket, and the winning number was...49! Our hearts suddenly started pumping blood into our veins at an alarming rate. We took out the ticket, to follow the winning series as well. Number 49 had a few different series, it was never just one. When we checked, it wasn't ours. Nooooo!!! Disappointment was huge. I was shocked and silent. They did extract number 49, the one I saw in my dream. It took my siblings a while to acknowledge what actually happened. Although we didn't win anything, the fact that I could collect the number from different realms, had been extraordinary and paranormal. The next day we bought the newspaper, just to have confirmation that we heard the presenter shouting my ticket number. It was 49, owned by someone from a different county, about 350km away! Did my consciousness travel to their house, and picked up the number? Was the ticket folded, with the series inside, making it impossible to read remotely? I took the newspaper to the farm, to show it to my parents. They didn't know what to think either. If I hadn't told them beforehand, it would've meant nothing, but it happened. How do you scientifically explain something that is not scientifically possible, but which is still occurring? Children are pure, and with a powerful connection with the matrix. As you grow older, that connection gets thinner and thinner. You are constantly occupied with something, and your brain becomes addicted to this lifestyle. This is why, society is constantly trying to corrupt you with something new. The secret to finding the right way to live is blocking outside interference often, and dedicating more time to meditating, to expanding your mental horizons and peace. Suppressing your left side of your brain -cognitive thinking- often is key. This is not meant to get you stupid, but to let your creativity run free more often.

We've all been told at least once, *don't think too much*, when making a decision. The higher the number of calculation, the bigger the chances you'll make mistakes, when having to make an important decision in a limited timeframe. This is one exercise to practise, and the other is to bring your hemispheres on the same frequency. This is how the detachment and travel of consciousness can occur. Maybe that was what I did. No matter how, when, and why I did it, it partially worked. I have found out about what might have happened, from a declassified CIA document, 23 years later...

What is your name?

When I was in the police force, from time to time, during general or local elections, police officers had to guard the polling stations, starting the day before. These were usually schools or councils. On this occasion, I've been assigned to this village school and kindergarten. It was great for me, as I was avoiding sleepless nights at the border, or in the checkpoint. I had my laptop with me, to watch movies, and also to continue developing my ideas about promoting my first book, *This is my Electronica*. The village was so quiet during the night, I almost wished that I was a smoker, to spend more time outside with the cute stray dogs. No matter where I was on shift, if there were dogs in the area, they'd always choose to do the shift with me. I was a magnet for dogs. I watched a few movies that night, and after figuring out how to pee into little people urinals, I went to sleep on the school benches. It was the perfect combo to herniate a disc. I dreamt of this girl going around in the classroom I was sleeping, looking at me, being captured by a feeling that she liked me. The vibe was quite strong. After a few hours, I woke up to check the doors. I had another wee, then went back to sleep. The girl came back, walking slowly around me, looking more and more curious. *"What is your name?"*, she asked me. It was then when I opened my eyes, becoming aware of the hair-raising experience. She was trying to build a rapport. "Shit!!!" I jumped off the benches, terrified by the clarity of the dream. After my first session of sleep, I didn't pay attention to the dream, and that had been a big mistake. I had no bad feeling about *her*, but I was still a human, so I had to be scared. There's no way around it. "Aaaaaaaaa!!!" Outside, the dogs probably couldn't understand why I was so desperate and restless. *"Hooman, go back to sleep, it's 3am!"* I went back inside only at the end of the shift, just to get my stuff. After a few days, I asked my colleagues living in that village, if they've ever heard about *special* events happening in that school. I never told them what happened to me. They were thinking I was a weird guy anyway. Because it was a *good* ghost, I've apologised for overreacting, in case I've offended *her*. I was alive, *she* wasn't. How could we ever have gotten along?

TV noise

Our farm was an old property. My mother grew up there with more bad memories than good, and her father hanged himself behind the house. Never go back to live in a house that caused you traumas. First time I went there I was six. It never felt comfortable. At that age, I didn't understand why we had to move to the countryside. I actually hated it, and being alone in the house caused me panic attacks. That silence, the clock ticking, everything was telling my young soul that I was not alone. I never felt the same in my father's parents farm. I found that property quite poetic, and perfect to transform into a museum with high-end gourmet restaurant.

It would've been a five stars archaic experience for sure. Nowadays, city folk would pay huge money to enjoy something like that. Anyway, now that I know how disconnected from nature and reality city people are, I consider my years at the farm a blessing, despite the horrors of a place with bad energies. When I started school there, older kids didn't like me, and always tried to kick my butt. Being one of the best students, and from the city, is not on the liking of rednecks. Without any obvious reason, girls liked me more too. Some lads were meeting me on the way home, trying to have a go at me. I've never been a kid to stray away from conflict, but some were stronger, and that terrified and angered me simultaneously. At the farm I started having my first nightmares, maybe because of those conflicts, or of the energies around the house. This one night I was seeing tv noise, with a black human shape walking towards me, but never actually reaching me. I was living in a perpetual and all encompassing tv noise, with this weird entity expressing its will to get close. Eventually, my mother woke me up. I was screaming in my sleep. Sweat was covering my face. I was thinking I've been awake the whole time, it felt like that. My mother told me, that I couldn't hear her shouting at me to wake up. I was really scared, and she slept next to me that night. She knew more than me about the energies of the house, but we were in a situation that didn't allow us to move back to the city. My father was to blame for it, but I couldn't know that, I was too little. I never wanted to be alone in that house, but sometimes it had to happen, because I wasn't old enough to go and work the crops with my family for a full day. I could manage the farm alone when I was nine though. This particular day, my mother, sister and brother went really far away to pick the corn from the field. It took them longer than expected to get home, and it turned dark. I didn't like it one bit. All animals were fed and sleeping, except this German shepherd we rescued from his former owner, that used to beat him. He was really connected with us, and highly protective. That night, to make it even worse for me, he started howling, in a way I've never heard him before. I was watching tv worried, and when he started being restless, I turned all the lights on. That was a different level of fear. My hair was raising. We knew from our grandparents, that when a dog is howling, it's not a good sign. It might mean that someone in your family is in danger. "Spic, calm down boy!" The dog was looking at me when calling him, then howling again. That evening I've lived in an excruciating fear for a few hours. It was so dark, I couldn't see anything beyond the gates. Our farm was at the edge of the village too, so there was only wild field ahead. When my mother was a kid, wolves would circle the property, trying to snatch lambs and other vulnerable animals. My family returned around 12 at night, but more scared than me. On the way back, they had to cross an area where a lot of villagers had devilish experiences. They told me that, as they were walking past those hills, along the loaded donkey-pulled carriage, from a complete silence, the shape of a fast carriage (similar with the carriages used in fast horse races) pulled by a horse appeared from thin air. Two men with powerful whips were driving it. It was pitch black, and my family could only hear the sounds of them wanting to charge. How the aggressors could see them, in the same night conditions, caused severe panic. They kept on swearing and driving around at high speed, snapping their whips from hell. The sound was really powerful. My brother and sister were carrying some sort of scythes for cutting corn stalks. They were ready to protect themselves. It was unusually dark, and no one had any light. How could they see my family, to attack them, was frightening. My mother started praying in her mind, and suddenly, with the snap of a whip, the attackers disappeared into the pitch black night. There was no sound of them galloping away, it all turned silent instantly. That had caused a lot of shock. When it all started, out of nowhere, the donkey engaged into pulling the weight unusually fast too. He didn't even start singing, as donkeys do. My brother was not one to get scared, but he looked more than shocked and exhausted. He drank a lot of wine that night. In a few days, my mother found out from other villagers, that it happened to them too, in the same exact place, with their horses getting scared and unmanageable, in the same type of unusual darkness. There were some places in the countryside, where bad stuff was happening to many villagers. They were all on the lookout, whenever they had to pass through there, and when the silence was unusual. You could feel the bad beforehand, as a premonition. Both came together, and terrified the people. You just had to pray, stay calm, and be aware.

Paper airplanes

The mandatory military service is the most boring place you could be in. So far, joining it voluntarily at 19, has been my biggest mistake in life. Half a year in, and I was named squad commander of this strategic guard, and later on, I also became a Sergeant. Straight after my appraisal, the tormenting boredom began. There was nothing to keep me entertained, just plain old nothingness. I was constantly tired. I could feel how my brain was melting and draining through my ear canals and nose. This specific day had been memorable. Boredom does have a limit. Beyond it, it's paradise. People in general, associate being bored with a bad state to be in. Wrong! Boredom is your brain waves calming down. If you manage to keep that state for long, you might just reach another level of consciousness. We are connected to other dimensions, there is no space in the non-physical. Daily life is disconnecting us through constant and accelerated entertainment. The analytical is almost 100% of our life. When is the last time you meditated? That specific day I'm referring to, I have reached a point of no return. I fell in this deep state of mental meltdown I had never experienced before, when all of a sudden I felt an easing of my condition, which occurred naturally. I felt like grabbing a notebook and a pen. My fingers kept on writing verse after verse, forming a comical poem about what the army meant, and also about our stupidity and clumsiness in that context. It felt brilliant, and I couldn't stop. Ideas were flowing all around me. I was laughing on my own at the ingenuity of my words. No one knew if they were funny for the others too. I didn't feel bored anymore, but excited, engaged, and with endless inspiration. I was limitless. At the end of my poetic endeavour, I've written around 372 verses, out of nowhere, and without a specific purpose. Following my almost cataleptic experience and resurrection, I felt alive, and someone else. I wanted to do some cooking, and even when higher officers came around to check on us, I was ready to confront them head on, if they were being aggressive. They enjoyed doing that, even when all was perfect. "I won't allow you to pick on my men! Talk to me, I'm their commander..." I felt new and refreshed. For a while, I kept on picking up all sorts of ideas from thin air, about anything and nothing in particular. Despite having months till liberation, I was feeling happiness. Probably I've never been more irrational, but it was all due to an episode of extreme boredom. That must've helped me achieve another state of consciousness. The transformation was there to stay, and after a few years, my creativity started giving me headaches, when planning not to pursue it. This became a burden, when I found out that there is no book in *Dacian* (Romanian) literature about DJing and electronic music. I've been passionate about the industry from early childhood, and now I was being haunted by the idea of writing a book about it. My brain got flooded with highly specific ideas, and words to use. When on duty in the coast guard, I kept on writing down every detail of my imagination, then polishing it at home. I was taking pills for my headaches. It was a flow I could not go against. When an idea gets into the brain, there's usually no going back. I managed to finish my first novel, *This is my Electronica*, in five months. 115,000 words in less than half a year. I'd say that's quite impressive for a beginner, with no writing skills whatsoever, and working full time. With every chapter, I was floating on imaginary worlds, from where I was collecting a continuation to the story of my personal life. I don't know why, but I wanted it finished and published before the end of March 2010. I'm a weirdo, I know, you're not the first thinking this about me. It got published eventually, on 31 March. I self-published it, after annoying this editor from a famous publishing house, who asked to see the full manuscript, but I wouldn't send it without assurance against theft. His reply was epic. They rejected me, and I had to go and pay for the printing myself. Imagine having 1,000 copies in your flat... It had to be done, for some reason.

A few years after embarking in a marketing endeavour on my own, I was re-reading the book, when I realised what I've written about in this specific chapter. My Dutch girlfriend had been trapped in an international airport, in Warsaw, due to a heavy rainstorm, while I was waiting for her in Ibiza, to witness one of my DJ acts the next day. She probably realised that I was planning to ask her to marry me, as I insisted she came, because she started crying. Comforting her over the phone wasn't doing much to help her. There was no way she could leave the country in time to attend the event, because all flights had been grounded till further notice. I told her to fly back home, as soon as flights resumed. While writing the chapter, I was imagining this black storm over Warsaw, that was causing havoc in airports, and forcing my girlfriend to be stranded and alone. I don't know why I chose that country and city. It was completely random. I just wanted to create drama and suspense. I published the book on 31 March 2010. On 10 April 2010, the Smolensk air disaster happened, during which the president of Poland, his wife and many statesmen died in a plane crash. They were flying from Warsaw to Russia.

Reading the chapter again, made me realise the paranormal of the situation. I did feel pushed by a force to get the book published before the end of March of that year, and then, the real darkness had set above Poland, involving an airplane, crying, and a powerful charge of immense magnitude. A plane crashing with so many diplomats had never happened before, in our entire history. I wrote that chapter four months before the incident. Did I create it, or just anticipated a disaster in that country? I guess I'll never find out...

We come in peace?

There are different instances of paranormal. It can also be something that you clearly see, not just feel, or dream. When I was working in the coast guard, during this shift in particular, I saw something that blew my mind away. I was really tired, after spending the whole day at the beach. My brain was shutting down after one hour into the shift. I told my colleagues not to count on me. Luckily, that night I've been posted right on the border, having to check a certain perimeter every hour. Back then, my shift officer was this tough guy close to pension age. Sometimes he was cooler than most colleagues on my shift, that thought they were cool just because they were thinking it. He was a good person, but he didn't like me much, for a specific reason. He never caught me sleeping on duty. All others were in his books, but not me. I always managed to wake up just before he arrived at our posts, whether it was the checkpoint or the actual border line. He was hunting me basically, every shift, to catch me on the wrong foot. This particular shift, I felt how I was going to fall from his grace. I had my own cabin, with a table big enough to mask me. I set my jacket on the floor, under the table, I borrowed a pillow from the checkpoint, and went to sleep. The table cover was creating perfect conditions. Throughout the night I could hear steps around the cabin, resembling the chief's gait. Probably because he couldn't see me in through the windows, he thought I was patrolling the border in the dark. Till morning, no one checked under the table. When I woke up, it was clear daylight. I pushed the end of the table cover up, so I could see the sky. The morning star was really bright. The sun wasn't up yet. I wasn't rushing, as the shift change was a few hours away. Suddenly, I could see another light on the sky, of the same size and intensity as the morning star (planet Venus), moving slowly and in zig-zags, towards the same area of the sky of the first planet. I started wondering if I was awake. Eventually, the light stopped its advance, and sat next to the morning start. We had two Venuses on the sky. *"What the fuck is going on?"* Both lights seemed as if they were above Bulgaria. I tried to take a photo of it with my phone, but the resolution of the camera was too low, to be able to capture the phenomenon. For the younger generations, the camera was VGA, a level up from .3gp. This was around 2009. I was trying to explain how that was possible. *"What is it?"* In order to be of the same intensity as Venus, the object should've been really big and out into space, or had such powerful lights as the stadiums. No matter how I was thinking it, it didn't make sense. And before being still, it moved on its own. I ran straight to the border point to call my colleagues, but it started dimming. They all thought I was mad. When they looked, all they could see was Venus, shining away beautiful. "Guys, I'm telling you, there was a light next to it!" People around the world have seen similar lights on the sky, but truth be told, no one believes those videos are real, until it happens to you. It was my turn to look weird. I was willing to expose myself that way. Usually, I'm highly aware of my surroundings. I would never point out something like that, if I wasn't sure about it. We didn't receive any reports about military flight training at the border. Someone had to know what that was, whether it's the secret services, or the military from both neighbouring countries. Normal people need to understand, that the airspace of a country is being monitored 24/7, by highly sophisticated radars, and actual people. Nothing can be missed, unless it is flying really fast, and at low altitude. This is part of each country's defence systems. If a foreign object enters the airspace, it is being picked up in a matter of seconds, and fighter jets are sent to intercept it in less than 10 minutes.

That object remained a mystery until one day, probably after a few weeks, when a colleague that laughed at my story had seen the same light himself, together with his patrol mate. "Aha! Now you believe me! Aha!!!" We were all wondering, having no knowledge to be able to make any sense of it. It couldn't have been an airplane. How can it do zig-zags? It was unusually bright too, and sitting next to the morning star, having the same intensity and size. The way it was dimming got us concerned too. Well, probably it was nothing to worry about, right? The government is there to speak the truth, and to protect us.

If you work in a system, and you see it's broken, but decide to do nothing, if you accept it hurting people and the overall human evolution, you are not a good human being. The future cannot be built by people like you.

CHAPTER 14

A THING ABOUT YOU

Music for this chapter
Lemin - Avant Garden
D. Ramirez & Mark Knight - Colombian Soul
Biesmans - Trains, Planes & Automobiles

Human existence is split into two stages: the innocence years and the revelation years. Innocence is characteristic to the first part of your life, and the last. How the information is being implemented is crucial to personal success. The revelation period will either take you back to innocence, or change you for good, putting you on a path of no return, of an eternal search for truth, and of decisive actions to change the world for the better. If the revelation years take you back to innocence, no one will be able to help you. You are kind of lost, for good. People in the two different groups will always go against each other. One group is voting for their favourite, the other does not vote, because they know voting will not change a thing. The two groups are toxic to each other, but only one is doing the right thing. When one group is saying no, the other is saying yes. They are like two boxers having a go at each other. Who is right? The one with a mortgage, or the other, that wants banks to be gone? Who is wrong? The one sacrificing his entire life for a job, or the other, who is using the job to achieve full independence? Who is right? The one who believes blindly that a coronavirus will kill them, or the other, who's doing proper research? If we keep living like this, we'll continue to die and get reborn, and die again and get reborn, in an infinite loop, until the destruction of human kind and of the world is complete. We are all being used as cannon meat. Cancer is a fight that shouldn't even exist. We are giving each other the cancer we are trying to cure.

Who are you? Treat this as if it's the most important question anyone has ever asked you. The answer can set you free, or forever entrap you. Most of you will probably respond unconsciously, *"I am Jessica Dormant"* or *"my name is Eugene Cant"*. I am *Julian Stance*, and I stand my ground against anything trying to have a negative impact on my present and future life, on my absolute sacred freedom. Because freedom is sacred, a right without the need to ask for consent. But most probably, this isn't my true name either, even if it represents the physical me. Hence, I'm asking you again, "who are you?". Did you ever think about what your real name could be? I mean *you*, the *sacred cloud.* When you descend upon this world, you're being given a name that your parents decide, but which might not be the real *you.* What is your name before you get born? This might sound crazy, if you don't believe in God, afterlife, reincarnation, or soul. If you are one of these people, I consider you highly inexperienced and uneducated. You cannot dismiss something so big, and think high of yourself in the same time. These two types of attitudes are incompatible. And for the ones on the other side of the discussion, no, your God is not greater than mine. God is our context, the source of the radiation forming the hologram that is you. But then again, probably you're letting yourself educated by society. You care more about how people see you, than how you see yourself, or maybe you don't believe in sacred, because you like to be known as a down-to-earth person with strong beliefs, that are heavily rooted in reality and common sense.

Is your reality the true reality? No matter what type of person you are, it's hard to not let yourself influenced by mass opinions, movements, lies, pseudo-truths, tradition, customs, news, the future. Marketing does work, you know. We get bombarded by information all around us, and instead of being educated about how to process it, we're being forced to accept it, without our own reason and filters. *"White people are racists."* This is an example of information that made its way into the modern world, more than a century after the last slaves have been released by white owners. Most white people never engaged in slave trades, and white people also stopped it, a long time ago. Be careful with this type of generalisation, no race will take it. You can also turn racist against your own race. It's all about who you are inside, not about how you look. Who are you, accepting information like this? You pick it up, and spread it like wildfire. Where is your processing ability? This president is bad, the other candidate would have been perfect. *"We want only black presidents. White people have had their time, now it's our time!"* Any time in history is for all races. If you're black, go to a mirror and ask yourself, when was the last time you've supported the cause of a poor white person, or of any other race that is not black. If you've never done it, or you feel like you would never do it, the society you live in is not the problem, you are. You want to live in a world only with black people? Look at Africa, and tell yourself that that is a good thing. Your children will be even more hateful than you, perpetuating a conflict that was never created by the whites. And having the BLM logo represented with fireworks at New Year's Eve is anything but inclusive, kind of showing the middle finger to anyone who's not black... You are being manipulated! This is a conflict on which the governments are thriving. Movements like BLM should never exist. No one should be integrated in any specific group, other than the human race. Not as long as thousands of black people in London are driving cars I personally could never afford, and occupy leading positions I would never have access to. If you don't know how to play the game, it doesn't mean someone is being racist with you. Not all black people can be rich or educated, and it's the same with white people. In this society, access to higher positions and wealth should be based on attitude, altitude and abilities. No race should be first in line, nor second in line. No matter the result of any elections, the other alternative would have been better. Why do you choose to live in this perpetual conflict, driven by forces that you do not want to acknowledge, and can't understand? If you find it difficult to fully comprehend something, stay on the side till you do, and then act. If I believe in a type of segregation, it is the separation between naive, inexperienced and intentionally uneducated people (self-education), and the rest. Let the clear minded take control and rule the world, while the naive should have no right to participate in society, but to vote, work and watch the telly. See what I've done there? If you think there is no corruption, you shouldn't be allowed to vote; there should not be a vote in the first place, if all is fair. The future cannot be built by people who vote. If you believe progress has not been stalled, you should not be allowed to have a voice. If you have an opinion about something, just because you chose to be opinionated, but lazy enough to browse through all the information available, you should not be listened to. Who are you, voting for the corrupt? Who are you, donating to charities that pay themselves first? Who are you, supporting cancer research, when cancer is planted into your food? Who are you, searching for one missing child, when hundreds of thousands disappear each year for blood transfusions, organs, slavery, soldiers, or even worse, experiments, and you never lift a finger to stop it? Oh, but you donate to charities that are trying to find missing children from 30 years ago! Who are you, debating a virus and sharing graphs with *spikes*, when you don't know anything about how viruses work, or how people are being killed in hospitals, just to scare everyone? Where is the life saving penicillin? Who are you, forcing someone with knowledge about the world to comply with your beliefs, people about whom you know nothing? Who are you, defending a world you have endless complaints about? Who are you, thinking that the government cares about your life, when they want you to work till pension age, and then hope you'd die before cashing in a penny? Who are you, getting a mortgage, getting married, and starting a family before owning anything? Who are you, having children just to get benefits? Who are you, having loads of children, just to overcome another race? Who are you, joining the armed forces, thinking you'll be able to help? Who are you, teaching your children to get a *good* job, and hold it till they die? Who are you, going into politics, after seeing what politics is? Who are you, building opinions only from watching the news? Who are you, living in society, in the city, in a trap? Who are you, forgetting about the pedophiles, because elections are more important? Who are you, paying your tax in time, thinking this will heal the economy? Who are you, leaving a massive debt to your unborn children? Who are you, the one owing so much money, despite doing nothing wrong? Who are you, supporting speed bumps on roads that should be clear of obstructions? Who are you, stopping the economy, and creating never seen before poverty, that will end up killing millions of healthy people? Who are you, killing someone with so much ease? Once again, "who are you?". "What is your name?"

As I've described in the chapter *Devil speaks perfect grammar*, some people can be possessed by unknown entities, that can double their voice. These people can be cured by priests with strong faith in God, and who believe that evil is real too. Forget about religion, I'm talking about faith. Faith never brought wars and mass murder, religions did, together with the ones that don't want you to have faith. Why wouldn't you be allowed to have faith in a divine power, in a *free* world? Because that divine power is in you too. A normal person could turn crazy in seconds at the sight; I guess I'm not that normal either, maybe I'm being *possessed* by the opposite. Once the name is found, the person becomes something else, until collapsing. No one knows if the spirit is truly gone or not. Only time can tell, and how the person behaves after that. It is a terrifying thing to see! Recently I was driving a woman in London, and during our random conversation, I pronounced the word *god*. She seemed nice and chatty, before suddenly turning silent. Then she made a random remark about the weather. I felt like she didn't want the conversation to continue, then she started making some weird sounds. I kept looking at her through the rear view mirror a bit scared, while she was staring out the window. I could not wait to see her out of my car. I obviously disturbed her demons with only one innocuous word. You probably wonder why I'd give you this example, how it can relate to what I previously said. Well, what is your real name? Since you're not using your brain and processing capacity when participating in society, thus choosing to leave yourself at the mercy of mass opinions and actions, hurting the thinkers and nonconformists, it means that someone else is driving you from inside, an evil spirit, because your true spirit would never hide the truth, it would constantly strive to find it, and act to protect it from the misleaders. We are all built from *truth*. Otherwise we'd all be stuffed animals on someone's furniture. Trust me when I say that we're not far from the latter. Why do you give up searching, and let your mind be something else, shaped, polished, but by the liars? You have a mind and soul to use them, not to lose them! When you see a bit of information, digest it, then act like a detective, before turning against someone for not conforming. By acting on impulse, you'll condemn future generations, your children, to a life of imprisonment. We are not made to have jobs, these should be bridges towards our personal escape from the trap that society is. Governments are obsolete, people in charge is a mistake. Each individual should be in charge of its own life. We should be allowed to make our own choices, as long as harming others is not involved. The future, as it stands, will not be like in the movies, it will shock, destabilise, and turn us against each other. Current society is feeding on conflict. If you appear in the fake news that you've hurt someone, you are guilty. You wake up one morning, and you don't know what is going on. All your friends run away from you, no one wants to deal with you, and you get isolated until you crash. You die, and no one even remembers you. You get erased from history, although you were completely innocent, just going about your daily life. You've been a successful experiment, and not one person even touched you, if you were *lucky*. Since we have this amazing power to produce negative chemicals when we are alone and isolated, why not strive to repel the negativism of society, and feed our lives and bodies with positive chemistry. It is not easy, nor difficult, it's a choice. What is wrong with your defence mechanism? Why are you using it against people that think before they act, people that will never harm you? Why are you so against the truth?

I trained my mind from an early age to receive the information, and fully understand it. What is the point of owning too much information about everything, if it's not properly understood? Who are you, telling me that my versions of the present and of the future are wrong? If you don't like this chapter, you are definitely living in a golden cage. It's not about waking up, but about looking around you, and understanding what is happening. Your eyes and your heart have to work together. Who are you, looking for jobs, and not enlightenment? Who are you, living the life of your parents, but in a totally changed world, incompatible with old, or any other type of doctrines? You all hate socialism, but you've never lived in a pure democracy, because people are at the top. True freedom is not possible with people in charge. You're being controlled from all directions, and today's socialism weapons have never been sharper. Do you think you're free to live as you wish? Society would come after you wherever you'd try to hide. To give you an example, imagine yourself as the creator of your own, first ever built spacecraft, capable to allow you to live in space, and explore on your own to the end of the universe, all without any aid from earth. Just you and your family, leaving earth behind, until you decide to come back. Do you think you will be allowed? All countries would come together, capture you, they would probably declare you insane, and lock you away, not before confiscating your spacecraft. No one is allowed to leave without *their* consent, we're trapped on this planet until *they* fall, and leave human kind to achieve its real potential. A world without compound interest, without asking for money from you before being even born. For this, I truly believe that everything has to change, and give the power to each individual.

Criminality is the easiest to tackle in this entire new equation, and the world I'm talking about has no need for law enforcement, nor justice. I brought crime into discussion because this is probably what you'd think of straight away. How we live now is just a fake image that we are tackling crime, but looking around you, do you really think someone cares about you being safe? We are all being sold a future with no space for human kind. We are living our own progressive extinction. Find the ones selling you short, and you'll have the answers. A chip in the brain means nothing, if yours is produced by Renault, and mine by Ferrari. I would still be smarter than you, in a select class of my own, now with outstanding control over you. Our brains should never have this type of technology in them, while existing in the current context. Our brains can communicate with each other anyway. Humans will always try to take advantage of the weak, because we are easily corruptible. The corrupters need to be extracted from the equation. The positive future we all dream of, can only be possible with the power in the individuals' hands. You need to learn how to meditate, how to completely empty your brain. Why do you think you're being kept entertained 24/7? A relaxed brain communicates with other brains, can surround the earth, or go to the end of the universe and back, in no time. It can collect information from other dimensions, and bring it back to improve your life and others'. If I'd have a pound for every time I felt like finding out the answer to something really big, during that state before deep sleep, I'd have a pocket full of coins. A trained brain can keep that information alive, when coming back to the conscious state. Train yourself to be you at all times, and put useless distractions last on the list. Stop needing a mentor, and to be spoon-fed the truth that is in front of you. Blindness is a condition, yours is a disease.

I have heard a lot of naive people asking me, *"but why would they do this to us?"*. This is the most widespread question asked by a person that refuses to think and see. Where is the proof?! Why would they do it? The government is full of corrupt people that, if they don't obey the clear instructions, they're out of politics or assassinated. Personally, I think that something bigger than humans is corrupting them so perfectly. How would you act, if one day a guy would put a gun to your temple, and ask you to do what they tell you? They'd promise you wealth, and an amazing life, with the price of your cooperation. If you refuse, they would wipe out your entire bloodline. In that situation, would you care about me not having what to eat? The big corporations want to squeeze everything from you, to make you stay put and silent. Banks control everything in society, from money printing, to the quality of pasta you eat. A few very rich people control the banks, because they own everything that you *borrow*. This is why everyone is saying, you should not own anything because it's not *profitable*. They are beyond money, this word doesn't mean anything to them, but an instrument for your entrapment. These are the ones deciding where the next war will be. Yes, everyone you do or don't know is conspiring against you. There is no doubt about it. Questionable conspiracy starts after this level. In your small world the non-proof conspiracy starts too soon, at lower levels. There is substantial proof up to the mentioned levels. From here, some believe that inter dimensional entities have hijacked our world, beings with no feelings or creativity, and started exploiting us. From my experience, and considering the recent scientific developments, I would say this is highly probable. They don't need to have physical shapes, but just consciousnesses able to control humans. This is why I was saying earlier that you might be driven, possessed by another entity that keeps you stupid, blind, and without will. Rumour goes that they got trapped here, and they don't like it. There are stories in religion and popular culture, that someone is trying to come into our world, or they did already, the fallen. My grandparents knew that the *yellow race* would dominate. Look at China nowadays. Spot on, I'd say. They never travelled, so how did they know?! If you look at history, compound interest started around the time of Christ. Maybe that is why He came to earth, to let us know about the dangers lurking in our future. If you're an atheist, just think of Him as a good person. Calm down! Why would you blame a person for telling people not to kill each other? Interesting is that, even after more than 2,000 years, we're still telling ourselves to open our eyes. Someone has to be right, and we need to stop being two separate camps. Common language is the answer! The future in total freedom cannot include law as well. Law is the framework for doctrine; democratic doctrine, liberal doctrine, communist doctrine, doctrine, right wing, left wing. No matter the system in place, humans are being killed intentionally.

Talking to some people recently, we got to this matter, of gradually getting rid of people. *"Yes, but, you know, we are a lot of people on this planet..."* Silently they agree with murder. My question for you, if you think this way, "what is the right number of people on the planet?". What if you and your family are next to have to go, to create space? *"You first, bitch, I'm healthier than you, mind, body and soul. You're taking my air. First, let's take out the people that agree with depopulation."* How does it feel? Billions of people on the planet does not kill the planet, a lot of people in cities is destroying it. The way we are forced to live is causing mayhem and destruction. There are some theories stating that, there is a limited number of human souls than can exist, and I tend to believe it. Think at all the water on this planet, the same quantity since the beginning, and you, your consciousness, being only a drop spilt from the ocean, which is the *Absolute*, God. It's a metaphor. Reincarnation would make sense with this theory too. If you travelled the world, you know I'm right. This planet can host billions upon billions of people. Not long ago, I had a dream during which, someone was telling me that earth can easily hold 30 billion people, as we live now. I woke up refreshed, and ready to challenge the ones shutting their eyes at murder. I hope I'm wrong, but this is my prophesy about why they want to kill us gradually - if the inter-dimensional entities are real, they allowed us to multiply to really high numbers, just to achieve their desired technological progress fast, so they can try to escape, or bring more of their own into our world, and once their plan is complete, to wipe us all out. Someone I know told me to look at the bible for an important clue, and it kind of makes sense, in almost all languages. There are four gospels in the bible, Matthew, Mark, Luke and John. "J" in Latin is capital "i". So we have MMLI, which in roman numbering is 2051. This might be a message, telling us about something massive, that will happen to us in that year, or between 2049-2051, MMIL-MMLI, however you'd want to move *John*. There are documentaries and studies kind of matching these dates, stating that around 2050, human numbers will be less than half of what we are now. If you have a bit of wit, you should've realised by now, that 2020 is the start of something big. Even powerful technocrats have publicly discussed about reducing the population with 15%-20%, or more than three billion, if we invest in *good healthcare*. If you look at the prognosis for the number of humans on the planet, in a few years the growth rate will turn negative. How come, if we have really good healthcare and prosperity? Does this make sense to you? This means somewhere between 3-4 billion people, in an environment and development of probably 10 billion by 2050. Why that would happen is a mystery, or maybe not. We shall see, a few years into the mass vaccination campaigns, with poison sold as antidote to a *coronavirus itch*. I'm not trying to go too much into the conspiracy mania, I just want you to open your eyes a bit, to see that something big is pushing us over the cliff. You don't want your children to hate you for conforming, do you? Your freedom is inversely proportional with technological advances, in the current context of our establishment. Remember this! Be careful which world you believe in most, because only one is so powerful, that it can punch right through the toughest influence of the other. Truth can melt any resistance, and it is irreversible.

My advice for you? Conceive your escape plan, make it the love of your life, spread love all around you, but be the *devil* in devil's plan. Keep it a secret! Do not talk about your individual escape plan around technology, close the notebook if you write something down, don't let it uncovered! Never talk to anyone about it, until the whole world is completely changed and unchained, and under no circumstance join protests, wars or mass opinions. Research everything! Once the shift is complete, wink at each other, and start building the new world, the world of perfect human beings, where no one is in control, or everyone is. It might seem like chaos, but it's the opposite, just open your mind to the possible. My way of life is this - do good and love, you might be *His* last man in the field. 2020 is your proof that money was never a problem, if you can get paid to stay indoors.

If you still don't think that you are being manipulated to act in a way that conforms with the masses, then close this book. Forget about it, shut your eyes, then open them again.

Congratulations, you beautiful human being! You live in a perfect world. Now back to work!

Human governance is, and has been the biggest mistake in our history as a species. By now, we should've successfully colonised at least one other planet, and created an indestructible connection with the Absolute (God), and each other. We keep on missing our soulmate due to a constantly broken connection with the Universal Matrix. What we are currently living is a mistake, that will eventually lead to the destruction of our genes, and ultimately to our extinction. Human governance was never a mistake though. The attempt to enslave human kind was ever present on this planet, for some unknown reason. It has nothing to do with human nature, it is not human.

References

The Polymerase Chain Reaction, by Kary B. Mullis, François Ferré, Richard A. Gibbs.

Dancing Naked in the Mind Field, Kary B. Mullis.

Coronavirus & Human Immunity in any medical journal, pre-2020.

www.bplgroup.com, for understanding proven century-old therapies for people with weak immune capabilities.

Data-Sheet of the mRNA vaccines.

mRNA technology uses and challenges.

Recombinant DNA.

America's Frontline Doctors, www.americasfrontlinedoctors.org.

The SPARS Pandemic 2025-2028: A Futuristic Scenario to Facilitate Medical Countermeasure Communication, Journal of a international Crisis and Risk Communication Research.

Event 201, the practice for a coronavirus pandemic.

Monsanto history and the effects of GMOs on the body and nature.

Epicyte company history and the Epicyte gene added to GMOs.

European commercial wine law, and the wine law of any country.

Global Trends 2040, A Publication of the National Intelligence Council (USA)

Remdesivir and it's uses.

The long-term effects and the dangers of an untreated high temperature (the myth of long-Covid).

Agenda 2030, Department for International Development (UK).
The list of mRNA serious adverse events, VAERS database, USA.
Vaccine technologies and their impact on the human body.
Notifications of Infectious Diseases - weekly reports, Public Health England.
Genomic Sequencing - what it is and methods in use.
MHRA & FDA histories, Big Pharma lobbying, and their relationship.
The Gateway Project, CIA.
W02014089290 - CRISPR-Based Genome Modification and Regulation.
The mechanics of Antibody-Dependant Enhancement.
Rothschild patent: US 2020/0279585A1.
International Space Law, United Nations Instruments - United Nations, Office for Outer Space Affairs.
www.freedomtaker.com
https://www.ema.europa.eu/en/documents/product-information/covid-19-vaccine-janssen-epar-product-information_en.pdf
https://www.fda.gov/media/146305/download
https://www.janssenlabels.com/emergency-use-authorization/Janssen+COVID-19+Vaccine-HCP-fact-sheet.pdf